Measuring Police Subcultural Perceptions

Zheng Chen

Measuring Police Subcultural Perceptions

A Study of Frontline Police Officers in China

Springer

Zheng Chen
Department of Basic Studies
National Police University of China
Shenyang
China

ISBN 978-981-10-0094-2 ISBN 978-981-10-0096-6 (eBook)
DOI 10.1007/978-981-10-0096-6

Library of Congress Control Number: 2015955388

Springer Singapore Heidelberg New York Dordrecht London

Printed on acid-free paper

Springer Science+Business Media Singapore Pte Ltd. is part of Springer Science+Business Media
(www.springer.com)

For Danni (Danni Sui) and
Henry (Yihang Chen) with love

Acknowledgments

I would like to express my gratitude to several individuals and organisations for their support and contributions to this study. My deepest gratitude goes to Dr. Chris Devery, who has been a great mentor and friend and whose wisdom, knowledge, and commitment to research continue to inspire and motivate me. I would also like to thank Dr. Ken Wooden, for his contributions, support, and encouragement throughout this process. He provided invaluable advice and direction for my research. I would also like to extend my appreciation to Dr. Susan Robinson, who guided me to the career of police research and helped me outline an ambitious timetable to complete this study. My thanks also go to Dr. Robert Trevethan who edited my draft in a very professional and helpful way.

I am grateful for the School of Policing Studies and Australian Graduate School of Policing and Security both at Faculty of Arts, Charles Sturt University. I would like to thank Associate Professor Rosemary Woolston, Professor Tracy Green, and Associate Professor Nick O'Brien who have kindly supported me and given me confidence in this research project.

I am forever grateful to my organisation, National Police University of China. I would like to thank all the Chinese front-line police officers who kindly participated in this study. This research could never have been achieved without their participation and devotion.

Finally, I want to express my deep appreciation and gratefulness to my wife Danni Sui for her continuous support, patience, and understanding. She has been taking care of the family and my son Henry Chen during my absence. I would like to thank my parents (Junsheng Chen and Lianzhi Zhang) and my parents-in-law (Zhijia Sui and Xiuying Huang) who have openly and always expressed their support, encouragement, and good wishes in our video conference meetings through the Internet and in all our lives. Thanks for your love, sacrifice, and patience. This manuscript is dedicated to them.

Contents

Abbreviations and Acronyms

ANOVA	Analysis of variance
CID	Criminal Investigation Department
CNKI	China National Knowledge Infrastructure
CP	Community policing
HERC	Human Research Ethics Committee
MANOVA	Multivariate analysis of variance
MPS	Ministry of Public Security (China)
PAP	People's Armed Police (China)
PLA	People's Liberation Army (China)
PP	People's police (China)
SPSS	Statistical package for the Social Sciences

List of Figures

List of Tables

Chapter 1
Introduction

1.1 Background of the Study

During the late 20th century, policing around the world has been subject to substantial change in response to changes in its political, economic, and social contexts, and also in response to changes in the political and social theories of policing in its various jurisdictional contexts. In China, these forces have been particularly powerful, as the country has experienced tremendous political, economic, and social change and these have impacted on the role and function of police. The mass-line was adopted as the dominant philosophy for policing since the founding of the communist new China in 1949. Created by Mao Zedong, the essence of mass-line policing was to mobilise the people and rely on the people to participate in maintaining social order and reducing crime (Wong 2009a). At that time, the relations between police and the people were close. The household administration system contributed to stable neighbours in urban areas with low geographic and residential mobility. In addition, traits in the Chinese traditional culture, such as collectivism and voluntarism, also promoted the cooperation and trust between police and the public (Wang and Wong 2012).

However, along with the implementation of the opening-up policy since 1978, China has undergone rapid social and economic development. A corresponding and major increase in crime initiated a strategic shift of policing style from the police-citizen cooperation mass-line to a series of strike-hard campaigns (Ma 2008). These campaigns initially produced a short-term effect, but the accompanying consequences, such as the abuse of police power (Dutton and Lee 1993), compromised procedural requirements (Ma 2008) and deterioration in police-citizen relationships (Du 1997), could not be overlooked. As a result, the focus of policing was transferred from social service to crime fighting (Wang and Wong 2012) and the police in China gradually accepted the role as crime fighters instead of service providers (Dutton 2000). In order to seek a more suitable policing strategy to improve police-citizen relationships and reduce the crime rate, the Ministry of Public of Security (MPS) launched the strategy of community policing as a new policy in 2002 (MPS 2002). As a dramatic change of philosophy, the concept of

Z. Chen, *Measuring Police Subcultural Perceptions*,
DOI 10.1007/978-981-10-0096-6_1

community policing has been adopted in many countries around the globe (Skogan 2008). Although community policing is a Western-based concept, officers in China do not find it difficult to understand because of its similarities with the traditional Chinese mass-line policing in terms of police-citizen cooperation (Ma 2008).

In order to initiate a successful implementation of community policing, it is vital to have the full support from the practitioners. This is far more complicated than declaring that community policing has been officially adopted. This concept may be used only as a cover for traditional policing because the real acceptance by frontline officers who actually perform the tasks and middle managers who supervise frontline officers is more important (Engel and Worden 2003; Vito et al. 2005; Wooden and Rogers 2014). Although there is not a widely accepted definition of community policing, some central ideas have been considered as its essential components, namely, a good police-citizen partnership, a decentralised organisational structure, and priority given to problem-solving and service for the community (COPS 2009; Miller et al. 2014; Skogan 2008). For a good police-citizen partnership, officers need to maintain harmonious relations with the community. Mutual trust and cooperation can be built only on genuine understanding and willingness. Organisational decentralisation may be fully realised only when frontline officers are granted more authority and permitted to participate in more decision-making procedures. It is also important for officers to accept these organisational changes on the basis of their freewill. Only on the basis of real concern for the community, will officers make good use of their authority to solve problems and provide service for people. Similarly, an effective problem-solving and service-oriented policing can be established only when officers are committed to the whole process. It is difficult to imagine that an officer with the crime fighter image and "us versus them" mentality could embrace community policing thoroughly. Do Chinese frontline police officers accept these principles? More empirical studies are still needed to answer this question. However, Western research has long been interested in these police occupational perceptions from the perspective of subculture.

Police officers are members of a unique occupational group and share a distinctive cultural orientation (Crank 2004). This specific subculture includes common perspectives, values, and assumptions (Nhan 2014). The characteristics in police subculture are distinctive compared with those in the general social culture. It is of great importance to understand police conduct and attitudes under the framework of police culture because of its intangible but powerful impact in the process of socialisation and professionalisation. Formed through the interactions among officers, the police subculture provides assurance and protection for officers against external danger and threats like a "protective armour shielding the force" (Reiner 2010, p. 122). For Brown (1981), the values of the police culture "derive from the hazards of police work and seek to minimise these hazards and protect members" (p. 85). Oldham (2006) commented on police culture: "Our culture is about all of the things that are good in life. We are the ones who people call when they need help; we are the ones who run toward problems and we are the ones who keep our domestic enemies at bay" (p. 21). Although positive aspects of the police subculture have been mentioned by academics like Oldham, it seems that much more attention has been given to the potential link between police subculture and negative attitudes and misconduct (Loyens 2009). According to Cochran and Bromley (2003), adherence to the police subculture includes the following negative attitudes (abridged):

- negative attitudes towards the various legal restrictions placed upon their efforts to effectively fight crime;
- negative, sceptical attitudes toward legal institutions and other elements of the criminal justice system;
- negative and suspicious attitudes toward police administration and the police bureaucracy; and
- negative, cynical attitudes toward the citizenry (p. 89).

In addition, many cultural themes of police subculture have been associated with police misconduct by researchers. These include solidarity (Shernock 2007), isolation (Clark 1965), cynicism (Niederhoffer 1967), authority (Goldstein 1967), and the police subculture as a whole (Ivković 2005; Pollock 2012; Prenzler 2009). The misconduct includes excessive violence (Armacost 2003; Lindsey et al. 2012), cover-ups, and even promotion of peer misconduct (Miller 2010; Shernock 2007).

1.2 Statement of the Problem

In addition to research about the links between police subculture and police misconduct, empirical studies have been conducted to investigate how the police subculture affects the way that police officers think and behave (Chan 2000; Novak et al. 2005; O'Loughlin and Billing 2000; Sever 2008; Terrill et al. 2003). Due to the powerful influence of the police subculture on police perceptions and behaviour, researchers have realised the importance of conducting studies about improving police performance and enhancing police accountability through the perspective of a positive police subculture. However, although a number of academic publications have appeared, police cultural studies are characterised by little consensus. Due to the complex and intangible nature of police culture, studies in this area tend to include various "definitions, methodologies, disciplinary orientations and focuses" with little consistency (Cockcroft 2013, p. 1).

1.2.1 In the West

Since the initial development of studies on police culture, researchers have made their contributions to describe a monolithic police subculture that is formed through the occupational socialisation in the police career (Paoline 2003; Terrill et al. 2003). From the classic description of police officers' "working personality" by Skolnick, to Crank's detailed analysis of more than twenty police cultural themes that characterised the concept of police, a focus has been placed on the shared components of police perceptions in a working environment with embedded uncertainties and risks (Crank 2004; Skolnick 1986). However, as police cultural studies develop, some researchers have begun to question the traditional monolithic description. Instead, studies have been conducted from the perspective of variations due to the specific characteristics of different organisations, police ranks, and individual factors (Brown 1981; Chan 1996; Paoline 2001, 2003, 2004; Reiner 1985; Waddington 1999a). Chan and colleagues have made a comprehensive criticism of the monolithic approach by emphasising the changing nature of the police culture (Chan 1996; Chan et al. 2003). When the traditional monolithic description of police culture tends to be marginalised and replaced by a new group of studies that emphasise changes and variations, some recent studies indicated that some key components of the traditional police culture remain untouched in modern policing and continue to exert great influence on police conduct and attitudes (Loftus 2010; Paoline and Terrill 2014; Skolnick 2008). The lack of agreement encourages more empirical research in the field of police cultural studies.

1.2.2 In China

Most of the existing literature about police culture was developed in the 20th century in the context of English-speaking countries (Loyens 2009). Although similarities in police subcultural perceptions might be expected due to the same working conditions, such as similarities between roles, functions, and relationships between police and the community impacting on occupational culture, different social cultural backgrounds may also generate variations. Therefore, as Loyens (2009) stated, more studies are still needed in the context of non-English-speaking countries. China is among those countries in which few empirical studies have been conducted to explore police subcultural perceptions. In the whole area of policing studies, Chinese policing research is a "much neglected field of study" (Wong 2007, p. 112). Therefore, due to the lack of scientific studies, there are insufficient contributions that could be generated, either theoretically or practically, from the literature for police reform (Wong 2009c).

Western researchers have widely discussed the negative influence of the police subculture on the successful implementation of community-oriented policing, such as the us versus them mentality, the top-down command structure, the crime-fighting image, and the trained craft of suspicious and cynical attitudes (Miller et al. 2014; Palmiotto 2011; Skolnick and Bayley 1988). Whether, and to what extent, these cultural perceptions will be evidenced among Chinese frontline police officers is not known. Empirical studies are needed to provide answers including the implications for future policies.

Different social structures and cultural backgrounds may breed different police subcultural characteristics. Chinese police officers are far less professional than their counterparts in the United States or other Western countries because they often regard themselves as moral authorities rather than law enforcement authorities (Jiao 2001a). This is partly due to the influence of Chinese traditional culture which emphasises moral principles rather than laws and regulations and emphasises collectivism rather than individualism (Jiao 2001b). It is suggested that most Chinese police officers are less cynical because they regard themselves as a part of the community and tend to socialise with community members; however, some are very cynical and suspicious toward citizens (Jiao 2001a). In addition, Chinese police officers are considered to be less conservative compared with American police officers but as authoritarian as them (Jiao 2001a). However, most of these comments about the police culture in China are not based on empirical studies. Wong (2007) summarised several obstacles for Western-based studies about Chinese policing, these being "a lack of research interest, resource, facility, access and secrecy" (p. 112). It is not an easy job for outsiders to get access to information or practitioners for surveying in the field of policing in China (Wong 2007). Within China, policing studies has just been developed since 2011 as an independent discipline under the name of public security studies by the Ministry of Education in China (Yuan 2012). Police studies are still in their preliminary stage with few systematic and scientific investigations (Wong 2009c).

In fact, most of the descriptions of police subculture in China remain at the level of theoretical or prescriptive statements, with few empirical and descriptive research studies having been conducted to explore what kind of subculture Chinese officers adhere to and to what extent they adhere to it. Studies of police subculture in China bear specific Chinese characteristics. They are focused on police team construction and promotion of police qualities (Cai and Liu 2011; Guo 2011; Ye 2011; Zhang 1993, 2007). Most theoretical studies of this type aim to develop macro-guidelines to establish a positive police culture. According to searches I have conducted within the two largest academic databases in China (CNKI and Wanfangdata), until early 2015, little empirical research was available on this subject. The differences of research focus between China and the West result from the contrasting social and cultural backgrounds (Zhang 1997). Some scholars in China have realized the necessity to apply the Western research of police subculture to help identify Chinese police culture and solve Chinese problems (Lin 2008; Yu 2011). Until now, the empirical research about police officers' cultural perceptions and whether or to what extent they adhere to the Western police subculture remains scarce.

1.3 Purpose of the Study

In this study, I intend to contribute to the growing knowledge of police subculture in China. Therefore, I made an empirical inquiry about subcultural perceptions among a sample of Chinese frontline police officers through a quantitative survey. As Schein (2004) claimed, "Determining which sets of assumptions apply to a whole society, or a whole organization, or a whole subgroup within an organization or occupation, should be done empirically" (p. 21). The research questionnaire in this study was designed on the basis of two existing research instruments that were developed and used by Western scholars within the theoretical framework of police occupational culture studies in the West (Cochran and Bromley 2003; Steyn 2007).

Justification for why the researcher intends to outline police subcultural perceptions of Chinese frontline police officers on the basis of the criteria and research instrument developed in the Western countries can be summarized in two points. First of all, studies of police culture in China are in the preliminary phase. Some scholars who are interested in policing studies have tried to construct the aims and the scope of police culture studies in China (Cai and Liu 2011; Guo 2011; Lin 2008; Ye 2011; Zhang 1993, 1997, 2007). They have realized the influence of police culture on morale and the overall effectiveness of the police force. However, few theoretical frameworks have been constructed and few empirical studies have been conducted to investigate police cultural perceptions in China. Therefore, the researcher conducted an exploratory study among Chinese frontline police officers on the basis of existing literature in the West. Secondly, although there are great differences between China and western countries in terms of social, political and cultural systems, frontline police officers as members of a unique occupational group, do face similar risks and challenges when they engage in law enforcement and community policing services for the public. Some key components of the police subculture have already been identified in countries of different social and political ideologies (Ernest and Arvind 2008). The study of Chinese police subculture using criteria of the West may provide a basis of comparative analysis of the similarities and variations between socialist China and the West. In addition, this study may also serve as the reference for designing specific research instrument and scales for Chinese police officers in further studies.

The main purposes of this study are threefold. First of all, I intend to gain a descriptive overview of subcultural perceptions among a sample of Chinese frontline police officers. Descriptive statistics should be able to provide an understanding of whether there is a widespread adherence to the key characteristics of the Western police subculture among Chinese frontline police officers. Findings in this study may also provide information for the academic development of Chinese police culture as an independent area of study.

Second, I attempt to find out whether a relationship exists between some individual and work-related characteristics and officers' adherence to police subculture. These demographic and work-related variables that I have chosen to investigate are age, gender, educational experience, tenure, type of police force, and being detectives or not. The findings of the potential correlations may provide some interpretations to police occupational attitudes.

Finally, the relations among these major cultural themes are also to be explored in this study. For instance, I aim to identify the correlations between police role orientations and other cultural themes such as solidarity, cynicism, isolation, traditionalism, and receptivity to change. The results of this analysis may provide evidence for the subcultural influence upon police role orientations and vice versa. Further implications could be derived from the findings to improve police training and administration for a better cultural environment that facilitates community policing and police performance.

1.4 Research Questions

The following research questions have been developed to explore police subcultural perceptions in China.

- Is there a widespread adherence to the police subculture suggested in the Western literature among Chinese frontline police officers?
- Among Chinese frontline police officers, are some demographic and work-related variables associated with police subcultural perceptions?
- For Chinese frontline police officers, are there significant relationships among the seven police subcultural themes suggested in Western literature?

1.5 Significance of the Study

1.5.1 Academic Significance

This study has potential to contribute to the knowledge of police subculture in China. Although the topic of police culture has been intensively discussed in the West, little empirical research has been conducted in China. As Wong (2009a) pointed out, the knowledge about Chinese policing is "sketchy, spotty, and superficial" and what is more needed is "reliable data than critical opinions" (pp. 1, 9). He further explained the status quo of policing studies in China through the much cited statement: "Everyone is entitled to his own opinions but not his own facts" by Daniel Patrick (Wong 2007, p. 121). For Sun and Wu (2010), one of the most obvious limitations of policing studies in China is the lack of empirical studies. There are remarkable differences between oriental China and the Western countries in the field of history, culture, politics, economy, and way of thinking. Most of our knowledge about police subculture is based on studies conducted in English-speaking countries (Loyens 2009). It is therefore worthwhile to extend our understanding about police perceptions in China and how Western findings in terms of police culture could be supported in the context of Chinese policing.

1.5.2 Practical Significance

The significance of this study also rests on the intangible power of police culture upon police attitudes, behaviour, and performance. Just as Sparrow, Moore, and Kennedy (1990) mentioned in their work, a key task of modern policing is to create a "more honorable, more realistic, and more productive" police culture (pp. 53–54). In addition, the reason that both academics and practitioners are unlikely to neglect cultural influence is due to the potential negative effects that have been discussed widely.

The police subculture suggested in the Western literature includes a strong orientation toward crime-fighting and negative attitudes about restrictions from legal institutions, police administrations, and the citizenry (Cochran and Bromley 2003). These attitudes may lead to police misconduct such as abuse of authority, illegitimate use of force, and selective enforcement (Armacost 2003; Corsianos 2012; Mollen et al. 1994; Wood 1997). Therefore, finding out whether and to what extent Chinese frontline police officers adhere to these characteristics of police subculture may help police administrators make improvements to prevent police misconduct from the perspective of police culture. The implications of this study are also important for leaders in police training departments and government agencies as they attempt to initiate reforms in police organisations. In addition, this study may provide valuable information for the successful implementation of community policing in China.

The concept of community policing was developed in the 1970s in the USA in order to "involve and engage the public" to assist in crime control and create a high standard of policing service and a better police-citizen relationship (Wong 2009b, p. 216). In 2002, the Chinese Ministry of Public Security and Ministry of Civil Affairs jointly promulgated *the Notice of on Strengthening the Construction of Community Policing* (MPS 2002). This represented the official launch of community policing in China. Different from the community policing in the USA, Chinese community police officers are assigned to neighbourhood committees as a relative stable way to deal with local affairs (Sun et al. 2009; Zhong 2009). The adoption of community policing aims to reinforce the relationship between police officers and neighbourhood committees to improve the function of social service. The adoption of community policing in China requires more cooperation from the public and higher levels of accountability and transparency of the police force (Palmiotto 2011). However, many core characteristics of traditional police subculture promote a cynical and negative attitude toward the public and help to strengthen the us versus them mentality between police and community members, such as protective solidarity, a code of silence, craft of suspicion, etc. (Cochran and Bromley 2003). For example, the more police officers stick to internal solidarity among officers, the more they feel isolated from the public; the more cynical and suspicious police officers become, and the worse their relationships with the citizens who should be served and protected by the police are. These may cause more tensions between police and the public. Studies have indicated that Chinese citizens have less trust for police than do their counterparts in the USA (Cao and Hou 2001). In addition, scholars who are interested in policing in China contend that Chinese police-citizen relationships need to be improved (Wu et al. 2011; Wu and Sun 2009). Although there is no widely agreed definition of community policing, a good police-community partnership and efforts and abilities to solve problems and provide service for the community are necessary (Brown 2014; Palmiotto 2011). The results from this study may provide an overall understanding of cultural attitudes among the sample of Chinese frontline police officers. Based on this, we may identify to what extent Chinese officers hold the corresponding attributes that are in line with the requirements of community policing and what negative cultural perceptions impede this process. For instance, results may help us to investigate to what extend Chinese frontline police officers adhere to the role orientation of service, and to what extent they are cynical and isolated from the public. Further suggestions could be made about improving police-citizen relationships and promoting the implementation of community policing from the perspective of a positive police culture.

1.6 Organisation of the Remainder of the Study

The next eight chapters contain the relevant literature, the methods used to conduct the study, the results of various analyses, a discussion of the findings, and conclusions of the study. Chapter 2 briefly introduces the theoretical context of this study: organisational culture and occupational culture. Chapter 3 provides a brief introduction of Chinese policing and how police subculture is closely connected with the successful transfer toward the community policing philosophy in China. Then, a review of police cultural studies and studies on several core cultural themes that form the foundations of the current study are presented in Chap. 4. Some demographic and work-related factors that have the potential to influence police perceptions are also discussed. Finally, a brief introduction of Chinese police cultural studies is provided in Chap. 5. Chapter 6 addresses the research questions, the research design, the survey instrument, the sampling method, an outline of data collection procedures, and the data analysis plan. Chapter 7 contains a description of the data used and the results in the current study. The statistical tests used in the five stages of data analysis and the corresponding results are provided in detail. In Chap. 8, discussions of the results for each of the research questions are presented in detail. Finally, Chap. 9 provides conclusions related to the key findings in this study; the implications and recommendations for police administrators, practitioners, and researchers; and the limitations of this research.

1.7 Summary

Scholars in the West have long noticed the influence of subculture on police perceptions and behaviour and conducted sizable studies to examine the intangible myth. However, along with social developments, there has been an increase of demographic diversity in the police force. According to some scholars, this demographic diversification could bring new characteristics to the traditional police subculture (Chan 1997; Paoline 2003). Other scholars contend that some key themes of police culture indeed remain unchanged because the nature of uncertainties embedded in policing work and the pressures related to the police role remain intact (Corsianos 2012; Loftus 2010). In China, policing studies are in the preliminary stage with few empirical studies having been conducted. Therefore, I intend to contribute to the existing knowledge of police subculture in China. I made an empirical inquiry on subcultural perceptions among a sample of Chinese frontline police officers through a quantitative survey. Based on the results of this study, policy suggestions could be made for improving police-citizen relationships and promoting the implementation of community policing from the perspective of a positive police culture. The next chapter introduces the theoretical context of this study: organisational culture and occupational culture. It begins with the origin of the concept of culture in the field of anthropology and sociology, followed by a specific context for this study—organisational culture and occupational subculture. After addressing the definition and components of occupational subculture, I focus on the forming of the abstract shared group of values in the same career—occupational socialisation.

Chapter 2
Theoretical Context: Organisational Culture and Occupational Culture

Research about police culture has been driven and theoretically supported by studies of sociologists that aim to comprehend police behaviour through the lens of the organisational culture perspective (Cockcroft 2013). Under the organisational culture approach, the cultural factors that influence the way that people think and behave is investigated and interpreted so that the "hidden and complex aspects of life in groups, organisations, and occupations" can be better understood (Schein 2004, p. 9). Although researchers using an organisational culture approach tend to emphasise culture within the boundary of organisations or departments (Paoline 2001), cultural phenomena in occupations could also be explained by this approach. This is because both organisational and occupational cultures are formed on the basis of shared history of members as ways to cope with outside pressures (Paoline 2001; Schein 2004; Trice and Beyer 1993). In police cultural studies, the concepts of organisational culture and occupational culture have been interchangeably used by academics (Bacon 2014; Cockcroft 2013, p. 16; Paoline and Terrill 2014, p. 4). In the classic work *Organizational Culture and Leadership* by leading sociologist Edgar Schein, he explained cultural phenomena at the level of groups, organisations, and occupations through the theoretical framework of organisational culture (Schein 2004). In this study, I have made an empirical inquiry of police subculture in China through the theoretical context of organisational culture and occupational culture.

2.1 The Concept of Culture and Subculture

The concept of culture was first developed by anthropologists toward the end of the 19th century (Haviland 1999). Tylor (1871) offered the first "clear and comprehensive" (Haviland 1999, p. 36) definition of culture as "that complex whole which includes knowledge, belief, art, morals, law, custom, and any other capabilities and habits acquired by man as a member of society" (p. 1). Early anthropologists and sociologists have explained the concept of culture as a collection of learned aspects that may symbolise the realm of human beings (Jenks 2005,

Z. Chen, *Measuring Police Subcultural Perceptions*,
DOI 10.1007/978-981-10-0096-6_2

pp. 8–9). Cultural studies from the perspective of sociology and anthropology now consider culture as "the whole way of life of a people" (Jenks 2005, p. 12).

For early anthropologists, culture was considered to be a specific construct embedded in human behaviour instead of that of other creatures (Jenks 2005, p. 9). Clifford Geertz (1973), a noted anthropologist, made a widely-cited description of the concept of culture:

> Believing, with Max Weber, that man is an animal suspended in webs of significance he himself has spun, I take culture to be those webs, and the analysis of it to be therefore not an experimental science in search of law but an interpretive one in search of meaning (p. 5).

This description not only addressed the human-specific nature of culture, but also emphasised its function of providing meaning for people's life and behaviour. Sociologists often use this description to assist their studies of culture (Jenks 2005).

For sociology, culture is regarded as "everything that is socially learned and shared by a group of people in a society" (Chalfant and LaBeff 1988, p. 28). Brinkerhoff and White (1988) defined culture as "the total way of life shared by members of a society. It includes not only language, values, and symbolic meanings but also technology and material objects" (p. 58). From this point of view, researchers in sociology divided the components into two types: material and nonmaterial. Material culture refers to physical objects or artefacts created by human beings, such as buildings, automobiles, tools, clothing, paintings, books, factories, and schools; nonmaterial culture refers to abstract creations such as ideas, values, beliefs, languages, norms, symbols, and customs (Robertson 1989; Theodorson and Theodorson 1990; Vander Zanden 1996). Everything produced in a society is included in the concept of culture. Culture determines our beliefs about what is important in life and it shapes our interpretations of what events mean and what our experiences mean (Knox 1990). Crank (2004) explained clearly how behaviour and perceptions can be justified through the "lens" of culture:

> Culture is how we act out our morals and social identities—it carries the values we bring to bear on what we see, our behaviors, and is present in the categories through which we organize the world seen and imagined. It is the implicit assumptions we make, and it is in the hidden edges and implicit meanings of the metaphors we use and take for granted. Culture is carried within us, not a thing set apart and reified from social action. … We share our thoughts, therefore culture exists. We act out our shared thoughts in self-fulfilling behaviors, and culture is confirmed (p. 3).

In addition, culture has been regarded as a way in which group members try to cope with shared problems and uncertainties, including how to survive and how to adapt to the environment and peers (Chalfant and LaBeff 1988; Trice and Beyer 1993). This is realised through the acquisition of appropriate norms, values, and beliefs that could be accepted within the culture (Trice and Beyer 1993).

Different scholars have offered opinions from different points of view. However, they did portray culture as a complex whole that is learned through interaction among people of a society, an organisation, or an occupation to cope with risks, uncertainties, and other embedded factors of the working environment that they have to deal with.

According to Theodorson and Theodorson (1990, p. 59), "variations among groups within a society are known as subcultures". Subcultures are part of the bigger social culture, but they are different from the social culture in many respects (Knox 1990). Members of a subculture embody the overall social culture but also share a number of distinctive values, norms, and lifestyles. They not only identify with their specific groups but also interact with other groups and the dominant culture (Calhoun et al. 1994, p. 63). Subcultures may be formed among people of the same occupation. The distinctive values, norms, lifestyles, and even slang language of the occupation unite group members and set them apart from the rest of the community (Chalfant and LaBeff 1988). From this perspective, police subculture refers to the cultural perceptions shared by police officers because of their shared working experience. Although officers share specific subcultural perceptions, they are also members of the whole society. They also embody the wider social cultural characteristics. For example, Chinese police officers were considered to be less cynical than their American counterparts due to the influence of Chinese traditional culture that values collective interests more than individual interest (Jiao 2001a). However, the two terms, namely, police subculture and police culture, are frequently used interchangeably. In this case, police culture indeed refers to the subculture of police.

2.2 Organisational Culture

As an important theoretical perspective of organisational studies, the history of organisational culture or organisational climate research can be traced back to the 1940s (Schein 1990) and has flourished since the 1980s (Hartnell et al. 2011; Ott 1989). Researchers have sought to find explanations through the new way of understanding organisations. The organisational school attempts to explain the phenomenon of organisational functioning and the behaviour and perceptions of the members of the organisation through new insights based on the assumptions about organisations and people (Shafritz and Ott 1987, p. 373). It is regarded to be a way in which researchers can probe into people's behaviour in an organisation as well as a metaphor for understanding human constructs within organisations (Smircich 1983). The study of organisational culture provides refreshing concepts to better understand existing knowledge about the way in which organisations operate as living entities. While traditional organisational theories tend to focus more on "systemic and structural issues" of an organisation, the cultural perspective is more interested in the "values, attitudes and beliefs" of members in the organisation and provides justifications for how people behave in an organisation (Modaff and DeWine 2002, p. 83).

Many scholars have contributed to the conceptualisation of organisational culture (Barley 1983, p. 393; Pettigrew 1979, p. 574; Sathe 1983, p. 6; Schein 1990, p. 111; Wilkins and Dyer 1988, p. 523). Schein (2004) offered the following definition that includes a relatively complete integration of the shared components:

> [Organisational culture is] a pattern of shared basic assumptions that was learned by a group as it solved its problems of external adaptation and internal integration, that has worked well enough to be considered valid and, therefore, to be taught to new members as the correct way to perceive, think, and feel in relation to those problems (p. 17).

From this definition, the core components are the learning process through shared experience, the socialisation process to pass on to newcomers, the defensive functions to cope with internal and external problems, and the accepted ways of behaviour and perceptions. These elements could be expanded to cultures of groups beyond the boundary of organisations, such as occupations. Schein goes on to explain that this definition needs to be fully understood with the help of several other "critical elements": "structural stability", "depth", "breadth", and "patterning or integration" (pp. 14–15). Structural stability means that the cultural assumptions shared by group members are stable and difficult to change once they are formed; depth refers to intangible power of cultures that usually functions unconsciously; breadth includes all aspects of group operations; and patterning or integration is vital to the concept of culture in that it ties all the elements in the group together as a "coherent whole" (Schein 2004, p. 15).

For Schein (2004), there are three levels of culture: artefacts, espoused beliefs and values, and underlying assumptions (p. 26). Artefacts include the organisational objects that can be visually identified, such as language, folklore, products, ceremonies, and clothes; espoused beliefs and values represent the articulated beliefs, norms, and values that group members use to express their culture including associations to the observable manifestations that may also finally become absorbed into the deepest level of culture; underlying assumptions are the deeper level of beliefs and perceptions that are unconsciously embedded and constitute the essence of culture (Schein 2004, pp. 25–26). These components of organisational culture would provide the justification for people's perceptions and behaviour (Sathe 1985, p. 10). These three levels of culture are closely connected with each other. For example, physical artefacts, such as uniforms or jargon, may symbolise some special meaning or metaphor for members of an organisation and these explanations are usually hard to be inferred only on the basis of the physical items. Articulated beliefs and values guide group members concerning how to behave and deal with certain problems that they may encounter. Some of these beliefs and values may eventually become taken for granted after being tested for a long period of time. Then they become the nondebatable assumptions that are abided by members unconsciously, justifying the way people think and behave.

These cultural elements continue to influence people's behaviour and perceptions to the extent that members of the organisation accept these cultural norms, values, beliefs and assumptions in an unconscious manner (Shafritz and Ott 1987, p. 374). In addition, these behaviour-shaping assumptions will also serve as a tool of integration, linking people into the social group (Louis 1987, p. 424). In the sociological context, organisation members are socialised with ways to communicate with other members and deal with outsiders; in the psychological context, individuals interact with social ideals, which will be individualised to guide their perceptions and behaviour (Louis 1987, pp. 424–425). Ott (1989) provided a widely-accepted functional definition of organisational culture as "a social force that controls patterns of organizational behavior by shaping members' cognitions and perceptions of meanings and realities, providing affective energy for mobilization, and identifying who belongs and who does not" (p. 69). However, there are both formal and informal socialisation processes for newcomers to be accepted as full members. Through formal socialisation, the "espoused beliefs and values" are formally taught to newcomers; the deeper level of culture, namely, the "underlying assumptions", will be revealed to only those members who have been acknowledged as insiders through informal field activities (Schein 2004, p. 26). In addition, organisational culture also serves as "psychological cognitive defense mechanisms" for group members to continue working with less anxiety (Schein 2004, p. 32).

These theoretical discussions of organisational culture are not limited within organisations. Cultural phenomena in occupations also fit well into the framework of organisational culture. Occupational culture researchers emphasise the culture developed through "social interaction, shared experience, common training and affiliation, mutual support, associated values and norms, and similar personal characteristics of members" of a certain vocation (Johnson et al. 2009, p. 320).

Literature depicts the existence of some essential features of the police subculture among police officers across police agencies. The components include a cynical attitude, traditionalism, siege mentality, isolation from the public, solidarity, authoritarianism, pragmatism etc. (Crank 2004; Herbert 1998; Loftus 2010; Reiner 2010; Skolnick 1986). However, the forming of the occupational culture is "shaped" by structural characteristics of police organisations. For example, the traditional central command structure and the paramilitary strict rules strengthen the crime-fighter role orientation and limit any attempts to implement change or innovation (Kraska 2007; Roberg et al. 2009). Manning (2007a) summarised several structural features that influence police occupational culture: inspectorial strategy of policing with minimal supervision, the special information distribution system with most information not widely publicised, the nature of policing with high risk and danger, police operations that are suffused with secrecy, and the "bottom-entry socialization" that makes it not easy to be promoted (p. 47). All of these features of police organisations are closely associated with the cultural norms within the occupation. The style of patrol with little outside supervision facilitates the code of secrecy, the downward chains of information and command may foster a paramilitary and traditional view towards police work, and the working environment featured with danger and uncertainty makes peers united and loyal to each other. Therefore, the formation of a police occupational culture cannot be separated from the bureaucratic, rule-oriented, hierarchical structure of police organisations (Manning 2007a, p. 52).

In addition, the police occupational subculture is consistent with the main components of the concept of organisational culture explained by Schein. Formed through the shared experience within the career of policing, widely accepted norms and values are created among police officers against the risks and uncertainties embedded in the nature of police work. The articulated rules of conduct and professional skills, together with the tacitly agreed forms of behaviour, are transmitted to newcomers through formal and informal socialisation at police academies and field operations by instructors and veteran officers (Corsianos 2012; Ford 2003). Besides the formal training of law enforcement techniques and procedures, police culture—the informal acquisition of norms, values, and behaviour tends to have more enduring importance (Van Maanen 1975). Whether a new police officer has gained the full membership of an insider could also be tested through the degree to which he or she has been equipped with the subcultural norms of police. The shared cultural influence of the police profession not only provides justification for police behaviour and attitudes at work, but also exerts an impact on their everyday life and social communications (Lindsey et al. 2012).

2.3 Occupational Culture

According to Trice and Beyer (1993, p. 179), "occupations are cultural entities". It is through the social interactions among people doing similar work that occupations come into being (Trice and Beyer 1993). People doing like tasks form occupational groups and develop common ways of dealing with pressures embedded in the vocation (Trice and Beyer 1993). Group members believe that the pressures and uncertainties mainly come from the world outside their occupation. Based on the similar work experiences and accumulated knowledge of the occupation, some widely accepted norms and values are formed among members of the occupational group. Everyone within the group needs to feel secure and to identify as a member within the group. It is the occupational culture that unites people together on a basis of both practical and emotional needs. Manning (2007b) has provided the following definition of occupational culture:

> An occupational culture is a means for coping with the vicissitudes or uncertainties arising routinely in the course of doing a job. An occupational culture is a reduced, selective, and task-based version of culture that includes history and traditions, etiquette and routines, rules, principles, and practices that serve to buffer practitioners from contacts with the public. A kind of lens on the world, it highlights some aspects of the social and physical environment and omits or minimizes others. It generates stories, lore, and legends (p. 865).

Trice (1993) summarised seven forces that promote the formation of occupational culture and "facilitate group identity" among members: "(1) esoteric knowledge and expertise, (2) extreme or unusual demands, (3) consciousness of kind, (4) pervasiveness, (5) favourable self-image and social value in tasks, (6) primary reference group, and (7) abundance of cultural forms" (pp. 26–41).

Police occupational culture, the unique cultural orientation shared by police officers, conforms to these seven characteristics to a great extent. For police officers, the lengthy and formal training process in the police academy and the learning of "real" police work in the field include rich information about the skills of police work, the expected way of dealing with work and getting along with peers, and other intangible norms within police subculture. It is the actual possession of the skills, knowledge, capabilities, and informal norms that induct police recruits into the world of police officers. An outsider will become an insider only when he or she meets all the formal and informal requirements that are defined by the occupational culture. In addition, in a profession with embedded danger and uncertainty, unusual demands are imposed on police officers. In order to cope with danger, uncertainties, and moral dilemmas, police officers need to relieve pressure through accepted ways of behaving within the organisation. The cynical attitude toward the public and the us versus them worldview are gradually formed as a result of the process of dealing with outside risks and danger and the stress they encountered because of the police work (Nhan 2014; Rivera-Vazquez 2014). The more that members learn how to deal with the demands, the more distinctive they regard themselves (Trice 1993, p. 29). The police identity sometimes even intrudes into their private lives. For example, officers may take the trained craft of suspicion beyond the professional context, and this may cause unpleasant feelings among family members or friends (Crank 2004). The rich cultural forms of police profession help to unite police officers as a cohesive occupational group, such as the cop jargon, the arduous process from police recruits to "real" police officers, the high commitment to loyalty, and solidarity within the police group.

2.4 Occupational Socialisation

Researchers who are interested in occupations and professions have tried to explain how an occupational culture could influence attitudes, personality, and behaviour of its members. In fact, the influences between occupational culture and occupational members are mutual, especially when newcomers keep coming in and are being socialised. The transmission of knowledge and values provides novices with cultural understandings of the occupation. However, newcomers will also bring their contributions to the existing occupational culture when they receive the socialisation.

Transmission of cultural perceptions from existing members to newcomers is realised in the process of socialisation, which is "one of the most central to the field of sociology" (Pavalko 1971, p. 80). According to Corsianos (2012), socialisation is so important that "people cannot mature intellectually, socially, emotionally, and psychologically" without it (p. 60). In sociology, socialisation refers to the process by which "people acquire the knowledge, attitudes, values, and behaviour essential for effective participation in society" (Vander Zanden 1996, p. 68). This definition shows clearly that group-expected perceptions are gained through social context. Some other definitions further explained the nature of socialisation and transmission of culture. Merton et al. (1957) stated that socialisation is "… the process by which people selectively acquire the values and attitudes, the interests, skills and knowledge—in short, the culture—current in the groups to which they are, or seek to become, a member" (p. 287). Trice and Beyer (1993) defined socialisation as "the process by which persons are inculcated with the substance and forms of a culture" (p. 129). Although the concept of socialisation has been applied to childhood socialisation to a large extent, it could also be useful for the whole lifetime to explain how adults acquire cultural essentials of a specific organisation or occupation, namely, organisational socialisation or occupational socialisation. According to Chan et al. (2003), socialisation is "the process through which a novice learns the skills, knowledge, and values necessary to become a competent member of an organisation or occupation" (p. 3). Sociologists are now more and more interested in occupational socialisation because they want to find out the relationship between occupational culture and effectiveness of employees (Calhoun et al. 1994).

When a person becomes a member of an occupation or an organisation, he or she will be required to know the anticipated way of thinking, behaving, and interacting with other members. In other words, the person will be socialised as a member of the occupation. Occupational socialisation is defined as "the process by which one generation passes on to another the technical knowledge, ideologies, and expected behaviour deemed necessary to perform an occupational role" (Trice 1993, p. 114). Socialisation to an occupation equips a person with

> not only specific job-related skills but also a set of values and ethics that applies to a person's work, the unofficial rules of the workplace that the person is entering, and knowledge of the ways that people in the organization are expected to relate to one another depending on their statuses and roles (Calhoun et al. 1994, p. 122).

Occupational socialisation is a process by which newcomers interact with members of the occupation and the occupational culture. In the process, some personalities of newcomers would be shaped to some extent by the occupation; at the same time, new tendencies may also be brought into the existing ideologies (Trice 1993). This is especially true for professions in which members are actively engaged in the socialisation, such as police officers and doctors. Police recruits need to spend much time and energy to pass the training in the academy and be accepted as a member of police in the field. Therefore, in the socialisation process, the interaction between police recruits and the occupational culture may have a lasting impression on both sides.

To be a member of an occupational culture, a newcomer has to go through the process of socialisation which is made up of formal socialisation and informal socialisation (Trice 1993; Van Maanen and Schein 1979). Formal socialisation is usually carried out through specifically designed training for novices themselves to let them know the "correct" way of thinking and behaving (Van Maanen and Schein 1979, pp. 44–45). For example, police recruits are required to attend the lengthy formal training in a police academy although they may consider it to be irrelevant from real police work (Van Maanen and Schein 1979, p. 45). Informal socialisation allows newcomers to learn the "local knowledge" and the widely shared informal norms through unplanned settings (Trice 1993, p. 128; Van Maanen and Schein 1979, p. 44). Learning through informal socialisation is so important for police recruits because many inside understandings could be gained only with the help of veteran officers in the field. According to a large survey of American police officers, more than 97 % of the respondents agreed that the influence of other officers in their early police career was an important source of information, and more than 87 % of the respondents agreed that most of their policing knowledge was learned "on the job" (Paoline and Terrill 2014, p. 158). During the process of socialisation, new police officers keep learning the appropriate way of doing, thinking, and feeling from insiders because these subcultural elements signify occupational membership as police (Corsianos 2012). Meanwhile, policing observers have also observed how many of the police subcultural themes are brewed in the process of police socialisation. It is suggested that the training in a police academy emphasises a crime control orientation and helps to develop the us versus them mentality among the recruits; field training makes them quickly learn the unwritten working norms and realise the difference between reality and ideal, and cynicism begins to develop (Nhan 2014).

Occupational socialisation is the process through which newcomers learn the accepted norms and values in the occupation, namely, the occupational culture. For police officers, all the behaviours and perceptions need to be understood through the help of the police culture, because the entire police work is conducted through the "lens of police culture", from structures of the organisation to perceptions of police officers, from police operations and practices to ethical decision-making and police training (Crank 2004, p. 3).

From the material presented in this section, the formation of police subculture could be adequately explained within the framework of occupational socialisation theory. Although in this study I do not intend to investigate the process of occupational socialisation, it is also necessary to make the whole theoretical context clear enough to be understood. In order to understand police subculture, it is necessary to understand the whole process of police occupational socialisation, because it is through this combination of formal and informal socialisation that officers learn the expected rules of behaviour and perception that help to cope with uncertainties and unite peers together.

2.5 Summary

In this chapter I have provided an explanation of the theoretical context of this study: organisational culture and occupational culture. Police subculture perceptions were investigated through the perspective of occupational culture because the key themes that constitute the concept of police subculture in this study are formed due to the shared experience of a group of people within the same occupation:

police officers. It is due to the specific working environment that is full of uncertainty and challenges, and the need to cope with the pressures and stress related to the police work, police officers are socialised into this cultural mystery. However, occupational culture could also and has to be theoretically supported by the more developed theoretical context: organisational culture that could be traced back to the theory of organisation. Scholars such as Schein have made thorough explanations about different levels of culture within organisations and occupations as well. In this study, I would like to explore police subcultural perceptions within the contexts of both organisational and occupational culture. In the next chapter, a brief introduction of the history of Chinese policing is discussed, including a brief introduction of police history, police system, police functions, and police strategies in China. In addition, the relationship between community policing and police subculture is also discussed.

Chapter 3
Policing in China

The purpose of this chapter is to address the context of this study, Chinese policing. A brief review of Chinese policing, including the history of policing, the police system, police functions, and police strategies, is discussed, followed by a discussion of the relations between community policing and police culture. This demonstrates why it is necessary to investigate police cultural perceptions in China, namely the need in the nationwide transfer toward the philosophy of community policing.

3.1 Development of Policing Strategies in China

According to Zhong (2009), the history of Chinese policing since 1949 can be divided into three periods: mass-line policing (1949–1980), strike-hard policing (1981–2001), and community policing (since 2002). In accordance with the three periods, different strategies were adopted as the principles of policing.

The main policy of policing in the first period is embodied in the idea of "for the masses, relying on the masses, from the masses and to the masses" which focuses on the mobilisation of the masses and gaining the support of the masses (Zhong 2009, p. 158). However, the main police functions such as patrol, crime prevention, and crime reporting and recording systems, were far from well-established during this period (Sun et al. 2009). In the first 30 years after the founding of the PRC, the fundamental policing strategy was the mass-line (Sun and Wu 2010; Wang and Wong 2012; Zhong 2009). The mass-line was introduced by Mao Zedong in 1943 as a communist ideology that emphasised the importance of listening to the masses, mobilising the masses, relying on the masses, and providing service for the masses (Wong 2009a). In the field of policing, as Wong (2009a) commented, the mass-line was considered to be "an ideological postulate, a revolutionary perspective, a mission statement, a leadership style, an organizational method, and an operational principle" (p. 191). The deep influence of mass-line principle in policing is also embodied in the naming of the police in China as

Z. Chen, *Measuring Police Subcultural Perceptions*,
DOI 10.1007/978-981-10-0096 6_3

People's Police. The relationship between people and the police was described as that between fish and water, indicating that the police would not succeed without the support of the masses. Within the framework of mass-line policing, the police performed law enforcement on the basis of a tight household registration system and some local mechanisms such as neighbourhood committees and workplace security units (Ma 2008; Sun and Wu 2010). The household registration system reduced residential mobility to the minimum, functioning as a surveillance network that promoted stability, conformity, and homogeneity in communities (Wang and Wong 2012; Zhong 2009). Besides the household registration system, the police were supported by neighbourhood committees set up in communities and security units set up in workplaces. Neighbourhood committees performed functions in nearly all the neighbourhood level aspects concerning residents' well-being. From the perspective of public security, neighbourhood committees could identify clues related to potential crimes on the basis of informal patrols, remind residents of potential crimes, and meditate disputes among residents (Ma 2008). In addition, workplace security units which were set up in all major work units were responsible for keeping security within the work unit and assisting the police with unit-related crimes. With the help of the household registration system, police officers had very close relations with local residents and they were responsible for much more than law enforcement. The police-citizen relationship was very good because police officers devoted themselves to the needs of citizens and citizens expected officers to participate in various aspects of their community life (Wang and Wong 2012; Zhong 2009).

Since the founding of the People's Republic of China in 1949, one of the main functions of the police was to oppress counterrevolutionary activities in order to consolidate the communist rule of the country. The police were actively involved in the support of communist mass political movements and suppression of the other side, the supporters of the nationalist party (Sun and Wu 2010). The police were far from a professional team of law enforcement as seen in Western countries, as the backbone of policing, systematic patrol, did not exist in China during the period of mass-line policing (Ma 2008). Although the Constitution and police regulations were established in the 1950s, the 10 year Cultural Revolution (1966–1976) almost changed all of China into a lawless state. Due to the decision of Chairman Mao, the newly established legal and criminal justice system in China was severely damaged and the whole society was controlled under the rule of man instead of rule of law in order to serve the aim of the Cultural Revolution (Sun and Wu 2010).

Along with the adoption of the opening-up policy and economic reform in 1978, China experienced a rapid increase in crime (Sun and Wu 2010; Zhong 2009). The practices of policing under the principle of mass-line gradually lost its effectiveness because the original geographic static structure of population was altered by an increase of population mobility from rural areas to urban areas in the new social economic environment. In addition, it became much more difficult than before to mobilise people to provide evidence for crime prevention and detection because of deterioration of police-citizen relationships (Wang and Wong 2012).

Therefore, the Chinese government began to adopt campaign-style policing by launching a series of strike-hard campaigns in order to reduce the rising crime rate. Particular types of crime became the target of this campaign. These were corruption, prostitution, pornography, drug offences, and gambling (Dutton and Lee 1993). There were three major campaigns from 1978 to 2002, targeting particular types of crimes for a certain period of time (Liang 2005; Zhong 2009). Liang (2005, p. 391) provided a detailed summary of the three rounds of strike-hard campaigns. The campaign launched in 1983 targeted gang fighting, rape, and hooliganism; the second round, from 1996, focused on armed and violent crimes; the third round was initiated from 2001 with the aim of cracking down on underworld organisations. In addition to the three rounds of strike-hard campaigns, some special operations with specific targets were carried out from 1998 to 2004. These included the special operation towards motor vehicle theft and robbery in 1998, the operation towards trafficking and abduction of women and children in 2000, and the operation towards robbery and looting crimes in 2002 (He 2006).

With regard to the crime control outcomes of the campaigns, statistical data did show some immediate reduction of the crime rate after each campaign, but rebounds always followed to take the crime rate back to its previous levels (Dutton and Lee 1993, p. 323; Liang 2005, pp. 393–394; Trevaskes 2003, p. 287). Many scholars commented on the negative effects of the strategy of campaign-style policing, including ruining the already low level of professionalism in Chinese policing (Dutton and Lee 1993; Ma 2008), worsening the already shortage of police manpower (Dutton and Lee 1993), various forms of police misconduct including the abuse of police authority and excessive punishment (Dutton and Lee 1993; Liang 2005; Trevaskes 2003), and a compromise of legal provisions due to the requirements of the campaigns (Liang 2005; Qu 2005). Some police academics and practitioners in China pointed out that strike-hard campaigns could have been used more effectively if they were under strict control of legal regulations (He 2006; You and Xie 2004). Social scientists analysed the underlying reasons that the campaign-style policing continued to exist despite its crime control effect being questionable. Dutton and Lee (1993) indicated that the main reason came from people's support of the government's willingness to curb crime. According to Trevaskes (2003), the adoption of campaign-style policing embodied the incompetence of government leaders in dealing with the problems accompanying the social and economic change in China. From the perspective of policing styles, strike-hard campaigns have an effect on role orientations of police officers. The role of crime control was emphasised and the role of social service was weakened (Dutton 2000; Wang and Wong 2012). In addition, along with the campaigns, policing in China became more punitive than preventive (Dutton and Lee 1993; Wang and Wong 2012).

Unlike the highly unprofessional policing in the mass-line period, Chinese policing has initiated some important steps toward police professionalisation during the strike-hard period. The Chinese government began to make attempts to bring police operations under the rule of law and regulations. After the devastating Cultural Revolution, the first Criminal Procedural Law was promulgated in 1979, making the police power and authority clear and legitimate for the first time (Ma 2000). In addition, the promulgation of the new police law in 1995 marked monumental progress in the Chinese criminal justice system and the history of Chinese policing. This police law clarifies some important provisions about the police in China, including police functions, powers, obligations, organisation, supervision, and police recruitment and training (Ma 1997; The People's Police Law of People's Republic of China 1995). However, although there was some preliminary progress towards rule of law, there is still a long way to go for a really professional police force in China. In comparison with their Western counterparts, Chinese police officers were granted great power due to the lack of well-written procedural requirements in Chinese laws and the longstanding culture that advocates low respect for the law (Sun and Wu 2010). Following Western police practices, the Chinese police started to establish police routine patrol system and the 110 crime report system in the 1990s, symbolising a move toward police professionalisation (Zhong 2009).

In 2002, the Chinese government began to adopt a community policing policy throughout the country. In contrast to community policing in the USA, Chinese community police officers are assigned to neighbourhood committees as a relatively stable way to deal with local affairs (Sun et al. 2009; Zhong 2009). The adoption of community policing aims to reinforce the relationship between police officers and neighbourhood committees to improve the function of social services. However, some studies suggest that community policing in China is based on a mixture of the ideas of mass-line policing and strike-hard policing (Wong 2009a; Zhong 2009). This implies that the mass principle and the prevention principle are functionally and structurally integrated into the police work in community policing in China (Jiao 2001a, p. 166).

In the era of rapid social and economic development, the Chinese government would like to find an effective policing strategy to adapt to the changing conditions and curb the ascending crime rate. Meanwhile, some Western countries have gained success by reforming traditional policing from a new perspective: community policing, which emphasises the role of people in crime control and crime prevention (Wong 2001). Therefore, Chinese police leaders began to absorb the advantages of Western policing experience to apply to the Chinese context. Since the late 1990s, some major cities in China have begun to adopt community policing as the guiding strategy for law enforcement before the nationwide implementation officially launched by MPS in 2002 (Zhong 2009).

Although there is not a fixed definition or model of community policing in the West, Chinese police practitioners do not find it difficult to follow because of its resemblance to the mass-line in China (Ma 2008; Wong 2009a; Zhong 2009). According to the requirements of MPS, a large group of officers were allocated to field police stations from higher level police departments and urban police bureaus deployed a certain number of community policing officers to communities according to the number of residents in a community (Ma 2008; Sun and Wu 2010). Community policing officers are responsible for a variety of duties that include education about the law, order maintenance, assisting neighbourhood committees in public security duties, and solving problems and emergencies in the community (Ma 2008). Meanwhile, police departments also try to reinforce the role of community service among officers by advocating "serving people wholeheartedly", which is also written in the 1995 People's Police Law and is in accordance with the mass-line. One of the main requirements of community policing is to establish a good police-citizen relationship and enhance public participation and support in policing (Chen 2002).

In China, the informal social control organisations were established since the founding of the PRC, including the neighbourhood committees and the workplace public security units. However, according to Chen (2002, p. 11), these local organisations should be labelled as "quasi-formal" because they are organised by the government on the basis of the Constitution of China. These "quasi-formal" organisations have played an important role in crime prevention and crime detection since the mass-line period. However, some other forms of informal force were believed to ruin the police professionalisation. These include social joint protection teams that were formed to compensate for the shortage of police power during the mass-line period. In order to build a professionalised police force, the Ministry of Public Security abolished the social joint protection teams in 2008 (Zhong 2009). Efforts were also made to establish more regulations for police officers in their law enforcement given that citizens were becoming more aware of their human rights and more sensitive about the legitimacy and appropriateness of police behaviour. The promulgation of *Procedural Regulations for Public Security Organs Handling Administrative Cases* is one of the attempts to put police operations under supervision of clearer rules (Sun and Wu 2010).

However, the image of police did not improve due to more regulations on their behaviour. Media reports and online social networking made police misconduct and abuse of power easy to be publicised and circulated. It is easier to say that a better police-citizen relationship is vital for community policing than to build mutual trust. Some scholars made comparisons between community policing strategies in China and in Western countries, especially the USA (Sun and Wu 2010; Wong 2001; Wu et al. 2011). It has been suggested that there are many shared features between community policing strategies in China and the USA, including a priority of community service, a favourable police-community relationship, a high level of public participation, and a tendency for decentralisation of police authority and decision-making power (Sun and Wu 2010, p. 288). The main difference is that American police play a dominant role with the help of the people while Chinese community policing entails a strong self-policing orientation by community members assisted by the police (Wong 2001, p. 206). Although it is suggested that community policing strategy has experienced a successful beginning (Ma 2008; Wong 2001, pp. 188–189), empirical studies are still needed to determine whether positive outcomes have eventuated (Ma 2008). However, some difficulties have already been raised by scholars and practitioners in the field of policing, including the imbalance of implementation of community policing policies throughout China, the lack of effective evaluation of community policing officer work, an over-involvement of non-policing activities, shortage of manpower of community policing officers, and low level of public participation due to worsened police-community relationships (Liu 2004; Xu 2008).

As Dai (2008) commented, it is rash to say that a policing style is dominant in China because of the occurrence of socioeconomic changes in a short period of time. Different policing strategies could be identified in the form of combinations because of the accumulation of new ideas and the influence of traditional Chinese culture and policing practices (Dai 2008, p. 225). This point is also evidenced in a couple of studies of Chinese policing (Jiao 2001a; Wong 2009a; Zhong 2009). It has been found that contemporary Chinese policing is indeed an integrated combination of police strategies that have been used during the periods of the mass-line and strike-hard campaign under the banner of community policing. Zhong (2009) commented that the community policing practices used in Shenzhen (a city in Guangdong Province) largely resembles those used in mass-line policing in terms of such factors as the underlying guidelines, government financial support, and evaluation methods. The then head of the Criminal Investigation Bureau of the Ministry of Public Security, Ting He (2006), officially stated that the Chinese police should continue implementing the strike-hard measures on the basis of obeying laws, human rights requirements, and scientific evaluation system. In 2010, the Ministry of Public Security started the fourth round of strike-hard campaigns, which comprises a continuous mechanism of strike-hard campaigns even in the period that has been officially characterised as being based on a community policing strategy (Pan 2010). This round of campaigns targeted seven types of serious crimes, namely extremely violent crimes by individuals; crimes involving guns and explosives; organised gang crimes; Internet fraud; trafficking women and children; robbery and looting; and prostitution, gambling, and drug-related crimes (Pan 2010). Therefore, community policing, the Western concept, might be adopted in China with Chinese characteristics.

3.2 The Police System and Functions in China

The current police system in China is based on the People's Police Law of 1995. The promulgation of the police law is regarded as one of the key measures that has been taken to promote the professionalisation and modernisation of Chinese policing. According to the People's Police Law of 1995, the Chinese police system (People's Police or PP) includes five police forces: public security police, state security police, prison police, judicial police in people's courts, and judicial police in people's procuratorates (The People's Police Law of People's Republic of China 1995). Each of the five police forces performs its own specific functions prescribed by the law and each has its own hierarchical organisation. Public security police are the largest part of PP, which account for 86 % of all the five police forces (Wong 2009a, p. 158). In China, public security police are the officers who people usually refer to when they mention police because they interact with citizens most in the five police forces. In addition, public security police are responsible for a wide range of functions including "investigating crimes, maintaining public order, directing traffic, conducting patrols, administrating the household registration system and the citizen identification card system, providing guidance to mass-line crime prevention and security organizations, and providing services to community residents" (Ma 2008, p. 17). The Chinese police system is both centralised and decentralised (Dai 2008; Sun et al. 2010; Wong 2009a). On the one hand, the Chinese police system is centralised because all members of the Chinese public security police force need to meet the professional standards, rules, and regulations set by the MPS. The same minimum requirements of recruitment, training, and promotion are implemented nationwide. Police operations of serious criminal or social order crimes are also under the guidance and direction of the MPS. On the other side, decentralisation is embodied in the responsibilities of local governments. Local governments are responsible for the administration of local police departments, such as providing budgets, setting local policing priorities and the size of local police force, and making arrangements for local police practices and operations (Dai 2008; Ma 2008; Sun et al. 2010; Wong 2009a). Jiao (2001a) made a comparative analysis of this characteristic between Chinese police and American police. For Jiao, the Chinese police system is more decentralised than the American police system because of the numerous police stations that are set up across the country in major communities. These field stations are responsible for social order cases and less serious criminal cases within certain areas. This design is in accordance with the party line, the mass-line, and the prevention line: principles of policing adopted by the Chinese government. However, American police officers regard law enforcement as the main responsibility, which emphasises professionalisation of policing (Jiao 2001a).

Besides regular public security police, there are several special teams of police under the leadership of the MPS: railway police, transportation police, civil aviation police, forest police, and antismuggling police. These special police are under the dual leadership of both the respective ministries and the MPS. For instance, forest police need to conduct law enforcement with the guidance of the Ministry of Forests and also abide by the regulations and rules set by the MPS. In addition to these five special police, there is another police force under the leadership of the State Council and the Central Military Committee: the People's Armed Police (PAP). Different from the People's Liberation Army and PP, the PAP have dual responsibilities: both military tasks and public securities involvement (Sun and Wu 2009). The dual responsibilities become the "greatest strength" of the PAP because they meet the requirements of both wartime and peacetime needs in a flexible way (Sun and Wu 2009, p. 118). In practice, the PAP perform duties of maintaining border security; safeguarding important government buildings, VIPS, and important public facilities; fire fighting; and emergency and disaster rescue (Ma 2008; Sun and Wu 2009; Wong 2009a).

According to the People's Police Law of 1995, there are 14 functions that need to be performed by the police in China. The functions cover a wide range of duties, from criminal investigation, social order maintenance, and traffic control to fire prevention, household registration, and safeguarding important officials

(The People's Police Law of People's Republic of China 1995). These functions are only for public security police. Therefore, Wong (2009a) commented that Chinese police perform a wider range of functions than any other police force worldwide. In addition to the above mentioned functions, there is a very important function that needs to be stressed: service. In the philosophy of Chinese policing, the mass-line principle is one of the key guidelines that is based on the idea of "from the masses and to the masses" introduced by Mao Zedong in 1943. According to the mass-line principle, the police and police authority come from the masses and the police should rely on the masses, mobilise the masses, and provide service to the masses (Wong 2009a, p. 185; Zhang 2010b). In China, there is a very popular saying about the police: "turn to police for help if you have trouble". It is clearly prescribed in Article 21 of the People's Police Law that the police should immediately come to the rescue when citizens are in dangerous situations; they should help citizens in settling their disputes (The People's Police Law of People's Republic of China 1995). However, this becomes a controversial topic in China. On the one hand, the MPS has officially announced the implementation of community policing nationwide, which includes a service-oriented principle and aims to establish a better police-citizen relationship. On the other hand, there is some discontent about too much police involvement in "non-police" work and the already demanding law enforcement work among frontline police officers (Cao 2003; Fu 1994; Gong 2004; Wang 2011).

Gong (2004) made a detailed analysis of the causes of police involvement in non-policing activities. The dual leadership system in China created the phenomenon that police officers not only need to follow the direction of the MPS in law enforcement operations but also need to perform some extra non-policing tasks allocated by local governments. The ambiguity of police functions in China also paved the way for police involvement in non-policing activities (Gong 2004). It is necessary and urgent to make a clearer distinction between community service in the community policing strategy and service in non-policing activities because police involvement may hinder the process of professionalisation and legalisation of policing in China (Cao 2003; Gong 2004). In addition, the use of police resources in non-policing activities also goes against the performance principles of economy, efficiency, and effectiveness. Although most police practitioners and scholars insist that non-policing tasks should be separated from police duties, some opposing arguments also exist. Zhang (2009) indicated that some of the so-called non-policing activities should fall into the scope of policing activities from the perspective of the stipulation of laws and the nature of public security organisations.

3.3 Following the Evolution of Western Policing

Although the socio-political environments between China and the West stand in contrast to each other, the development process of Chinese policing has followed the Western trend. It is useful to have a brief look at the evolution of policing development in the Western world. The origin of modern police can be traced back to the London Metropolitan Police created in 1829 through the efforts of Robert Peel who has been referred to as the "father" of modern policing (Archbold 2013). The contribution of Robert Peel includes an emphasis on crime prevention, the preventive patrol, paramilitary organisational structure, the necessity of wearing police uniforms, and the famous nine principles for the police force (Walker and Katz 2013). Although these contributions helped to build the modern police force in London, many new approaches were not in practice until many years later. In America, modern police forces were established in 1840s. In 1844, the first metropolitan police department in America was formed in New York (Archbold 2013). Most of the characteristics of American policing were borrowed from their British counterpart, including the organisational structure, the preventive patrol, and the crime prevention mission (Walker and Katz 2013). American policing in the 19th century was greatly influenced and dominated by local politics; politicians had powerful control over police agencies to maintain their political power (Archbold 2013). The selection standard of police officers was how well they were connected with politicians; it was also common for police chiefs to be appointed or changed based on political considerations. Reform efforts were needed to remove politics from American policing and establish an independent and professional police force.

A great reform movement in American policing was initiated in the 1920s–1930s, with the main characteristic of professionalisation (Hu 2004; Wang and Sun 2003). Just like Robert Peel who is considered to be the main contributor for the founding of modern police, August Vollmer is regarded as the pioneer of American police professionalism (Walker and Katz 2013). As police chief in Berkeley, California, from 1905 to 1932, Vollmer made great efforts to improve police recruitment standards, promoting education and training for police officers and arming officers with technology in their routine patrols (Scaramella et al. 2011). In addition to raising personnel standards, the reform movement also targeted new organisation management methods, including centralised administration, specialised police units, and an increase in the number of officers (Scaramella et al. 2011). With the progress of professionalisation of American policing, the main role of the police was gradually focused upon crime control. In reality, the progress of professionalism was far from smooth because it is quite common for police organisations to resist any reform efforts. However, these reform efforts of professionalism paved a way and pointed out the direction for other police departments to follow. Another direction of development in American policing is characterised by technology-driven police modernisation. The use of patrol cars, radio communications, and telephones in patrol have greatly revolutionised traditional policing in America (Walker and Katz 2013). However, the unexpected impact of modernised police car patrol was the isolation of police officers from the public. The progress of police professionalism, the use of technology in police patrols, the specialised units, and the centralised organisational structure all led to more distance between police and the public.

To improve police-citizen relations and build a positive partnership in police work, the contemporary philosophical transfer toward community policing came in the 1980s. This move was aimed at reducing the gap between the public and the police and establishing a community-oriented instead of a crime-fighting-oriented style of policing. The advent of community policing and problem-oriented policing are due to the fact that the police could never deal with crimes and other security problems without the help and cooperation of the public (Scaramella et al. 2011). In America, an office was established within the Department of Justice to facilitate of adoption of community policing nationwide. This is the Office of Community Oriented Policing Services (COPS Office). In the UK, the program of Neighbourhood Policing incorporates the main features of community policing, emphasising a close and strong partnership between the police and the community (Rowe 2014; Tuffin 2008). In addition to the USA and the UK, a community policing strategy has been adopted as the basis for police work in many countries around the world with various localised principles in practice. These countries include Japan, Sweden, South Korea, South Africa, the Netherlands, Nigeria, Gambia, India, and Afghanistan (Verma et al. 2013).

From the above summary of Western policing evolution, it is evident that the development of Chinese policing is following the trend of Western policing, from being politically driven to independent, from non-professional toward professional, from crime-control-oriented toward service-oriented, and from traditional toward modernisation. The development of modern policing in China has occurred in just over half a century, while it took Western powers nearly two centuries to evolve the process. Therefore, there are specific Chinese characteristics in the development of policing: a mixture of different policing strategies. This is largely due to the fact that each evolution stage in Chinese policing suffered the fate of lack of sufficient time to develop well (Hu 2004).

3.4 Community Policing and Police Subculture

Aiming to establish a partnership with the community to solve crime and disorder concerns, community policing has been one of the most dramatic and innovative shifts in policing philosophy and strategy in many parts of the world (Kappeler and Gaines 2009; Morabito 2010). Police academics and practitioners have defined it differently, but there is still not a widely accepted definition of community policing due to the complex nature of the concept. However, most of the definitions have included the following three main elements: community involvement, problem solving, and organisational decentralisation (COPS 2009; Miller et al. 2014; Skogan 2008). The following is one of the most comprehensive definitions of community policing:

> Community policing is a philosophy of policing, based on the concept that police officers and people working together in creative ways can help solve contemporary community problems related to crime, fear of crime, quality of life, and neighborhood conditions.

> The philosophy is predicated on the belief that achieving these goals requires that police departments develop a new relationship with people by expanding their role in the community, allowing ordinary people the power to set local police priorities, and involving them in efforts to improve the overall quality of life in their neighborhoods. It shifts the focus of police work from responding to random crime calls to proactively addressing community concerns (Kappeler and Gaines 2009, p. 5).

Kappeler and Gaines (2009, p. 4) presented a theoretical framework for community policing from four major facets: the philosophical facet, the organisational and personnel facet, the strategic facet, and the programmatic facet. This is shown in Fig. 3.1.

For the philosophical facet, there are seven main requirements to establish a community-oriented policing style:

- Broad police function and community focus: shift from a crime-fighting-oriented policing to a policing with broader police functions, including fear reduction, order maintenance, and community health
- Community input: provide qualified service according to the needs of the community
- Concern for people: show emotional concern for people
- Developing trust: build trust with community members through more communication, and get better cooperation from them
- Sharing power: hear people's demands
- Creativity: involve ideas from the community to innovate police service
- Neighbourhood variation: recognise and follow neighbourhood variation when enforcing the law (Kappeler and Gaines 2009, pp. 5–12).

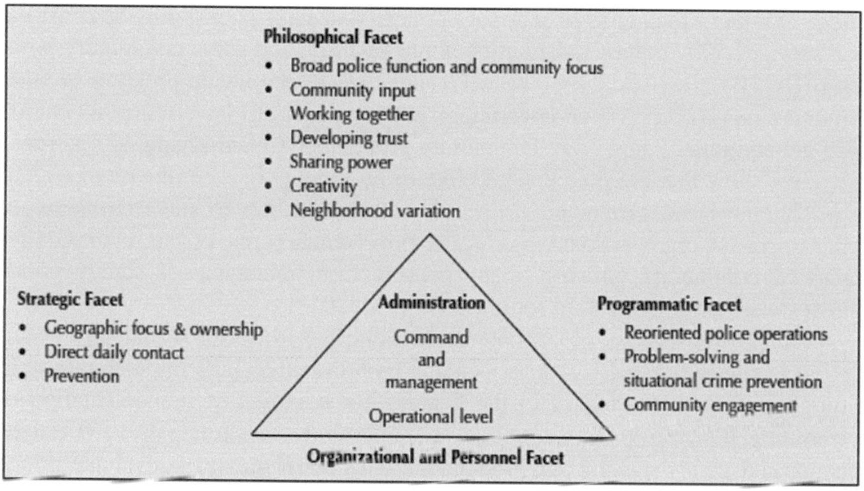

Fig. 3.1 Theoretical framework for community policing. Adapted from Kappeler and Gaines (2009, p. 4). Copyright 2009 by Matthew Bender & Company, Inc

The organisational and personnel facet requires a structural change of police organisations and decentralised police authority to serve the community more responsively. The strategic facet translates the above principles into three concrete guidelines for police work. First, officers are given a fixed geographic area in order to become familiar with the people and social problems in that area. Second, foot or bicycle patrol is recommended rather than car patrol to achieve direct, daily, face-to-face contact. Third, crime prevention is accorded great importance to transfer from reactive policing to proactive policing. The programmatic facet provides the detailed tactics for community-oriented police work. First, police operations are reoriented toward community problems. Therefore, the police are required to make use of various methods, such as foot patrols and surveys, to initiate interactions with community members to meet their needs. Second, the police are required to identify solutions to community problems through thorough procedures, from identification of the problem, analysis of the problem, to solving problems and evaluations. Third, in order to effectively involve community members into policing, the police should make use of different social organisations and activities to establish partnerships. These organisations may include governmental and private agencies, community committees, and sports or educational activities (Kappeler and Gaines 2009).

Since the official adoption of community policing by the MPS in 2002, the Chinese government has made efforts to put the Western concept into practice. In 2006, the MPS issued the *Decisions on the Community and Rural Policing Tactics* (MPS 2006). This order aimed to readjust police assignments according to the geographic characteristics of neighbourhoods and deploy community policing officers to fixed neighbourhoods. In 2007, according to the requirements of the MPS, police departments carried out the program of *Police-Citizens Gather in Police Stations* which aims to seek for opinions and suggestions, provide consultation services, disseminate information about security, and solve community problems (Du 2007). In late 2008, the MPS launched a nationwide program of *Walk through Communities* which encourages police officers to have more interaction with the community and solve community problems (Xu and Zhang 2008). These programs show that the police would like to promote police–community communications and build partnership with community members to solve problems. In order to realise organisational decentralisation, which is one of the main requirements of community policing, many officers from municipal or county police bureaus were assigned to field stations (Wu et al. 2011).

Although the strategy of community policing has not been sufficiently evaluated, it is suggested that it at least benefits both the police and the community in a number of ways. In regard to the benefits for community, implementation of community policing gives the public an opportunity to participate in decision-making and policy-making activities concerning policing, and to evaluate police performance from the perspective of community members; in addition, citizens do have less fear of perceived crime and social disorder when the new policing style makes them feel confident about police care. With regard to the benefits for the police, community policing may help the police gain community support and understanding of their work, and build morale and work satisfaction among officers (Skolnick and Bayley 1988).

The successful implementation of community policing has to be realised with the help of full support from both the police officers and the community members. First of all, police support for community policing is essential. The philosophy of community policing requires officers to see themselves as part of the community rather than separate from the community. The police should have broad role orientations and consider solving community problems as their primary responsibility. It is only through genuine concern for citizens that trust could be developed and partnerships can be built between the police and the community. Then community members would be willing to become actively involved in cooperation with the police. In addition, the support from the public is also necessary for community policing, because the successful implementation of community policing relies on the extent to which citizens would like to participate in, cooperate with, and provide help in crime prevention and problem-solving (Wu et al. 2011). However, one of the most striking obstacles to the implementation of community policing is the influence of traditional police subculture (Skolnick and Bayley 1988). An occupational subculture featured with a strong us versus them mentality, a cynical attitude toward the public, a preference for a crime fighting role and discrimination of community service, specific group loyalty and protective solidarity, a paramilitary and centralised organisation structure, and a rigid top down chain of command, contains too many elements that are contrary to the principles of community policing. According to an empirical study conducted by Chappell (2009) among 54 police officers in a police department in the USA, some officers expressed strong cynical attitudes toward the idea of community policing and never considered it seriously. The police subculture that is featured with cynicism and an us versus them mentality may negatively influence police interactions with citizens. At the same time, dissatisfaction with police encounters is negatively associated with public support for community policing (Joseph et al. 2003).

In addition, because community policing challenges the fundamental values of the police subculture, the resistance to it may be easily maintained because officers simply do not want to face dramatic change (Kappeler and Gaines 2009). One of the key tasks of successful implementation of community policing is to change the police occupational culture from a traditional crime-oriented one to a community-oriented one (Peak and Glensor 1999). Therefore, it is vital to change the existing subcultural perception that strictly distinguishes the police from the citizens and establish good police-community relations through reorientation of policing aims from crime control to solving problems of community and policies of increasing citizen participation and building mass rapport. In addition, it is also important to decentralise police authority and let officers be receptive to the changes brought by community policing. In China, although studies show that the new strategy has gained positive feedback from the public (Wu et al. 2011), the implementation of community policing remains at a preliminary stage and faces many challenges. For instance, a worsened police-citizen relationship makes it difficult for the police to mobilise the masses and gain their support (Du 1997).

In addition, the contradiction between providing overall service for people and the inability and manpower shortage of police to be involved in non-policing activities arouses complaints from police officers and leads to deteriorated police–citizen relations (Gong 2004; Zhang 2009).

For the successful implementation of community policing, it is important to know how officers perceive their role in the new strategy of policing and whether they have been prepared to receive more community support and scrutiny. It is the aim of this study to explore the degree of adherence to traditional police subculture among Chinese frontline police officers and to present corresponding suggestions for policy making and police training.

3.5 Summary

This chapter introduces the development of policing strategies, the police system and functions, and the implementation of community policing in China. Since the founding of the People's Republic of China, the history of policing can be roughly divided into three stages: mass-line policing, strike-hard policing, and community policing (Zhong 2009). Mass-line policing is the application of communist ideology into the strategy of policing, advocating the support of citizens in policing and a good police-citizen relationship (Wong 2001). Along with the opening-up of China, the rate of crime rose rapidly. Therefore, a series of strike-hard campaigns were initiated by the government toward some specific types of crime. Crimes were temporarily controlled by the campaigns, but other problems appeared along with these campaigns, such as abuse of police authority (Dutton and Lee 1993; Liang 2005; Trevaskes 2003) and a compromise of legal provisions due to the requirements of the campaigns (Liang 2005; Qu 2005). In 2002, the Chinese government launched the nationwide adoption of community policing strategy. Although community policing is a Western concept, Chinese police officers find it familiar because of its similarity to mass-line policing. The successful implementation of a new policing strategy is impossible without the support of police practitioners. It is important to find out whether and to what extent there is adherence to the police subculture suggested in the Western literature among Chinese officers, because many of the cultural themes are indeed contradictory to the requirements of community policing. In the next chapter, a detailed review of police cultural studies in the West will be provided, with a focus on the core themes of police subculture and the potential influence of some demographic and work-related variables.

Chapter 4
Studies of Police Culture in the West

The chapter focuses on the existing studies of police culture. The review begins by considering the historical development of police cultural studies, followed by discussing some core cultural themes summarised by policing scholars; after that, the demographic and work-related variables that have potential influence on police cultural perceptions are reviewed.

4.1 A Review of Studies

The study of police culture can be traced back to the early 1950s (Cancino and Enriquez 2004; Paoline 2004; Terrill et al. 2003; Westley 1953). However, the concept of police culture remains "loosely defined in the criminological literature" (Chan 1996, p. 111) because scholars have tried to comprehend this concept from different angles and academic interest. The attempts to define police culture each provided a unique perspective of justifying police behaviours and perceptions. Manning (1989) defined police culture as "accepted practices, rules, and principles of conduct that are situationally applied, and generated rationales and beliefs" (p. 360). Reiner (2010) put forward the following definition: "Cultures are complex ensembles of values, attitudes, symbols, rules, recipes, and practices, emerging as people react to the exigencies and situations they confront, interpreted through the cognitive frames and orientations they carry with them from prior experiences" (p. 116). For Chan (1997), police culture can be regarded as "a layer of informal occupational norms and values operating under the apparently rigid hierarchical structure of police organizations" (p. 43). In the *Dictionary of Policing*, Waddington (2008) provided the following definition: "the mix of informal prejudices, values, attitudes and working practices commonly found among the lower ranks of the police that influences the exercise of discretion" (p. 203). Although these definitions emphasise different aspects of the creation of police culture, such as modifying accepted police attitudes and behaviour, clarifying different layers of police culture, and the coping mechanisms that help to ease the tension and reduce risks, none of them could be regarded as a widely-accepted definition (Cockcroft 2013).

Z. Chen, *Measuring Police Subcultural Perceptions*,
DOI 10.1007/978-981-10-0096-6_4

Cockcroft (2013) summarised three points that add to the difficulty in defining police culture. First of all, the role of police officers includes various kinds of work from crime control, public reassurance, traffic management, offender management, and order maintenance, to different kinds of community service. The complex contents of policing with a nature of solving problems make police culture difficult to characterise. The second point is the negative label which has been attached to the police culture in the literature (Cochran and Bromley 2003; Mollen et al. 1994; Wood 1997). Many studies have identified the relationship between police cultural perceptions, such as group loyalty and the code of silence, and police misconduct such as cover-ups or corruption (Armacost 2003; Kappeler et al. 1998; Mollen et al. 1994; Petter et al. 2011; Prenzler 2009; Punch 2003; Raines 2010; Wood 1997). Westmarland (2008) pointed out that police culture has been used as an "explanation or excuse" for some misconduct of police officers (p. 253). Some positive aspects have been put forward, but they are very limited in comparison to the negative ones. As a mechanism to cope with risks and uncertainties, the police culture provides officers with a fixed pattern to reduce stress and enhance feelings of comfort (Brown 1981; Chan 1996; Paoline 2001; Waddington 1999a). It is also reasonable to suggest that police recruits are socialised into the expected norms of attitudes and behaviours in everyday police work with the help of a police culture (Manning 2007b). Finally, we have seen great change to not only policing but the social and political systems. The great change makes it even more difficult to address a definition of police culture in a widely accepted way because it is reasonable to suggest that the connotation of police culture changes as well.

Researchers have long noticed the impact of the norms and values created from the unique cultural orientation shared by police officers. Studies of police culture mainly fall into two perspectives: occupational and organisational (Paoline 2001). The former considers police culture as shared beliefs, behaviours, and norms among members of the police profession; the latter attaches importance to the police organisation in which officers form their common assumptions and behaviour. The fundamental difference between these two approaches is that one takes the work people do as the main driving force for the shared values and the other takes the organisation that people work for as the main driving force. However, in practice, the two terms "organisational culture" and "occupational culture" are often used synonymously (Bacon 2014, p. 106) because policing as an occupation cannot be studied separately from the organisational structure of the police.

Most studies regard police culture as an occupational phenomenon for all police officers (Paoline 2001). Since the seminal work of Westley (1953) in the 1950s, researchers have become more and more interested in the study of police culture. Ethnographic studies have paved the way for the traditional descriptions of a single police culture. The traditional view defines a monolithic police culture that features as the significant coping mechanism to help officers deal with the hazards and uncertainties created in the occupational and organisational environment (Paoline 2003; Terrill et al. 2003).

As an intrinsic nature of the occupational environment, police officers may have to face various unpleasant situations, situational uncertainties, and danger (Crank 2004; Kappeler et al. 1998; Reiner 2010; Skolnick 1986; Westley 1970). The stress and uncertainties of policing result in one of the strongest occupational subcultures (Violanti et al. 2007). Scholars have tried to explain one or several components of the "coping mechanism" created in the police world. Westley (1970) emphasised the use of secrecy to protect the interests of the whole occupational group: "secrecy among the police stands as a shield against the attacks of the outside world" (p. 111). The code of silence has attracted the attention of both academics and practitioners as a symbol of solidarity among peers against the outer world. Westley also described a sense of isolation against the public among police officers. Social isolation promotes group solidarity and the combination of these two leads to an us versus them mentality. The above subcultural perceptions can provide an explanation for the use of force by police officers in that police officers might use violence when they feel that their authority is challenged because the us versus them mentality functions as a cultural catalyst. Another contribution made by Westley is that he is the pioneer to explain the concept of police identity and how it is formed through police work (Greene 2010). This is a sociological analysis of the making of a unique group of people who devote their life and career to policing, quite beyond a descriptive analysis of police work (Cockcroft 2013).

Banton is another leading contributor to the study of policing in the 20th century. His work, *The Policeman in the Community*, has attracted many sociologists to policing studies through a comparative study of police work and police culture in Scottish and American contexts (Banton 1964). Although this book did not use police occupational culture as the main topic, all the contents relate to how cultural norms shape police attitudes and behaviour. Banton is one of the earliest scholars who emphasised the importance of the use of discretion for police officers, including how they use discretionary power and its intangible cultural norms (Cockcroft 2013; Westmarland 2008). One of the reasons that policing is so unique an occupation is that some level of discretion is embedded in the nature of the work. Discretion is a necessary element in policing as police cannot enforce all the laws all the time. When police officers need to choose whether to take action or not and what kind of actions to take when there is no supervision, it is reasonable for them to follow the occupational cultural norms to respond (Cockcroft 2013). For policing, "the law in theory and the law in practice" are different and police culture renders interpretation for how police officers choose (Westmarland 2008, p. 255). While Banton (1964) was more interested in how officers try to use discretion to conduct law enforcement in a moral manner, other observers have been concerned about the inappropriate use of discretion which leads to selective enforcement and other forms of misconduct through the influence of the police subculture (Klockars 1985a; Sparrow et al. 1990; Waddington 1999b).

Skolnick (1986) made another pioneering contribution to the depiction of police culture. He described police culture as a "working personality" formed as a consequence of the key elements of police work: danger, authority and efficiency (p. 42). Although Skolnick used the concept "personality", the sketch of "working personality" actually refers to a sociological phenomenon rather than a psychological one (Reiner 2010, p. 118).

As one of the main elements of "working personality", danger or the risk of danger in policing is always an unavoidable topic. Compared with other high risk careers (such as mining), the real danger encountered by police officers does not seem particularly hazardous. What threatens police officers is the unpredictable potential risks (Crank 2004). A survey of 91 police officers in the USA in 1983 clearly showed that police see their jobs as a paradox (both safe and unsafe) because they know that serious injury or killing are uncommon while potential threats are inherent in the work (Cullen et al. 1983). The training from the police academy to the field reinforces the perception of danger among police officers through various stories of dangerous encounters and negative personal experiences (Kappeler et al. 1998). This perception of danger among police officers promotes the forming of the protective cultural mechanism against the uncertainties.

Authority is another principle "variable" of police role (Skolnick 1986, p. 44). Police officers are accorded power to use coercion over others with probable reasons, such as in self-defence or in defence of another individual or group. A sense of authority is usually maintained when duties are performed or even merged into part of the life of officers as an authoritarian personality (Lindsey et al. 2012). In fact, authority and danger are interdependent: police officers face danger if they encounter resistant offenders during their exercise of authority. However, they still tend to initiate more actions in the areas that they believe to be more problematic and challenging and toward suspects who resist violently (Ingram 2007; Worden 1996). In addition, the more police officers encounter situations in which they have to use coercion to assert their authority, the more they perceive the occupational environment to be hazardous. The sense of authority and the use of coercion may also promote isolation of police officers from the general public.

In addition to danger and authority, efficiency is the third driving force that creates a police culture according to Skolnick. The needs of "production" may push police officers to neglect the protection of offenders' rights during law enforcement (Skolnick 1986). However, Reiner (2010) considered the outside pressure of police officers to be efficient has been "overemphasised" because the role of crime-fighting is primarily labelled by the police themselves (p. 119).

Another widely discussed element of police culture is solidarity which is closely associated with social isolation. Unlike other occupations, police officers share an unusually high level of solidarity due to the policing work itself and the occupational environment (Paoline 2001; Skolnick 1986). Policing as a job with intrinsic danger requires group loyalty and cooperation among peers. Internal solidarity functions like a shield protecting the whole occupational group against unpredictable risks and the challenges from the public. The protective solidarity has been widely associated with police misconduct, such as cover-ups (Crank 2004; Reiner 2010) or even complicity (Muir 1977). The group loyalty sets officers apart from the rest of the community, resulting to the us versus them mentality. The craft of "suspicion" and the sense of authority also separate police from non-police (Paoline 2001; Reiner 2010; Skolnick 1986).

Skolnick made a thorough explanation of some key components of the police culture through his empirical sketch of aspects of police attitudes and perceptions created through their work. He is among one of the earliest scholars to point out how the main components of "working personality", such as danger, solidarity, authority, and isolation, interact with one another and promote the overall police culture formation as a coping mechanism of risks created in the occupational environment. By presenting "working personality", Skolnick did not intend to imply that all police are alike. Instead, he insisted that variations of police culture exist at both the individual and group level. What he meant was that the combination of danger, authority, and efficiency forms a unique occupational group with these "cognitive tendencies" (Skolnick 1986, p. 42).

In contrast to the above researchers who have described police cultural attitudes and behaviour in a soft or moderate manner, Van Maanen adopted a "warts and all" approach (Westmarland 2008, p. 262). This can be identified from the derogatory terms he used to describe the "asshole" at the very beginning of his classic article *The Asshole* (Van Maanen 1978). He made an explicit depiction of how police officers classify people they deal with into three "ideal types" and label them as "suspicious persons", "assholes" and "know nothings":

> "suspicious persons"—those whom the police have reason to believe may have committed a serious offense; "assholes"—those who do not accept the police definition of the situation; and "know nothings"—those who are not either of the first two categories but are not police and therefore, according to the police, cannot know what the police are about (Van Maanen 1978, p. 223).

The important contribution of Van Maanen to describe the above classification and the corresponding manner of dealing with them by police officers is that this made a clear illustration of police subcultural norms and their impact. It is clear that the classification and the interpretations of it are not due to the social mandate of the police. To some extent, this shared understanding among police officers toward the way to deal with certain types of people is not only accepted by officers but also by the society because of the accepted discretionary power (Dempsey and Forst 2012). This work also showed the level of importance that officers attach to the sense of authority. Assholes are those who engage in behaviour that threaten the authority of officers. What officers are supposed to do is to teach them a lesson and rectify their behaviour.

While the works mentioned previously put an emphasis on the depiction of the shared components of police culture, we then see a shift of research focus to the study of variations of police culture.

As a pioneer of describing police cultural variations, Reuss-Ianni (1983) conducted an in-depth study of police officers in two precincts in New York City and identified two cultures of policing: street cop culture and management cop culture. Street cops believe that they are a distinctive group of people who face risks and uncertainties to guarantee the security of people and society in general; they believe that they know exactly about the police work and that they should receive support and respect from the public and the administrative departments; they contend that officers need internal loyalty and interdependence to work, and that discretion should be an important component of the police world (Reuss-Ianni 1983, pp. 6–7). In contrast, for Reuss-Ianni, management cop culture "seeks to maximise the bureaucratic benefits of efficient organisation, rational decision-making, cost-effective procedures, and objective accountability at all levels of policing" (p. 6). Management officers emphasise all of policing under the social, political system and suggest that products should be quantified and measured in a scientific and efficient way. Reuss-Ianni made a thorough analysis of the reasons for the fragmentation of the police culture, including corruption investigations carried out by the Knapp Commission (1973), rights protection for disenfranchised minorities, higher education levels, and better incomes (pp. 5–6). Reuss-Ianni made a clear illustration of the two incompatible police cultures and gave sound explanation after the observational research. However, just as Paoline (2001) pointed out in his work, Reuss-Ianni did not mention the possible overlapping of cultural perceptions among each of the two groups, because some of the street cops may adhere to some of the components of management cop culture. Like Reuss-Ianni, Manning (1989) also contended that police officers of different ranks adhere to different subcultures. He identified three segments of culture: low participants, middle management, and top command. Low participants are similar to what Reuss-Ianni called street cops. Manning made the cultural perceptions of management cops clearer than Reuss-Ianni did by the further division of middle management and top command. Besides pointing out the two police cultures, Reuss-Ianni made another contribution to police culture studies by summarising 21 precepts of street police that is called "Cop's Code":

1. Watch out for your partner first and then the rest of the guys working that tour.
2. Don't give up another cop.
3. Show toughness.
4. Be aggressive when you have to, but don't be too eager.
5. Don't get involved in anything in another guy's sector.
6. Hold up your end of the work.
7. If you get caught off base, don't implicate anybody else.
8. Make sure the other guys know if another cop is dangerous or unsafe.
9. Don't trust a new guy until you have checked him out.
10. Don't tell anybody else more than they have to know; it could be bad for you and it could be bad for them.
11. Don't talk too much or too little. Both are suspicious.
12. Don't leave work for the next tour.
13. Protect yourself. (If the system wants to get you, it will.)
14. Don't make waves. Supervisors pay attention to troublemakers.
15. Don't give them too much activity. Don't be too eager.
16. Keep out of the way of any boss from outside your precinct.

17. Don't look for favors just for yourself.
18. Don't take on the patrol sergeant by yourself.
19. Know your bosses. Who's working and who has the desk?
20. Don't do the bosses' work for them.
21. Don't trust bosses to look out for your interests (Reuss-Ianni 1983, pp. 13–16).

These postulates indicate that police solidarity is attached great importance in the police subculture. Most of the subcultural requirements remind officers to stand in line with their peers to protect each other from outside risks, even from their bosses.

In addition to the description of dichotomy of street cop culture and management cop culture, some scholars focused their attention on the cultural variations among different police types, such as uniformed police and police detectives. Both Young (1991) and Hobbs (1988) investigated the specific cultural norms of police detectives of CID (Criminal Investigation Department), and made comparisons with uniformed officers. Young could conduct an in-depth ethnographic study of the real police world because he was a member of the police and had an insider view. He experienced the shift of position from a uniformed officer to a police detective in CID. He described the different cultural norms, values, and even dress-styles. Flexibility of work, casual dress, and the importance of "statistical detections" all help to support how different the culture of police detectives is from uniformed officers (Young 1991). For Hobbs, the socialisation process of CID gives officers a distinctive introduction to the work and culture of police detectives. He also emphasised the unique characteristics of the East End of London where he conducted his research and its influence to policing styles there. Both of these scholars illustrated the existence of cultural variations among different police types and the distinctiveness of police detectives.

Most of the studies discussed explored the shared characteristics or variations of police culture from the perspective of occupational culture and socialisation. From that perspective, the forming of police culture and the attitudes and behaviour shaped by this culture could be identified within the occupational group of police as a coping mechanism in the face of the pressure and the risks of the occupation. Researchers who favour the perspective of organisational culture emphasise the influence upon police culture of institutional structures and the management level judgement. James Q. Wilson is one of the representatives of this perspective. Although he focused on the differences of police behaviour instead of police culture, as the name of his classic work *Varieties of Police Behaviour* suggests, the combination of behavioural variations in different organisational contexts supports the existence of different policing styles and police subcultures. Wilson (1968) identified three styles of policing through his study of police departments in eight American communities: the "watchman" style, the "legalistic" style, and the "service" style. For him, the watchman style departments bear a high level of tolerance towards "minor violations", such as "traffic and juvenile offences", and toward certain groups of people, such as young people and black people. In this style of policing, the role of order maintenance is accorded more value than the role of law enforcement. In contrast to the watchman departments, he continued to explain, the legalistic departments emphasise the role of crime control and professional law enforcement. In this style of policing, formal procedures take precedence and the space of police discretion is minimised. The service style departments tend to be in the middle, focusing on both law enforcement and order maintenance in an informal way of intervention. In this style of policing, there is a high level of agreement between community members and the police that the role of providing service is central. There are two main contributions of this classic work. First, Wilson identified the variations of policing styles among different police agencies. Second, he pointed out the influence of the expectations of communities and the orientations of police administrators to the adoption of policing styles and the formation of police subcultures. However, just as Paoline (2001) mentioned, this work failed to explain the possible existence of different orientations of policing in one police department and what kind of style should be adopted for communities with complex or mixed demands.

Along with the discussions of police culture passing from traditional policing to contemporary policing, the focus has been shifted from a monolithic depiction to multiple police cultures in different occupational and organisational environments. More recent accounts of police culture aim to put the concept of police culture in a more complex framework through which variations, changes, and the relationship between police culture and the bigger social culture could be explained with an integrative view. Janet Chan is one of the representatives of contemporary scholars in the field of police cultural studies. She has criticised the traditional accounts of police culture for their failure to explain the variations of police culture, the active role of officers in the forming of police culture, and relationships between police culture and the external context (Chan 1997). Based on these arguments, Chan (1997) proposed a new framework under which police culture could be reconceptualised on the basis of a combination of a multiple cultures perspective from Sackmann's and Schein's cognitive perspective of culture (Sackmann 1991; Schein 1985), active role of individuals from Shearing and Ericson's phenomenological treatment of culture (Shearing and Ericson 1991), and the concepts of "field" ("the structural conditions of police work") and "habitus" ("cultural knowledge") from Bourdieu's relational theory (Bourdieu 1990). In this framework, officers are no longer passive learners of police culture. The formation and change of police culture are subject to changes in the structural conditions and whether officers are adaptable to those changes (Chan 1997). The most important contribution of Chan lies in that she established a model that can explain the active role of individuals and the changing police culture in the context of an outer environment. Like Chan, Waddington (1999a) also questioned traditional accounts of police culture and attempted to explain police culture in a descriptive way instead of connecting it with misbehaviour. Another important issue that he proposed is the differentiation between canteen and operational cultures. To what extent an officer's oral descriptions of culture are identical to their cultural behaviour and how the two influence each other are important topics that failed to attract enough notice (Cockcroft 2013). Both Chan and Waddington criticised the traditional model of exploring police culture and tried to explain this phenomenon in a way that took the external context into consideration. However, this more "condemnatory" manner has to be based on the existing knowledge of key components of police culture, although the scope of some key characteristics may begin to diminish or change in the changing societal environment.

Recently, researchers have conducted some empirical studies to support the existence of variations of police cultural perceptions on the basis of quantitative statistical classifications (Cochran and Bromley 2003; Ingram et al. 2013; Paoline 2001, 2004; Paoline and Terrill 2014). Cochran and Bromley (2003) measured police subcultural perceptions in terms of their role orientations toward crime control and community service, and other cultural themes including cynicism, traditionalism, and receptivity to change. Using cluster analysis and discriminant function analysis, they identified three cultural types with different levels of adherence, named "Sub-Cultural Adherents", "COP Cops", and "Normals" (Cochran and Bromley 2003). Paoline (2001, 2004) found seven distinct groups of officers on the basis of the similarities and differences of their occupational outlooks. Five of these types were very similar to those identified in previous typological research, namely, Traditionalists, Old-Pros, Law Enforcers, Peacekeepers, and Lay-Lows; two additional groups were named Anti-Organizational Street-Cops and Dirty Harry Enforcers (Paoline 2004). A recent quantitative study conducted by Paoline and Terrill (2014) surveyed 2109 police officers across seven police agencies in the USA. The researchers collected police responses to 13 main police cultural dimensions and analysed the degree of agreement about these cultural themes. Results supported the existence of support for some main characteristics of traditional police subculture among the officers. These included the crime fighting role orientation, loyalty, perception of danger, and perception of police authority. However, cultural variations were also identified about their attitudes about such things as social isolation, police administration, community policing, and suspicion. Unlike previous ethnographic qualitative studies that described the delicate aspect of police culture, the use of quantitative statistical techniques are useful in providing a general picture of a large sample of officers with regard to their cultural perceptions. In addition, this may also pave the way for further statistical calculations that may assist in further interpretation of the complex cultural phenomenon. This study is also based on this perspective of inquiry in that I would like to make use of quantitative research design and statistical analyses to describe police cultural perceptions in China and also to draw some conclusions from investigating the associations between police subcultural perceptions and some demographic and work-related factors.

4.2 Traditional and Contemporary Police Culture: Similarities and Variations

From the discussions above, it is possible to conclude that studies of police culture mainly fall into two periods. Earlier scholars, such as Westley (1970), Skolnick (1986), and Banton (1964), put the focus on depicting a widely shared police culture, although some of them did comment on the existence of cultural variations. Since the work of Reuss-Ianni (1983), more and more researchers shifted their attention to the differences within police culture. Research focus turned to explain variations and the continuous changing nature of police culture in the context of a complex and changing society. In fact, many researchers have questioned the monolithic view of police culture as suggested in some of the literature. However, it is necessary to absorb the essence of core characteristics of the police culture depicted by earlier scholars before contemplating dimensions of contemporary police culture. Previous findings of police culture do provide a valuable reference for policing studies in general. Although variations of police culture have gained a wide acknowledgement, the influencing factors and the extent of differences still require theoretical and practical evidence to support them. Similarities or shared characteristics of police culture have also been identified in different cities and even countries (Ernest and Arvind 2008), because similar recruitment and training processes, similar risks and uncertainties, and similar tasks such as crime control and order maintenance, tie police officers around the world together (Cockcroft 2013, p. 38; Westmarland 2008, p. 257).

Just as Reiner (2010) suggested in his work, even if different police subcultures exist, there are shared "values, norms, perspectives, myths and craft rules" because officers do face "similar basic pressures that shape a distinctive and characteristic culture, discernible in many parts of the contemporary world" (pp. 116–117). The shared problems and risks lead to the survival of these core elements because of a "psychological fit, with the demands of the rank-and-file cop condition" (Reiner 2010, p. 118). Similarly to Reiner, Crank (2004) suggested that the reason that some cultural themes are shared by most frontline officers is that they "respond to similar audiences and share similar functional concerns" (p. 57).

Paoline (2003) has made an analysis that pointed out the relationship between the occupational culture and variations: "the forces of fragmentation should be working to erode a single monolithic police culture, but not totally dissolve it" (p. 210). Some studies have been conducted to explain the changes of police culture and to indicate that changes will continue to occur (Chan 1997; Loftus 2009; Sklansky 2006). The driving forces mainly include the acceptance of more women, racial minorities, and college graduates into police force, and the adoption of new philosophies of policing such as community policing (Paoline 2003, p. 208). Sklansky (2006) suggested that diversification of police practitioners has led to the end of a monolithic police subculture and has also weakened police group solidarity as well as police isolation from the public. On the other hand, a recent study conducted by Loftus (2010) suggested that the main themes of traditional police subculture remain "untouched" today because police officers still face the same pressures. Although, along with the passage of time and changes in the sociopolitical environment, the explanatory power of traditional accounts of police culture has diminished, some key characteristics of police culture do survive and "have extend into the contemporary policing landscape" (Loftus 2009, p. 191). Skolnick (2008) also recently contended that some key components of police culture, such as authority, secrecy, and use of force, are enduring even in contemporary policing. Similar to the above two commentators, Corsianos (2012) has suggested that the police subculture tends to remain "intact" although the police force has experienced more demographic diversity (pp. 61–112). From these contributions, it is obvious that the phenomenon of police culture can easily be oversimplified by emphasising either its changing nature or the enduring traditional cultural themes. In addition, it is necessary to discuss contemporary police culture within a specific social context, such as the under-investigated Chinese policing.

4.3 Themes of Police Subculture

In the following section, several core themes of police subculture summarised by Western scholars and police practitioners are discussed with regard to their definitions, their causes, and the effects they have on police perceptions.

According to Reiner (2010, pp. 118–132), the core characteristics of police subculture include cynicism (pessimism), suspicion, isolation (solidarity), conservatism, machismo, racial prejudice, and pragmatism. A number of scholars have accounted for the shared components of police culture through a mixture of different cultural themes (Manning 1989; Reuss-Ianni 1983; Shearing and Ericson 1991). Indeed, for every culture, there are always a number of cultural "themes". These themes are "dynamic affirmations", which are "declared or implied, and usually controlling behavior or stimulating activity" (Opler 1945, p. 198). According to Kappeler et al. (1998), cultural themes are central to police organisations because they regulate the pattern of "social interactions" of group members (p. 100). For Crank (2004, p. 53), cultural themes are essential "building blocks" that represent common activities of most police departments. Crank (2004) summarised the following 21 themes of police subculture: dominion, force, militarisation, guns, suspicion, danger and its anticipation, unpredictability and situational uncertainty, turbulence and edge control, seduction, police morality, common sense, masculinity, solidarity, racism, outsiders, individualism, deception, deterrence, bullshit, death, and police funerals. These cultural themes may reflect behavioural, dispositional, and social structural aspects of police work.

4.3.1 Isolation

Isolation is "an emotional and physical condition that makes it difficult for members of one social group to have relationships and interact with members of another group" (Kappeler et al. 1998, p. 100). Many observers have listed isolation as one of primary themes of police subculture (Clark 1965; Meyer and Steyn 2009; Reiner 2010; Skolnick 1986; Swanton 1981; Westley 1953, 1970). It is a product of the coping mechanism through which police officers have to deal with the problems they face in both the organisational and occupational environments (Paoline 2003, p. 203). In 1950s, Westley (1953, p. 35) identified the unamiable relationship between police and the public and attributed police brutality and secrecy to their social isolation. In his classic work *Violence and the Police*, Westley (1970) made a systematic analysis of police isolation on the basis of survey data collected from 77 members of the public and 85 police officers about their attitudes toward each other. Westley concluded that both police officers and community members show a high level of hostility toward each other. Clark (1965) systematically analysed the causes of police isolation and the corresponding positive and negative consequences. According to him, the causes of police isolation come from the resentment of people who have been or expect to be policed, the negative influence of police misconduct, the nature of policing to enforce sanctions, and the requirements of police agencies (pp. 307–308). In addition, Clark measured the degree and the nature of the isolation in policing through a survey of 611 police officers in the United States and the UK. This study demonstrated the feeling of isolation among police officers, with slight differences between the two countries. However, a large proportion of the officers felt that they were isolated from the public (Clark 1965). Skolnick (1986) included some vivid expressions of how police officers feel isolated from the community and how difficult it is for police officers to keep good relationships with outsiders, showing a clear us versus them mentality (pp. 49–51). Swanton (1981) distinguished two types of determinants resulting in social isolation: social and work settings. Both the community and the police may initiate isolation in the social setting. From the public there are a perceived opposing relationship between the nature of police work and police-citizen friendship, a resentment towards sanctions from the police, some people's attempts to curry favour with officers, and the socially unattractive police personality (Swanton 1981, p. 18). Officers themselves also tend to be insulated because of their perception of the hostility from the public. Harris (1978) described some people's contradictory feeling of valuing police work and avoiding close contact: "the respectables hire the police to do their dirty work for them" (p. 273). Another source of isolation comes from the police work. Shift work and irregular working hours, the somewhat suspicious and cynical police personality, and the need of police to keep distance from the public, all become barriers to maintaining good relationships with the public (Swanton 1981, p. 18). Kappeler et al. (1998, p. 100) added another determinant that leads to social isolation of police, namely, regarding outsiders as potential threats to their security and authority. Therefore, to maintain social distance is regarded to be a way to shield from potential risks. On the basis of previous explanations, Paoline (2001) contended that social isolation is one of the "defining characteristics" of police culture (p. 18). He attributed social isolation of police to the occupational environment and the accompanying coping mechanism of police officers: the perception of danger, the sense of authority, and the craft of suspicion (p. 18). The intrinsic nature of danger and uncertainties require group loyalty and cooperation. The more officers perceive policing work to be dangerous, the more they highlight the sense of authority and internal protective solidarity. Together with the trained craft of suspicion, all of these attributes promote the us versus them mentality and lead to social isolation.

4.3.2 Solidarity

Closely related to social isolation, a strong sense of solidarity has frequently been noted as a dominant and distinguishing theme in police subculture by many commentators (Banton 1964; Cockcroft 2013; Crank 2004; Goldsmith 1990; Kappeler et al. 1998; Miller 2010; Reiner 2010; Shernock 2007; Skolnick 1986; Skolnick and Fyfe 1993; Westley 1970). According to Shernock (2007), solidarity is "the unique sense of identity, belonging, and cohesion that one develops as part of a group of colleagues who share in common social roles, interests, problems, concerns, and even lifestyles" (p. 994). Internal solidarity has been traditionally explained as a coping mechanism to protect officers against the embedded danger and uncertainties of police work and social rejection (Kappeler et al. 1998). The dangerous work environment requires close cooperation and a high level of trust from fellow officers. Social isolation and the us versus them mentality resulting from the nature of policing and unfriendliness of both police officers and the community further promote group loyalty. Many expressions have been used to emphasise this unique strong sense of solidarity in the entrenched police subculture. These include "camaraderie, cohesiveness, fealty, the brotherhood, honor, the blue curtain, esprit-de-corps, and brother and sister cops" (Cockcroft 2013, p. 60). Police solidarity is created and reinforced through academy training, field training, and common work experiences (Crank 2004, pp. 237–238; Mollen et al. 1994, p. 55; Shernock 2007, p. 994; Van Maanen 1973). For example, an officer testified to the Mollen Commission about the start of socialising to the protective secrecy: "It starts in the Police Academy, and it just develops from there. … It starts with the instructors telling you never to be a rat, never give up your fellow officer." (Mollen et al. 1994, p. 55). In the process of occupational socialisation, police recruits learn the idea that citizens are unsupportive and fellow officers are the only people who can be relied on (Crank 2004; Shernock 2007; Skolnick 1986).

To some extent, this kind of solidarity is beneficial for the police force because it paves the way for teamwork and cooperation and builds the confidence that is important for a sense of mission and commitment (Shernock 2007, p. 998).

Although positive influences of police solidarity have been identified, more attention has been focused on its negative consequences. According to Shernock (2007), police solidarity may ruin supervisory control, loyalty to the community, and officers' professional ethical perception because police solidarity is loyalty to colleagues rather than loyalty to police departments, communities, or ethical standards (pp. 994–998). The widely accepted negative impact of police solidarity is that it becomes a shield for misconduct, cover-ups, and complicity (Crank 2004; Reiner 2010; Shernock 2007; Skolnick 1986; Skolnick and Fyfe 1993; Westley 1970). Various minor violations are considered to be accepted and covered up under the protection of the mask of protective solidarity. These violations include violence, accepting or even extorting a small amount of money or refreshments, small thefts, and different kinds of abuse of power (Crank 2004, p. 250; Shernock 2007, p. 998). It has been suggested that in this police subculture, an officer usually has no other choice but to keep quiet when he notices illegalities of peer officers, although this act may be far beyond his moral limit. It has been repeatedly noted that if an officer breaks the "code of silence" to be the "whistle blower", he or she will be immediately ostracised and labelled as a "rat" (Cockcroft 2013; Crank 2004; Mollen et al. 1994; Shernock 2007). According to the New York Mollen Commission Report, Lieutenant Robert McKenna addressed his view of the consequences of reporting peer misconduct:

> The cops are ostracized at times. They're held away. They're pushed off to one side. They're kept away from the rest of the group. I could almost say it'd be like the effects of a divorce. You're separated from your family. You're alone over here. Your family, the cops, are over there (Mollen et al. 1994, p. 54).

Gradually, the high degree of misconduct endurance fosters not only cover-ups of peer deviance but also complicity based on both officers' own violations and fellow officers' violations (Shernock 2007, p. 998).

Instead of a uniform description of solidarity, some scholars identified variations with regard to gender (Shernock 2007), education (Shernock 2007), rank (Reiner 2010; Reuss-Ianni 1983), and type of labour (Cain 1973; Young 1991). The identification of the two different subcultures of street cops and management cops provides the basis for different degrees of solidarity within and between these two groups (Reuss-Ianni 1983). Reiner (2010, p. 122) made a further analysis of how management cops need to balance between covering up and confronting with misconduct of street cops because they need to deal with the public. Similarly, the division between detectives and uniformed police officers may also influence the degree of inter-group solidarity (Cain 1973; Young 1991). In addition, other indicators such as female police officers and officers with higher educational qualifications may also threaten police solidarity (Shernock 2007, p. 999).

4.3.3 Cynicism

Many observers have mentioned that there is an attitude among police officers that includes a general distrust and a lack of hope toward citizens and the criminal justice system—cynicism (Buerger 2007; Burke and Mikkelsen 2005; Cockcroft 2013; Crank 2004; Crank et al. 1987; Graves 1996; Lotz and Regoli 1977; Niederhoffer 1967; Poole and Regoli 1979; Reiner 2010). Niederhoffer (1967) is the first observer who made an explicit description of police cynicism:

> Cynicism is an ideological plank deeply entrenched in the ethos of the police world, and it serves equally well for attack or defence. For many reasons the police are particularly vulnerable to cynicism. When they succumb, they lose faith in people, society, and eventually in themselves. In their Hobbesian view the world becomes a jungle in which crime, corruption, and brutality are normal features of the terrain (p. 9).

Buerger (2007) provided a relatively loose definition:

> Police cynicism is a widely acknowledged, little quantified property of the police subculture. It is a belief that the world—or at least the criminal justice system—operates according to rules that are opposite to its publicly articulated principles. The concept summarizes an ingrained belief that there is no altruism, everyone is out for themselves at the expense of anyone who gets in the way, and everyone lies—especially to the police (p. 370).

The sources of the cynical attitude lie in the occupational environment of police work. Many components of police subculture and the interaction among these components contribute to this attitude. They include the mission-oriented perception, the trained craft of suspicion, the sense of social isolation, the pressure to be efficient, and a permanent gap between expectations and the reality of the police world (Buerger 2007; Cockcroft 2013; Reiner 2010). The sense of mission of most frontline police officers attaches great importance to law enforcement, the detection of criminal activities, and the successful prosecution of criminals. For Reiner (2010), cynicism is the "Janus face of commitment" (p. 120). The sense of mission and the requirement of efficiency to some extent result from an intrinsic motivation of the police force and the police subculture (Reiner 2010, pp. 120–121). However, the reality of policing may disappoint officers. Citizens are not as supportive as police expect them to be, supervisors and administrators may not stand in line with them all the time, and the courts seem to be too lenient when the original judgements of police are not supported (Buerger 2007; Cochran and Bromley 2003). Another trait closely associated with the formation of police cynicism is suspicion. To cope with potential danger in the occupational environment, police officers have developed the "craft of suspicion" through both training and self-experience (Crank 2004; Rubinstein 1973). Many observers have mentioned suspicion as one of the core characteristics of police subculture or a character of police personality (Crank 2004; Kappeler et al. 1998; Reiner 2010; Skolnick 1986; Westley 1970). Reiner (2010, p. 121) noted that "suspicion is a response to the danger, authority, and efficiency elements in the environment, as well as an outcome of the sense of mission". According to Crank (2004), officers need to have a carefully honed level of reasonable suspicion when they interrogate a citizen.

Together with observational skills, reasonable suspicion may become a powerful tool to sort out latent wrongdoings. However, as a necessary occupational craft of police, suspicion is undoubtedly considered to be an undesirable attribute in society as it may lead to the social isolation of police officers from the broader organisation and community. When police officers routinely deal with possible "liars" who only provide information that police already know, it is natural for officers to form the negative and cynical view toward citizens, police administration, the criminal justice system, and even everything else (Buerger 2007).

The negative influence of police cynicism has attracted much attention among social scientists. One of the main impacts is the ruin of the moral foundations of police officers (Cockcroft 2013). Any efforts of reform aiming to reduce police misconduct and enhance ethical standards may meet great obstacles due to cynicism. In addition, a cynical attitude shows different levels of distrust of human nature, jeopardising efficiency and morale of police team (Graves 1996; Poole and Regoli 1979). Police cynicism may also harm police-citizen relationships and the implementation of community policing because citizens resist cooperating with police officers who consider them to be liars (Buerger 2007). However, some scholars have tried to identify some positive influences of police cynicism. A cynical view may sometimes serve as a way for officers to reduce the tensions caused by the occupational environment and what they regard as failures in law enforcement (Reiner 2010). It is also possible that officers who adhere more to a cynical and suspicious attitude may be better prepared for unexpected incidents (Caplan 2003).

Like other cultural themes such as isolation and solidarity, the cynical attitude is also transmitted through the process of occupational socialisation (Buerger 2007; Crank 2004). The formal socialisation in police academies and the informal socialisation in the field provide newcomers with sufficient opportunities to understand and finally accept this perspective. According to Niederhoffer (1967, p. 100), the whole socialisation process of cynicism takes at least 5 years among newcomers. He designed a 40-item research instrument to measure cynicism. He classified four stages of development of police cynicism: "pseudo-cynicism", "romantic cynicism", "aggressive cynicism", and "resigned cynicism" (pp. 98–99). In the first stage, police recruits easily learn this attitude because they try to follow the manner of perceptions and behaviour of experienced officers. Both Niederhoffer (1967) and Wilt and Bannon (in Crank 2004, p. 325) regarded this attitude only as the starting point of socialisation instead of real cynicism. As time passes, the socialisation level of cynicism develops with a progressive increase of maturity, from romantic cynicism, which refers to the primitive formation after 5 years of service, to aggressive cynicism (around 10 years of service) and resigned cynicism (the last few years of service) which shows a more steadfast attitude with the accumulation of more individual and occupational experiences (Niederhoffer 1967, pp. 98–99). In addition, Niederhoffer identified other variables that might influence the level of cynicism. These include position, education level, race, and type of labour.

A number of researchers have measured cynicism among police officers using the research instrument designed by Niederhoffer and its modified versions (Crank et al. 1987; Lotz and Regoli 1977; Poole and Regoli 1979). As a result, it has been suggested that police professionalism and adherence to cynicism are inversely related (Lotz and Regoli 1977; Niederhoffer 1967; Poole and Regoli 1979). This measurement scale has received much research interest of other commentators and has also received some criticism concerning its validity and generalisability (Hickman et al. 2004; Langworthy 1987). One obvious fact is that most of the empirical studies were conducted in the 20th century following the pioneering work of Niederhoffer. It has also been suggested that the research focus has shifted from investigating the concept of cynicism to a more complex examination of police job satisfaction under the influence of multiple factors (Buerger 2007, p. 373). Nevertheless, it is interesting that a relatively recent ethnographic study of police cultural perceptions in the UK conducted by Loftus (2010) indicated that a cynical view toward citizens and the legal system is still easily identifiable among police officers.

4.3.4 Traditionalism

Klockars (1993, p. 158) explained that for police traditionalism is a "political position they are structurally obliged to assume and whose ideology they are occupationally inclined to embrace". Being the representatives of the government, what the police need to do is usually to defend the status quo. Therefore, it is easy for police officers to develop an inclination of being traditional (Klockars 1993). For police officers, this inclination of traditionalism is mostly embodied in their organisational perceptions. Most police organisations are characterised by a paramilitary design with an hierarchical pyramid structure (Roberg et al. 2009; Scaramella et al. 2011). Exposed in the unique paramilitary organisations, police officers tend to become receptive of traditionalism under the influence of a strong crime fighter image and the rigid style of militarism, resisting changes and innovations (Cochran and Bromley 2003). LaGrange (1998) summarised seven typical characteristics of traditional paramilitary police organisations:

- Central command structure
- Rigid differences among ranks
- Terminology similar to that of the military
- Frequency use of commands and orders
- Strong enforcement of rules, regulations, and discipline
- Discouragement of individual creativity
- Resistance of system to change (LaGrange 1998, p. 318).

There are clear rank structures and a strict top-down chain of command in police departments. The clearly defined lines of authority are indicated by the uniform colours and police ranking accessories (Scaramella et al. 2011). The top-down communication negatively influences the communication between same-level units and the communication from frontline officers upward (Scaramella et al. 2011). Frontline officers are usually not involved in the decision-making of policy setting due to their low ranking, although they are responsible for most of the police work on the street. Therefore, the paramilitary structure may discourage the enthusiasm and performance of frontline officers (Franz and Jones 1987). This paramilitary subculture is also closely connected with the traditional mental priority upon law enforcement and use of an aggressive manner by many police officers (Kraska 2007).

Although the philosophy of community policing has been widely adopted in America and other Western countries, a trend of increasing militarisation in the police force has been documented by empirical studies (Kraska 2007; Kraska and Cubellis 1997; Kraska and Kappeler 1997; Phillips 2014). Kraska (2007, p. 508) considered the phenomenon of militarisation in American police to be indicative of some kind of implicit "resistance" or "corrective" to the pressure of implementation of community policing strategies. One of the phenomena that has been identified as proof of the rise of paramilitary style of policing lies in the increasing number of paramilitary units such as SWAT (Special Weapon and Tactics) and PPU (Police Paramilitary Unit) (Kraska 2007; Roberg et al. 2009). This trend is obviously against the essence of community policing: "from less militaristic to more militaristic, from generalist to specialist, and from service- and problem-oriented to aggressive crime fighting" (Roberg et al. 2009, p. 102). In contrast, community policing requires a more flattened structure to grant more power of decision-making to frontline police officers; decentralisation of police authority may allow frontline officers to have more decision-making power in their police work; and creativity in problem-solving will be encouraged, while a sense of responsibility for their work and for the community will also be enhanced among frontline officers (COPS 2009). This obviously contradicts the centralised police organisation structure and the subculture brewed in the paramilitary police organisations. It will be on the list of the reform agenda for police administrators when they initiate the community policing strategy.

In China, police departments share the paramilitary organisational structure of Western police (Wong 2012). Traditionally, the Chinese police force was closely linked with the People's Liberation Army (PLA), the military force in China (Wong 2009a). The organisational structure, the military discipline, and the military doctrines were all borrowed from the military. In addition, many police officers in China have the experience of service in the PLA. As a paramilitary-bureaucratic organisation, Chinese police agencies are characterised by all the essential elements mentioned above, such as the top-down chain of command, the hierarchical ranking system, and the strict discipline. However, it is still unclear whether there is a strong adherence to traditionalism among Chinese officers. It is important for us to have an idea of the subcultural perceptions among Chinese police officers through empirical studies, on the basis of which useful suggestions could be made for police administrators and police training instructors to facilitate the implementation of community policing.

4.3.5 Resistance to Change

For organisations in a society that experiences rapid changes and development, creative and innovative thinking are essential. However, it is pointed out that "the most common characteristic of change is people's resistance to it", because changes may bring the "feeling of stress and fear of the unknown" (Roberg et al. 2009, p. 124). Police officers are considered to be even less receptive to changes at work than are other people due to the traditional quasi-military organisations that they are exposed to every day (Lingamneni 1979; Roberg et al. 2009). Many police departments have experienced or are experiencing a significant shift from a traditional policing style to a service-oriented policing style, namely, community policing. This shift obviously broadens the functions of police in providing services for citizens. In addition, the implementation of community policing needs not only a shift of the police orientation from crime control to community service but also purposeful organisational change, such as decentralisation of police authority (Cochran et al. 2002). All of these efforts may encounter resistance from police practitioners. Lingamneni (1979) summarised three main factors that lead to resistance to changes at work in police agencies: "authoritarian-totalitarian system of organisational structure, leadership styles and attitudes of the police chiefs and ideology or dogma" (p. 19). First of all, the paramilitary structure of police departments is relatively more likely to resist potential change than is the structure of other organisations. Police officers in Western countries, especially in the USA, are granted "limited authority to afford maximum individual freedom" and are expected to "enforce the law only" (Jiao 2001a, p. 174). Police officers tend to be conservative and stick to "the straight and narrow path to right living" (Jiao 2001a, p. 175). Therefore, the tendency of "cover yourself" keeps officers away from innovation. Second, traditional police subculture entails internal norms and values that may hamper reform efforts. The police subculture functions like a defence mechanism against outside pressures and uncertainties. Once the shared values and norms are formed, they will be "extremely difficult to change" (Schein 2004, p. 31). This means that, if changes happen, they will generate "large quantities of basic anxiety" (Schein 2004, p. 31). It is always expected that officers simply conform to and not question the ideology in police organisations (Lingamneni 1979). It has been suggested that officers who hold attitudes that are in line with traditional depictions of police subculture show a lower level of receptivity to change (Cochran et al. 2002, p. 511). In addition, the attitudes of police leaders are also likely to play an important role in deciding the perceptions of frontline officers and the final consequence of any innovative effort. If police officers adhere to a traditional police subculture that resists any reform efforts, it is difficult for the implementation of community policing to be successful because the support from frontline police officers is essential for any reform attempt in policing strategies.

4.3.6 Police Role Orientations of Crime Control and Service

Traditional police subculture suggested in the Western literature entails a strong preference for the role of crime fighting, a sense of mission, and a tendency to use aggressive policing tactics (Cochran and Bromley 2003). Crime fighting is given high priority and regarded as the real police work in the police culture, while other police functions such as order maintenance and community service are considered secondary or even a waste of time (Klockars 1985b; Paoline 2003, 2004; Paoline et al. 2000; Rumbaut and Egon 1979; Sparrow et al. 1990; Walker and Katz 2005; Westley 1970; Wilson 1968). In this police subculture, police officers consider themselves to be "the only real crime fighters" and focus on the deterrence of crime (Sparrow et al. 1990, p. 51). This crime fighter image is labelled by the police themselves (Walker and Katz 2005, p. 6). Sparrow et al. (1990) provide a clear illustration of the importance of the crime fighter image for the police:

> The image lies at the heart of the police value system; indeed, it is its foundation stone. This image is what police chiefs talk of at award dinners and budget time; it is what police officers talk of with their "civilian" friends. It is the face of policing wishes to present to the public. It is real, or at least honest, as far as it goes; the police really do believe it (p. 50).

There are several reasons that crime fighting is considered to be the core mandate of the police. First, police officers would like to prove to the public that they are efficient by showing that they have done "something important" (Walker and Katz 2005, p. 6). In addition, police aim for the social recognition that they have the exclusive expertise in the field of crime control and law enforcement (Manning 1997). Police agencies make every effort to reinforce this role orientation of crime fighting. Crime-related topics are accorded great importance during police training, the department is organised by law enforcement specialisations, crime control is one of the main aims of police statistics, and career promotion is heavily based on law enforcement performance (Bittner 1974, pp. 238–239; Wilson 1968, p. 69). In addition to the police themselves, the crime fighter image is widely "cultivated and propagated" by the media and government officials (Bittner 1974, p. 238; Rumbaut and Egon 1979, p. 262; Walker and Katz 2005, p. 6).

This role orientation of crime fighting may have many negative consequences, because the reality of police work is far more complex and comprehensive than mere crime fighting. According to a study of police service and citizen demands conducted in America, only 19 percent of calls for police service from citizens are crime-related (Walker and Katz 2005, p. 7). In addition, policing involves a high level of discretion that requires skills of decision-making on the basis of experience and capability rather than simply arresting criminals (Walker and Katz 2005). Walker and Katz (2005) summarised three consequences of the crime-fighter image. First, this image may lead to an incorrect evaluation of police work because it overlooks many other functions of policing. Police officers in contemporary societies usually need to take more responsibilities than public imagination, such as "crime fighting, crime reduction, dealing with anti-social behaviour, tackling terrorism, public reassurance, traffic duties, immigration control, school work, offender management, event security, disaster management, making people feel safer and so on" (Millie 2014, p. 53). Second, an unrealistic high expectation of crime deterrence efficiency is formed as a result of the propaganda of the crime fighting role of police. In addition, police officers may also be trapped in this contradictory situation where beliefs and behaviour don't match (Walker and Katz 2005, pp. 6–7).

Together with this crime fighter image is a preference for aggressive policing tactics and a negative attitude toward legal and procedural restrictions that are perceived as obstacles of the effectiveness of law enforcement (Cochran and Bromley 2003; Paoline et al. 2000). Aggressiveness in policing is "a matter of taking the initiative on the street to control crime and a preoccupation with order that legitimises the use of illegal tactics" (Brown 1981, p. 223). According to Sparrow et al. (1990, p. 51), "it is impossible to win the war against crime without bending the rules". Among these rule-bending behaviour, excessive and illegal use of force is one of the most frequently mentioned topics (Crank 2004; Kappeler et al. 1998; Skolnick and Fyfe 1993; Terrill et al. 2003; Westley 1953).

Although above studies have identified police subculture as traditionally involving a preference of the role orientation of crime fighting and aggressive policing tactics, many studies have discovered variations of police role orientations (Broderick 1987; Brown 1981; Cochran and Bromley 2003; Muir 1977; Paoline 2001; White 1972; Worden 1995). Due to subcultural variations in different occupational and organisational environments, different styles of policing are formed correspondingly (Paoline 2001). These typologies are mostly based on police attitudes toward role orientations and other elements of police culture.

White (1972) conducted one of the earliest typological studies of police role orientations. She identified four police role types: the "tough-cop", the "crime-fighter", the "problem solver", and the "rule-applier" (White 1972). Each role type is "empirically specifiable by the perceptions and the behaviour of the role occupants" (White 1972, p. 65). Tough cops are strong adherents of the traditional accounts of police culture. They believe in a tough policing style that emphasises the outcome of crime control with the help of violence and stereotyping. Problem-solvers consider the central role of policing is to offer assistance and to solve problems for people. Crime-fighters consider the role of fighting crime to be their principal task and believe that process is more important than outcomes. For White, rule-appliers are of great interest because they consider neither fighting crime nor providing service as the foremost tasks. What they intend to do is following commands and trying to "operate by the book" (p. 72).

Based on the model of a "professional politician" established by Weber (1965), Muir (1977) proposed a typology by defining a "good" policeman. For him, the key elements of whether an officer can be good are to what extent his "passion and perspective" are in accordance with the professional model. The virtue of "passion" measures an officer's ability to integrate the use of coercion with a moral aim; the virtue of "perspective" refers to whether an officer adopts a tragic rather than a cynical attitude toward the suffering of people. In the words of Muir (1977), a professional police officer is someone feeling "morally reconciled to using coercion" and reflecting "empathetically upon the condition of mankind" (p. 54). In addition to the "professional" type, he summarised three non-professional types: "enforcers" (high passion, low perspective), "reciprocators" (high perspective, low passion), and "avoiders" (low passion and perspective) (p. 55).

Broderick (1987, p. 5) established a typology of police officers based on their perceptions of "due process of law" and keeping social order. Officers who are more in favour of keeping the social order rather than due process are labelled "enforcers"; those who believe that due process is more important than social order are "optimists"; officers who attach equal importance to the two dimensions are "idealists"; and those who place low emphasis on both social order and individual rights are "realists" (Broderick 1987, p. 5).

Similar to the above mentioned scholars, Brown (1981, p. 224) also developed a four-fold typology of police officers: "Old Style Crime Fighters", "Clean Beat Crime Fighters", "Service Style", and "Professionals". Not as abstract as the typologies of White and Muir, Brown classified officers on the degree of their "aggressiveness" of crime control and their "selectivity" of law enforcement (p. 223). "Aggressive" officers embody many of the characteristics of traditional police culture. They contend that crime control is central to policing and some minor violations of norms could be legitimate for the sake of outcomes. "Selective" officers have their own preference in the process of law enforcement. For them, felonies are "the only violation worth pursuing" (Brown 1981, p. 225). Officers who are very aggressive and selective are classified as "Old Style Crime Fighters"; those who are aggressive and non-selective are classified as "Clean Beat Crime Fighters"; highly selective and non-aggressive ones are labelled as "Service Style" officers; those who are neither selective nor aggressive are classified as "Professionals" (Brown 1981).

Reiner (1985, p. 106) summarised a composite on the basis of existing typological studies: "an alienated cynic, a managerial professional, a peacekeeper and a law-enforcer". For him, this classification shows the variations between street and management officers and between detectives and uniformed officers, while also representing individual differences related with police work (Reiner 2010).

Based on the previous typologies, Worden (1995) also developed a composite including the dimensions that had been proposed by the previous four scholars. In his composite, "tough cops" represent most of the characteristics of the traditional police culture, with a cynical attitude toward the public and legal restrictions that are deemed to obstruct the crime control function of policing; "clean-beat crime-fighters" are those officers who are similar to tough cops in their priority of law enforcement and are different from them in their persistence of the due process and individual rights; as the name suggests, "avoiders" refer to the type of officers who wish to spend only a small amount of energy in their work and have a low level of commitment to the work; "problem-solvers" have a strong preference for the role of providing service and solving problems for the community instead of crime control and law enforcement; "professionals" are "the most well-rounded and balanced" of all the types, with equal commitment to the roles of law enforcement and community service and positive opinions toward the public and the legal system (pp. 58–60).

Based on the composite typology of Worden and other existing typologies, Paoline (2001) developed a seven-fold typology through his survey study among around four hundred officers in two police departments in the USA. Different from the previous typologies, the seven-fold typology is generated through quantitative cluster analysis on the data collected with interpretations from Paoline. Among the seven types of officers, five of them are similar to the classification of Worden: "Lay-Lows" versus "avoiders", "Old-Pros" versus "professionals", "Traditionalists" versus "tough cops", "Peacekeepers" versus "problem-solvers", "Law Enforcers" versus "clean-beat crime-fighters" (Paoline 2001, pp. 93–109). Two other types are "Anti-Organisational Street-Cops" and "Dirty Harry Enforcers". The former stands in the middle of "Lay-Lows" and "Traditionalists", with strong negative attitudes toward supervisors and highly positive attitudes toward citizens. The latter resembles "Traditionalists" and "Law Enforcers" in that they prefer aggressive policing and dislike due process of law enforcement.

Following the research model of Paoline (2001), Cochran and Bromley (2003) conducted an empirical study to examine the degree of adherence to the police subculture among a sample of officers in the USA and designed a questionnaire made up of five work orientation scales—crime control, service, cynicism, traditionalism, and receptivity to change. They constructed and validated a taxonomy of police officers through advanced statistical analysis techniques, dividing their orientations into three groups—"Subcultural Adherents", "COP Cops" and "Normals" on the basis of the degree of adherence to the police subculture (Cochran and Bromley 2003).

The above mentioned studies have identified differences between police officers in terms of role orientations and policing styles. Typological studies show that officers from various groups may not share some attitudes, values, and norms commonly associated with the police culture or they may embody them differently (Paoline 2004). In China, few empirical studies have been conducted to investigate the role orientations of frontline police officers. Because that police subculture is within the entire Chinese social culture, it is often assumed that the service function is one of the central tasks of police in China (Jiao 2001b; Wang and Wong 2012). Chinese traditional culture emphasises collectivism, voluntarism, and group orientation (Wang and Wong 2012, p. 40); the mass-line policing, adopted in China as the guideline for policing since 1949, also requires a high level of cooperation between the police and the people (Zhong 2009).

Therefore, it is suggested that Chinese policing is more service-oriented than the Western policing style and this has led to a closer police-citizen relationship (Chen 2002). However, since the Chinese government adopted its opening-up policy, the economy developed quickly and Chinese society changed accordingly. In order to deal with the rise of crimes in China, police departments conducted many strike-hard campaigns. In addition, the trend of professionalisation also reminds officers to rethink the contradiction between their legitimate functions and what they have been expected to do in reality (Dai 2001; Wang and Wong 2012). As a result, Chinese policing has become more punitive and crime control has become the central task of the police. One of the negative outcomes of police professionalisation in China is that the close relationship between police and the people tends to be loosened (Sun et al. 2009; Wong 2001). Police-citizen relations in China have worsened since the 1980s, and people have less trust in the police than they did previously (Du 1997). Comparative research has indicated that Chinese people generally have less confidence of police than do their American counterparts (Cao and Hou 2001). The official launch of community policing in China in 2002 signalled clearly that Chinese police aim to adopt a service-oriented proactive strategy and regain support and trust from the public. It is therefore meaningful to understand role orientations of Chinese frontline officers through empirical studies because the support of police practitioners, especially frontline officers, is crucial for the philosophical shift to a community- and service-oriented strategy.

4.3.7 The Interactions Between Police Subcultural Themes

The subcultural themes are not supposed to be separated from each other; instead, there should be some close associations among them so that the whole subculture could be a group of coherently united components that are hard to be altered. This is important for police administrators in that if the subcultural themes are closely correlated with each other or some of them are correlated with some other themes, it is necessary for police administrators to consider the police subculture as a whole instead of some separate themes when they plan to make some positive changes to the existing subculture.

The police role orientation of crime fighting has also been associated with other police cultural themes such as isolation, solidarity, traditionalism, and cynicism, because the crime fighter image is central in the police subculture (Sparrow et al. 1990). The more officers consider themselves to be the only real crime fighters, the more they stick to group loyalty and remain isolated from the public. Packer gave (1968) some principles for the policing model that focuses on crime control and one of them mentions that there is "a presumption of guilt" (p. 161). Therefore, a cynical attitude is easily formed: Those "who are beaten must have deserved it; all defendants must be guilty" (Pollock 2012, p. 103). An officer who is crime-fighting-oriented also tends to prefer the traditional paramilitary organisational structure of police departments because all the essential characteristics of the traditional police organisations are indeed facilitating a "war" against crime, such as the centralised authority and the strict discipline (Roberg et al. 2009). Similarly, adherents of the crime fighter image are also relatively less receptive to changes, especially such as the strategic shift from a crime fighter to a service provider. Conversely, the role orientation of crime fighting may also be reinforced by other subcultural themes, such as cynicism, traditionalism, isolation, and solidarity. Although policing analysts have made these arguments to describe the close relations between the crime fighting role orientation and other cultural themes, empirical evidence is not enough to support the above assertions. In addition, if the crime fighter image is significantly correlated with the other parts of the subculture, will the role orientation of service also be inversely correlated with them? The study conducted by Cochran, Bromley, and Swando in the USA indicated that service role orientation is positively associated with receptivity to change for police officers (Cochran et al. 2002). For other associations, empirical studies are needed to give an answer.

It is reasonable to link police solidarity with social isolation and cynicism. Cynicism, the negative attitude toward the public and the legal system formed and reinforced in police work, is commonly regarded as being socially unattractive and makes it difficult for officers to form friendship with outsiders (Swanton 1981). Therefore, it is more likely that officers become more integrated with other police officers and less into the public. In this sense, police internal solidarity is further reinforced. Police officers who adhere to a cynical attitude also find it difficult to accept innovative changes and reforms because they believe that all new programs would suffer from the same fate of failure (Buerger 2007). The paramilitary organisational structures in most police departments tend to make people resist change. Therefore, it is expected that officers who prefer the traditional police organisational structures would be less receptive to changes at work. Will officers who adhere to police traditionalism be more likely to have higher levels of solidarity, isolation, and cynicism? Will officers who are receptive to changes be less socialised into the three subcultural themes? There is still very little empirically based knowledge to answer these questions.

4.4 Individual and Work-Related Characteristics and Police Subculture

Traditional depictions of police subculture in the West describe a relatively overwhelming adherence to a set of beliefs generated through the socialisation process under the occupational and organisational environment of policing. Recent studies have become more and more focused on the variations of police cultural perceptions and the explanation of how police culture changes in a changing society that is far more complex than in the past. Some observers have conducted empirical studies in order to find out to what extent contemporary policing still mirrors traditional police subculture and what factors correlate with cultural attributes of modern policing (Loftus 2010; Skolnick 2008). Social scientists have also been interested in the causes of variations of police cultural attitudes and behaviour in terms of different individual and work-related characteristics. It is reasonable to assume that officers who are women, from racial minorities, and who are college graduates will show a relatively lower level of adherence to the traditional police culture than do other officers,but these assumptions have not been sufficiently supported by empirical studies (Bacon 2014; Cochran and Bromley 2003; Pauline 2003; Pauline et al. 2000; Reuss-Ianni 1983). In addition, it is reasonable to assume that newcomers are less socialised into the police subculture than are their experienced counterparts (Chan et al. 2003). According to Niederhoffer, the socialisation level of police cynicism could be classified into four stages based on the length of service (Niederhoffer 1967, pp. 98–99). The degree of police cynicism varies when tenure changes. Similar to cynicism, police officers' role orientations are also associated with their tenure. Paoline (2001) made a detailed analysis of this relationship on the basis of previous typological studies. It is reasonable to assume that officers who strongly adhere to the role of crime fighter would be more experienced rather than newcomers (Broderick 1987; Brown 1981; Muir 1977; White 1972). Some researchers have made observations concerning the relationship between police cultural perceptions and some individual and work-related characteristics including gender (Britz 1997; Cochran and Bromley 2003; Paoline et al. 2000; Worden 1993), race (Britz 1997; Paoline et al. 2000), educational background (Cochran and Bromley 2003; Paoline et al. 2000; Reuss-Ianni 1983; Worden 1990), age (Britz 1997; Cochran and Bromley 2003), tenure (Britz 1997; Cochran and Bromley 2003; Paoline et al. 2000), rank (Reuss-Ianni 1983), and whether officers are detectives or non-detectives (Hobbs 1988; Young 1991). However, empirical studies of the above mentioned topics are very limited. Most of the results did not support the previous assumptions. Furthermore, no empirical study could be found in the context of Chinese policing on this topic. More empirical studies in different contexts, such as Chinese policing, may contribute to a clearer understanding of the factors influencing police cultural variations in the mist of ambiguities and contradictions between assumptions and scientific conclusions.

4.4.1 Gender

Police culture has been traditionally described as a culture dominated by the beliefs of male officers (Crank 2004; Reiner 2010; Westmarland 2001; Young 1991). The masculine orientation includes "the avoidance of anything vaguely feminine, the attainment of success and social status, a manly air of toughness, confidence, and self-reliance, and an aura of aggressiveness, daring, and violence" (Crank 2004, p. 231). This cult of masculinity has become a cultural theme rooted in the police subculture and leaves "no real place for a woman" in the world of policing (Young 1991, p. 251). In the occupational environment of police work, masculinity echoes with a need to deal with the uncertainties of policing and an internal solidarity to protect officers against outside risks and to maintain police authority. Since training in the police academy, police recruits have received an emphasis of masculine characteristics such as physical strength, along with skills of weapon use and fighting, through formal or informal socialisation (Crank 2004, p. 230; Prokos and Padavic 2002). This resonates with an interview of a female officer conducted by Heidensohn (1992): "from the training school, the atmosphere had been that you were second-class police because you were really going to sit-around fiddling with children and young people" (p. 120).

There are many negative consequences of masculinity in police subculture. First, the literature has provided evidence of different kinds of police misconduct regarding female citizens, victims, offenders and officers, such as sexual harassment (Cockcroft 2013, pp. 65–66; Crank 2004, p. 230). Second, female officers may suffer from marginalisation by their male counterparts and fewer promotion opportunities resulting from gender discrimination (Cockcroft 2013; Heidensohn 1992). In addition, the masculine orientation associated with aggressiveness and physical action does not match the implementation of community policing that emphasises good police-citizen relationships (Dejong 2004; Eterno 2006). Statistics in the USA have indicated that the percentage of female police officers has dramatically increased in the last couple of decades, but its influence upon police behaviour and attitudes seems to be unclear (Sklansky 2006). One of the reasons may be that female officers sometimes need to force themselves to meet the requirements of the masculine police subculture in order to avoid marginalisation (Sklansky 2006). It is suggested that female officers sometimes need to force themselves to avoid being friendly and behave aggressively in order to meet the accepted norms in the police subculture (Martin and Jurik 2007).

Since the advent of community policing, the focus has been shifted from the crime-fighting function to a softer policing style that emphasises good police-citizen relations. Researchers have contended that female officers have more potential to fulfil the tasks of community policing such as solving problems, mediation, and establishing good relationships (Belknap 2007; Miller 1998, 1999; Miller and Bonistall 2012; Miller and Hodge 2004). Although these skills are not regarded as real police work in the philosophy of traditional crime fighting and law enforcement, they may play an important role in community policing. Community policing emphasises "communication, familiarity, the building of better rapport and trust between police and residents, informal problem solving, and the fostering of citizen-police cooperation" (Miller 1998, p. 165). Under these principles, conflicts may be solved through dialogue, meditation, and other informal methods instead of aggressive methods. From this perspective, female officers may be able to make stronger contributions to community policing because they grasp these feminine traits better (Miller 1998). According to an Australian study, female officers were found to prefer "information exchange, support behaviours and rejecting comments" in interactions with citizens, while their male counterparts took a more "dominating role" (Wilson and Braithwaite 1996, p. vi). Another study conducted by Rabe-Hemp in America yielded mixed results: Female officers were less likely to be engaged in extreme controlling behaviours, but they did not use more supporting behaviours than did their male counterparts (Rabe-Hemp 2008). In addition, gender was found to be very weak in regard to its influence upon police perceptions (Poteyeva and Sun 2009).

In China, the recruitment of female police officers began in 1929 in Shanghai (Huang 2013; Zhang and Li 2006). Along with the rapid economic development and the adoption of reforming and opening-up policies, women gradually receive more and more opportunities to be employed into professions that have been traditionally dominated by men. The Ministry of Public Security of China has made a policy requirement that female police officers should account for 10–15 % of all police officers (Ling and Liu 2002, pp. 53–54). According to *Women and Men in China*—a yearbook edited by the National Bureau of Statistics of the People's Republic of China, the number of female police officers accounted for 13.7 % of the total number of 2 million Chinese police officers in 2011 (Jia 2012). This shows an increase of 3 % compared with the number of female police officers in 2002 (10 % of 1.6 million) (Rong 2013). In addition, police universities and academies also keep a steadily increasing rate of enrolment of female students and cadets. Two national police universities, namely China People's Public Security Police University (CPPSU) and National Police University of China (NPUC), planned to enrol 254 female students (accounting for 11.2 % of the total enrolment of 2260) (CPPSU 2015) and 140 female students (accounting for 10 % of total enrolment number of 1400) (NPUC 2015) in 2015. Some provincial police colleges and municipal academies at times have an even higher rate of female cadet enrolment. For instance, 112 female students were enrolled by Hunan Police College in 2012, accounting for 16 % of total 700 students enrolled (Rong 2013).

Although the enrolment of police universities and academies paves the way for a steady increase of female police officers in China, there are still many constraints. One of the main obstacles is the lack of appropriate positions for policewomen in the traditional masculine police world. Most female police officers are engaged in office work such as household registration management, women and child protection, or provincial and state police departments (Huang 2013). In addition, it has been revealed that female police officers in China prefer assignments, such as office work, that meet traditional gender expectations (Ling and Liu 2002); similar results were obtained from studies conducted in Taiwan, indicating that less than half of the surveyed female police cadets believed that female officers should be assigned the same tasks, such as patrol and criminal investigation, as their male counterparts (Chu and Tsao 2014). However, police administrators and researchers in China have realised that female police officers should have played a more important role due to their unique feminine traits. In addition, the expansion of female police officers will usher in new trends to contemporary police culture. It is possible that female police officers will help to form a more service-oriented police culture to help to change the traditional masculine police culture that regards crime fighting as the main target.

In this study, I would like to find out to what extent gender is associated with officers' adherence to police subculture in China. Based on the previous research and observations, it could be assumed that female officers would adopt a more service-oriented style of policing than do their male counterparts. In addition, some scholars have suggested that female officers tend to be engaged in less excessive force and various police misconduct (Garcia 2003; Roberg et al. 2009). It was also pointed out that female officers are less cynical toward citizens and less aggressive in law enforcement (Garcia 2003; Roberg et al. 2009). Therefore, I intend to investigate how gender is associated with police subcultural perceptions in China. If gender is found to be correlated with the police subculture, further suggestions could be made to promote the implementation of community policing through the perspective of a wider acknowledgement of feminine traits in policing by their male counterparts and police administration.

4.4.2 *Education*

Educational background has also been identified as a determinant that might influence police subculture (Cockcroft 2013; Punch 2007). Policing is traditionally portrayed as an occupation that is mainly based on practices and experiences rather than systematic accumulation of academic knowledge and formal education (Muir 1977). Therefore, police departments are not attractive to people with high educational qualifications; in addition, some police agencies impose obstacles for college graduates to be recruited to the police force (Cockcroft 2013; Fielding 1988). What is emphasised as the appropriate "working knowledge" is "practical, communal, 'common-sense' knowledge"; academic knowledge is regarded as "irrelevant", or even "dysfunctional" (Punch 2007, p. 109). What is considered to be accepted cultural norm is Cop's Code emphasising the importance of conformity, solidarity, and secrecy; "to be educated" means being "deviant" because it may challenge the existing norms (Crank 2004; Punch 2007, p. 110; Reuss-Ianni 1983).

In contemporary policing, science and technology have received great respect when international terrorism, cross-border crime, and high-tech crime appear in the ear of globalisation. Nowadays police officers are becoming more educated than they had been previously (Archbold 2013). This new trend will inevitably bring change to the existing police culture. Punch (2007) conducted a study about the impact of college education on police culture on the basis of a British program of sending officers to receive university education. He contended that college education may lead to "significant and positive" change to the existing police culture (p. 125). Through the interviews of officers who received education in university and returned to the police force, he observed that they were equipped with skills of critical thinking to "challenge the status quo" and "view the world differently" (p. 120). The influence of educational background on police officers' cultural perceptions has received the attention of social scientists who have been interested in such things as education's impact on police attitudes toward job satisfaction (Johnson 2012; Paoline et al. 2015), role orientations (Paoline et al. 2000, 2015), cynicism (Alpert and Dunham 1997), and aggressive policing (Carter and Sapp 1990; Paoline et al. 2000). It could be expected that police officers with a tertiary educational background would be less inclined to adhere to the traditional police culture than would their less educated counterparts. Paoline et al. (2000) made a detailed analysis of expectations about the influence of educational background on police cultural perceptions:

> Educational experiences might result in a greater appreciation of the multiple functions that police perform in modern society, of limitations on police authority, and of the social, economic, and psychological forces that shape the problems and behavior of the people with whom they have contact. Therefore one might expect that college-educated officers would subscribe to broader role orientations than their less educated colleagues, that they

> would have more positive attitudes toward citizens, and that they would be less aggressive. College-educated officers also might expect to be more autonomous in exercising discretion, and to accept bureaucratic constraints with less equanimity, than would less highly educated officers, thus we might expect them to be more favorably disposed toward selective enforcement (p. 585).

However, the above reasonable arguments have not been sufficiently supported by empirical studies. In China, the educational background of frontline police officers has been greatly enhanced. According to statistics of the Ministry of Public Security of China, police officers who have a college associate degree or above accounted for 57.3 % of total police officers in 2003 (Liu 2003). This has brought a greater diversity of educational background among Chinese frontline police officers. Therefore, in this study, I intended to find out whether educational background may bring differences to police cultural perceptions in China through empirical inquiry.

4.4.3 Age and Tenure

It is reasonable to expect that age and level of experience would be associated with the degree of adherence to police subculture (Cochran and Bromley 2003). Some studies have been conducted to investigate the relationship between different components of police culture and age or length of service. Brecher (2009) conducted an empirical survey study about two groups of police officers in Illinois, USA: the active and the retired. It was found out that older officers, compared with their younger counterparts, attached greater importance to community commitment, a paramilitary structure of police department, and the self-identification of police role (Brecher 2009). However, according to Brecher, although different generations of police officers show variations in their police cultural attitudes, age and tenure factors could be considered as only weak indicators. Another empirical study conducted in India also suggested that tenure does not significantly influence police role orientations and ethical perceptions (Scott et al. 2009). Although it is expected that officers with less service experience in the police force will adhere less to some themes of the police subculture such as social isolation, cynicism and internal solidarity, studies pointed out that adherence to some certain theme (such as cynicism) is actually far from simply positively influenced by tenure. As mentioned earlier, Niederhoffer (1967) made a four-stage classification of the process of cynicism socialisation among police officers: "pseudo-cynicism", "romantic cynicism", "aggressive cynicism", and "resigned cynicism" (pp. 98–99). He discovered that the level of police cynicism rises along with the socialisation in the first stage of a police career and then remains at the highest level in the period of 7–10 years of service experience before declining. This is also supported by some other studies (Lotz and Regoli 1977; Regoli 1976). In this study, I intend to find out whether age and tenure would significantly influence police subcultural perceptions in the Chinese context.

4.4.4 Type of Police Force

In China, the hierarchical structure of the police force is set up within the framework of the government's structure. At the top of the hierarchy is the Ministry of Public Security (MPS) which is a component of the State Council. The MPS is responsible for directing and coordinating police operations throughout the country. Under the MPS, there are provincial police departments in provinces, autonomous regions, and municipalities that are directly under the control of central government. Under provincial departments, there are municipal police bureaus that control police operation in each city and report to provincial police departments. Under municipal police bureaus, there are district or county police sub-bureaus. Police stations are at the bottom of the police system, located in communities all over the country.

Police departments at each level are accountable to both their immediately higher police department and the local government to which they belong For example, a municipal police bureau would be responsible for the police operation within their territory and be accountable to the provincial police department and the municipal government. From the perspective of duties, the MPS is usually in charge of setting professional rules and regulations, directing and coordinating major criminal investigations, and providing scientific and practical guidance to local police departments. A provincial police department is responsible for organizing and coordinating serious criminal investigations, directing and supervising police operations within its territory, and setting provincial rules and regulations. Municipal police bureaus, district police sub-bureaus, and police stations all directly engage in criminal investigations and public order maintenance. Police stations usually deal with public order cases, district police sub-bureaus handle criminal cases within the district, and municipal police bureaus are responsible for serious criminal and public order cases. However, the above division of responsibilities is not very clear-cut.

Therefore, in reality, police officers from different levels of police agencies have different duties and responsibilities. It is reasonable to expect that variations of police cultural perceptions could be formed among officers of different types of police force. In this study, this factor has been taken into consideration to find out whether different levels of police departments will discriminate police adherence to components of subculture.

4.4.5 Detectives Versus Non-detectives

As discussed in Sect. 4.1, police detectives have unique cultural norms and values compared with uniform officers because of the nature of their work. The most obvious difference between police detectives and non-detectives is represented by their clothing (detectives do not wear uniforms as other officers do) and daily work variations. Police detectives are not restricted by regular police uniforms and fixed work times; instead, the efficiency of successful detection functions like an intangible frame that defines their subculture (Young 1991). They are responsible for piecing together clues to find out how crimes have occurred, while uniformed officers regard an arrest as the end of most operations. Young experienced the cultural differences between the two groups of police officers on the basis of his own role transition from a uniformed officer to a detective in CID. According to his experience, uniformed police officers despise the ineffective crime detection of police detectives and the "uncontrolled nature" and the "apparent freedom of movement" of CID work (Young 1991, p. 81). Young also felt that crime detection in the CID actually turns out to be some "paper exercise of statistical detections" which are used to placate the general public regarding their fear of high crime rates (p. 83). For Young, these two groups of police officers have "different perceptions of police reality and their own structures of significance to maintain" (p. 82). Similar to Young, Hobbs described the unique set of informal rules in the occupational world of CID officers through a three-year ethnographic study of police detectives in the East-End of London (Hobbs 1991). For Hobbs, only a very small proportion of crime detections are due to real detective work, while the rest of the work could be considered to be a game between the police and the policed with regulations known by both.

In China, police detectives are responsible for criminal investigations, including the procedures from crime scene investigation, evidence collection, trace examination and analysis, to criminal cases detection. Besides common criminal cases, they are responsible for drug-related cases, organised cases, terrorism cases, and financial cases. They work in criminal investigation departments of different areas of the police force, from the Criminal Investigation Bureau in the MPS, provincial criminal police general commands, and municipal criminal police commands, to district or county criminal police units and local criminal police squads. Police detectives are one of the main components of Chinese frontline police.

In China, few studies have been conducted to examine subcultural perceptions of police detectives. According to the search in CNKI, the largest academic database in China, the only related academic article is *On the Professional Culture of the Criminal Police and its Impact on the Investigation,* by Yujuan Yang, from China People's Public Security University. Yang (2011) analysed the main characteristics of police detective subculture and their impact on criminal investigation on the basis of Reiner's theoretical accounts of police culture and the Chinese context. According to Yang, the professional culture of police detectives in China consists of three main components: "a sense of mission of maintaining justice", "the cohesion of unity and coordination", and "the idea of advocating power" (p. 50). This explanation is a combination of Western theory in police culture and the specific Chinese policing context. However, Yang failed to present the differences between the cultural perceptions of police detectives and non-detectives in her study. In addition, this depiction of police detective subculture is not on the basis of empirical studies. Therefore, in this study I would like to examine the subcultural variations between police detectives and non-detectives in China.

4.5 Summary

It has been well documented that police officers are socialised into a strong and steady subculture due to the embedded nature of danger and uncertainties, and the accompanying stress in the occupation (Nhan 2014). Since the seminal work of Westley in the 1950s, many researchers have tried to investigate the mysterious collection of cultural themes that may determine the making of a police officer (Banton 1964; Cain 1973; Crank 2004; Muir 1977; Reiner 1985; Skolnick 1986; Van Maanen 1973; Westley 1953). However, as time passes, the diversification of the police force has become a major characteristic in contemporary policing (Sklansky 2006) and, as a result, more and more observers have shifted their attention from a monolithic police subculture to the variations and changes (Chan 1996, 1997; Cochran and Bromley 2003; Paoline 2001, 2003, 2004). This line of inquiry has pushed police cultural studies toward new theoretical and practical sophistication. Nevertheless, some current studies keep informing us that demographic diversification and socioeconomic development have not changed the traditional depiction of police cultural themes because many of the core components are still clearly evidenced in contemporary policing (Loftus 2010; Skolnick 2008). In addition, most of the existing studies were based on the context of English-speaking countries (Loyens 2009), and few studies have been conducted in China with regard to police cultural perceptions.

This chapter discusses the occupational subculture of police officers by reviewing relevant studies of police culture from the traditional monolithic perspective to the contemporary perspective that emphasises variations and changes. Seven core cultural themes are discussed separately with an emphasis on the definitions, causes, and influences. After a detailed review of the literature about police cultural studies, some demographic and work-related variables that are believed to have potential influence on police cultural perceptions are then discussed, namely gender, education level, age, tenure, type of police force, and being detectives or not. In Chap. 5, I would like to discuss the status quo of Chinese police cultural studies, with a focus on the differences between Chinese and Western definitions of police culture.

Chapter 5
Studies of Police Culture in China

In China, policing researchers and practitioners began to be interested in studies of police culture in the early 1990s (Zhang 2010a, p. 55). Since then, many scholars have published their views on topics such as enhancing police culture cultivation (Cai and Liu 2011; Guo 2011; Zhang 1993), positive and negative police culture (Lin 2008; Yu 2011), and the relationship between police culture and police image (Ye 2011). However, studies of police culture in China differ significantly from those in Western countries (Zhang 2010a).

5.1 Definition of the Police Culture in China

The phrase "police culture" in China has a different connotation from that in Western countries. Even within China, it is hard to tell the exact meaning of police culture and reach an agreement in academic circles. At the very beginning, police culture can refer to a generalised concept of cultural and art undertakings related to the police, including arts, film production, research, media report, propaganda, and education and training (Zhang 2010a, p. 54). This way of defining and using the phrase "police culture" can be traced back to the remarks delivered by Luo Ruiqing, the first minister of MPS, in 1958 (Luo 1994). Along with the development of social sciences in China, scholars gradually developed multiple levels of understanding about police culture. With the influence of Western sociology, Chinese scholars begun to look at the concept of police culture from the perspective of sociology and further classify culture into material and non-material components (Zhang 2010a, p. 58). From the following definitions offered by a Chinese scholar, it is easy to recognise how similar it is to the Western discussions referred to above:

> Material police culture refers to the physical objects related with the police, including equipments, buildings, uniforms etc.; nonmaterial police culture refers to all the abstract creations related to the profession of police, including values, ideas, qualities, morals, and regulations, rules, codes of conduct, arts, and education (Zhang 1991, p. 67).

Z. Chen, *Measuring Police Subcultural Perceptions*,
DOI 10.1007/978-981-10-0096-6_5

Some scholars have proposed further sub-classifications, including material culture, behavioural culture, system culture, and spiritual culture (Zhang 1993). This typology indeed classifies nonmaterial culture into system culture (referring to all aspects of the policing system, including organisational structure, police functions, policing strategies, and police authority), behaviour culture (referring to the relationships among police officers and between the police and the society embodied through behaviour), and spiritual culture (referring to values, morals, arts, language, theories, education etc.) (Zhang 2010a). Although scholars have developed various layers of meaning for the term police culture, the dominant idea of police culture among police practitioners is still the earliest definition from Luo Ruiqing, namely, the combination of arts, sports, music, education, recreation etc. This could be vividly illustrated by part of a news report from the official Xinhua News Agency, titled *Senior Chinese Leader Stresses Cultivation of Police Culture* (Ding 2011). The following paragraph is part of this news article which reported that Zhou Yongkang, the then top Chinese leader who was responsible for criminal justice departments in China, emphasised the importance of the cultivation of police culture to improve police performance when he watched an exhibition of calligraphy works, paintings, and photographs by police officers.

> The exhibition displays more than 300 pieces of calligraphy works, paintings and photographs which are works from the public security sector to portray the work and the life of policemen. Zhou said that police should tap their potential to create excellent artistic works, enhance the influence of police culture, and cultivate their inner qualities as well as law enforcement capabilities so as to promote harmonious relations between the police and the public (Ding 2011).

5.2 Aim and Method of Studies of Police Subculture in China

Studies of police subculture in China are heavily influenced by the aim of fostering positive police culture to enhance team construction. They are focused on police team construction, and promotion of police qualities rather than empirical studies of police cultural attitudes and perceptions. Most theoretical studies of this type aim to develop macro-guidelines to establish positive police culture. Policing scholars in China tend to use qualitative methods to construct theoretical frameworks and concepts that serve as a guideline for policing practices (Zhang 2010a, p. 70).

5.3 A Brief Review of Studies in China

Zhang (1993) put forward one of the earliest theoretical descriptions of police cultural conception in China. Zhang defined police culture as "the compound of materials, spiritual outcomes and behavioural patterns created and developed by all police officers in the historic development process of police work (translation)" (p. 22). He contributed to the first systematic conceptual framework of police culture in China in his book *Studies of Police Culture* published in 1997. Zhang (2007) emphasised that the key problem of police cultural studies in China is the lack of agreement of many theoretical constructs. He mentioned that the sustainable development of police culture should be realised through the establishment of the central aims and the grasp of correct orientation of police culture cultivation. He suggested that the cultivation of police culture should be strategy-oriented, public order-oriented, and performance-oriented. To be strategy-oriented means that the aim of police culture cultivation is to set up a correct value system for Chinese police officers; to be public order-oriented means that police culture should be in accordance with effective crime control and order maintenance; to be performance-oriented means that cultivation of police culture aims to build a highly professional and effective police force (Zhang 2007, pp. 13–15).

Another typical Chinese depiction of police culture can be seen in the article by Gong (2010), entitled *On Police Culture Cultivation in the New Era*. In this article, Gong focused on the necessity of police culture cultivation and the direction and methods of police culture cultivation. For Gong, the importance of police culture construction lies in four aspects: enhancing the overall qualities of the police force, improving police management efficiency, strengthening internal cohesion, and creating a good image. He contended that the direction of police culture cultivation should meet two requirements: the requirement of political propaganda and the requirement of police professionalisation.

According to the search in the largest Chinese academic database CNKI in May 2015, there are 131 academic journal articles that include "police culture" in their titles. A detailed analysis of these articles suggested that 66.4 % of them (87 articles) include construction or cultivation (jianshe or suzao in Chinese) in their titles. These studies mostly were of a similar type to those mentioned above, describing the importance of establishing positive police culture for the sake of team construction or political and ideological purposes. The remaining studies concerned topics such as the relationship between police culture and police-community relations, a theoretical examination of police culture, the establishment of police culture studies as a discipline, associating police culture with police training or political propaganda, and the introduction of Western studies of police culture.

Some scholars discussed Western police cultural studies by reviewing Western literature and comparing the similarities and differences between studies in China and the West. For instance, Zhang (1997, 2010a) made a detailed comparison between police cultural studies in China and the West in regard to the discipline, development, contents and focus, and research methods. Other researchers made introductory reviews of Western studies and suggested that Chinese scholars learn from them (Xue 2010; Zhao 2010) or take the essential and discard the dross (Jiang 2012). Although some scholars have made suggestions that Western police studies could be used as a reference for the Chinese context, the related studies have just appeared and remain at the stage of review and introduction. According to the analysis of Chinese policing literature, I did not find any empirical studies about police culture, let alone a quantitative empirical study.

The very limited research available in China tends to offer a theoretical and ideological portrayal of prescriptive guidelines for the police. However, many theoretical statements are not based on facts or empirical evidence (Wong 2007). Many scholars have pointed out the lack of empirical studies in China (Dai 2008; Sun and Wu 2010; Wong 2007, 2009a). Therefore, one of the most needed tasks for Chinese policing studies is to provide empirical observations instead of opinion-based theoretical arguments.

5.4 Summary

In China, the studies of policing remain at a preliminary stage, with very limited scientific empirical studies available (Wong 2009c). In addition, the definition of police culture is quite different from the one in Western literature. Most existing police cultural studies in China are prescriptive in nature rather than descriptive. Some scholars in China have already realized the importance to apply Western theories on police culture to the Chinese context.

The methodology adopted in this study is discussed in the next chapter. It begins with a presentation of the research questions and a description of the research design, followed by information about the data collection procedures and a description of the research instrument. In addition, information is provided about the ethical requirements that were taken into consideration before the commencement of the study. Finally, a brief plan for the data analysis is provided.

Chapter 6
Methodology

Because few empirical studies have been conducted in the area of police culture in China, this study is exploratory in nature. In this chapter I discuss the research methodology used to measure police subcultural perceptions in China. I first detail and expand on the research questions already introduced, then set out the research design. Then detailed information about the research instrument and sampling is provided. The following parts address how research data were collected with a careful consideration of ethical issues. Finally, the plan for data analysis is explained in detail.

6.1 Research Questions

This study is intended to investigate whether there is a widespread adherence to the police subculture suggested in Western literature (Chan 1996; Cochran and Bromley 2003; Crank 2004; Loftus 2009; Paoline 2001; Reiner 2010; Skolnick 1986; Westley 1970) using the criteria of role orientations toward crime control and service, level of cynicism, traditionalism, receptivity to change, solidarity, and isolation among a sample of Chinese frontline police officers (Cochran and Bromley 2003; Steyn 2007). This study also explores the relationship between individual and work-related variables, namely, age, gender, educational level, tenure, type of police force and being detectives or not, and police subcultural perceptions. Finally, the possibility of associations among the seven subcultural themes, such as between role orientations (crime control and service functions) and other subcultural themes (cynicism, solidarity, isolation, traditionalism and resistance to change) will be explored.

The following research questions have been developed to explore the above issues.

- Is there widespread adherence to the police subculture suggested in the Western literature among Chinese frontline police officers?
- Among Chinese frontline police officers, are some demographic and work-related variables associated with police subcultural perceptions?

Z. Chen, *Measuring Police Subcultural Perceptions*,
DOI 10.1007/978-981-10-0096-6_6

- For Chinese frontline police officers, are there significant relationships among the seven police subcultural themes suggested in Western literature?

6.2 Research Design

A quantitative methodology was chosen for this study for several reasons. First, the primary aim of this study is to investigate police perceptions in China in regard to the key themes of police subculture suggested in Western literature. Quantitative method allows the researcher to have an exploratory and descriptive examination of "what is actually happening in the real world" (Bachman and Schutt 2010, p. 17). In addition, quantitative data could be collected from a relatively large sample of participants. This may also assist in having a clearer picture of police perceptions in China. Second, a quantitative approach provides opportunities for further explanatory analysis to explore the potential correlations between these subcultural perceptions and some individual and work-related variables. In this study, some qualitative data are also collected as compensation for weaknesses of quantitative data. The open-ended data are classified for analysis. They may provide further explanations and details for quantitative results.

Surveys are "the most widely used methods for collecting data in criminal justice research" (Bayens and Roberson 2011, p. 105). According to Bachman and Schutt (2010), three characteristics make survey research popular in the field of social sciences: versatility, efficiency, and generalisability. First, most topics in the social sciences are able to be researched through well-designed surveys. Second, survey research provides a relatively quick and economic way to collect and analyse data. Third, one of the aims of scientific studies is to generalise the research outcomes to a larger population. Surveys are sometimes the only feasible way to conduct a study representing the attitudes and characteristics of a large population (Bachman and Schutt 2010, pp. 205–206).

A scaled response survey instrument was used because it provides measurable results. The process of quantification may help researchers to conduct studies on larger populations and to obtain scientific results with validity and reliability through the application of statistical procedures (O'Leary 2010, p. 106). Survey research is commonly used in the field of criminal justice, such as attitudes toward police or crime severity (Hagan 2006). Survey research can be used for the purposes of making descriptive assertions, explanatory statements, or exploratory investigations about some populations (Bayens and Roberson 2011). For descriptive purposes, survey studies may provide a "systematic, standardized, and quantitative manner" with which to probe the dimensions of police perceptions (Klockars et al. 2004, p. 269). This study aims to describe the police subculture of a large sample of officers and give explanations through statistical analysis. A survey study allows the researcher to gather information from a number of people through sampling procedures and then test the relationship among variables that may be representative of the population of interest. In addition, it offers a convenient and economical way to use “quantitative or numerical description of trends, attitudes, or opinions of a population” through sampling (Creswell 2003, p. 153). This initial quantitative survey study also paves the way for the following statistical analyses for explanatory purposes.

There are also some criticisms about the use of survey in social research. The main criticisms are that survey questionnaires are highly structured and even “sterile, ritualistic and rigid” (De Vaus 1995, p. 8). Therefore, studies using survey method may be difficult to get access to the context of decision-making of the respondents; creative thinking would also be limited due to the lack of qualitative analyses (De Vaus 1995). In order to overcome the weakness in this regard, open-ended questions were provided for respondents to make comments they wanted to. The qualitative comments provided by the participants could assist in explaining the quantitative responses.

6.3 Survey Instrument

The complete research instrument used in this study is provided in Appendix A. It consisted of two sections. The first section sought information about seven individual and work-related characteristics of the respondents, namely, age, gender, education level, length of service, type of force, being detectives or not, and province in which the respondent worked.

The second section sought information about the degree of adherence to the police subculture in seven domains that had been suggested in Western literature. These domains were obtained from the survey questionnaires designed by Cochran and Bromley (2003) and Steyn (2007). The survey instrument designed by Cochran and Bromley was intended to measure the degree of adherence to police subculture among a sample of officers in the USA. In this study, there were five scales: role orientation toward crime control, role orientation toward service, and levels of cynicism, traditionalism, and receptivity to change. The instrument designed by Steyn was based on previous studies in the West and was intended to find evidence of police cultural themes of solidarity, cynicism, and isolation among new police officers in South Africa. Both of these questionnaires were tested for validity and reliability. On the basis of the above two questionnaires, a 40-item over 7-scale self-report inventory is constructed. Due to size and time limit, the author deleted some items which include overlapping contents and some items which are not highly relevant to Chinese context. The wording contents of the remaining 40 items were unchanged. Each item required participants to respond to five Likert-type categories ranging from “strongly disagree” to “strongly agree”.

The following domains were assessed;

- role orientation toward crime control (6 items),
- role orientation toward service (5 items),

- level of cynicism (6 items),
- level of traditionalism (5 items),
- receptivity to change (5 items),
- level of solidarity (6 items), and
- level of isolation (7 items).

After each domain, there was an open-ended question for the participants to address further comments related to the previous statements. It was anticipated that the open-ended questions might compensate for the weaknesses of close-ended questions because they allow participants to comment on the related topics in their own way and add some further information that is relevant but not covered in the previous questions. The qualitative data were analysed as further materials supporting the quantitative data.

The questionnaire was translated into Chinese. In order to ensure the validity of the translated questionnaire, back translation is adopted by researchers who are native speakers of Chinese and fluent users of English as well. In addition, the questionnaire is coded and no names or any identifying information are required in this study.

6.4 Sampling

Due to the availability of participants, this study adopted a selective sampling design. Bachman and Schutt (2010) summarized the main situations when non-probability sampling methods are adopted: studies without a population list, preliminary or exploratory studies, and studies concerning a small population (p. 127). For this study, it is almost impossible to target all Chinese frontline police officers as the population and conduct random sampling because of the large population and the difficulty of getting approval and conducting the nationwide survey.

Although a selective sampling method is chosen, the researcher has made much effort to enhance the representativeness of this sample. Participants in this survey study are frontline police officers who were attending training programs in a national police university in China. This university offers undergraduate to high school graduates, postgraduate education, and training programs to frontline police officers nationwide. Each year there are around 1000 frontline police officers who undertake training in the university from all over China. It would be convenient, reliable and representative to select frontline police officers here as research participants. First, they come from the northern part, the southern part, and the central part of China. They are diverse in terms of such things as age, gender, and length of service (details are shown in Section of 7.1.1). Therefore, the police officers here to some extent reflect the characteristics of Chinese frontline police officers. Second, it would be possible to administer the questionnaire survey face-to-face instead of mail or telephone survey. This could enhance the response rate and the authenticity of the answers. Third, it is convenient and economical to administer the survey in one place instead of travelling around China. It would be difficult to obtain all the permissions from each local police department to conduct the survey in local police departments around China.

When the survey study was conducted in the university, there were 500 frontline police officers who were attending training courses there. Before the commencement of this survey, I applied for and obtained approval for this research study from the police university in China. The police trainees were classified into six classes according to the topics of their training programs. Each class was allocated with a supervisor who was responsible for coordinating all the studying and life affairs during their stay in the university. In order to reach as many participants as possible, I contacted all six supervisors and decided to take advantage of the breaks between two sessions of lecture to conduct the study. In all, 401 frontline police officers agreed and participated in this survey study.

The details of this sample are discussed in the chapter of results. Although the sample is not balanced in many aspects, such as fewer female officers, and fewer officers with postgraduate degrees etc., these generally represent demographic characteristics of Chinese frontline police officers. One of the weaknesses of this sample of police trainees is that there are fewer senior officers who attend training programs than relatively junior ones. In regard to the geographical representativeness of this sample, there are officers from 29 provinces all over mainland China except Shanghai and Hainan. This is the advantage of national police universities that recruit trainees nationwide. Although efforts have been made to make this sample representative, it remains a convenience sample. This is one of the limitations of this study.

6.5 Data Collection Procedures

Data collection is very important for the study because "empirical research is only as good as the data on which it is based" (Punch 2005, p. 100). I distributed the questionnaires by hand to the frontline police officers who were receiving training in the Chinese police university in 2013. There are some reasons why I did not choose online survey or email distributed survey. First, the adoption of hand-delivered survey was expected to enhance response rate to a great extent compared with online survey or email distributed survey. Second, hand-delivered surveys would give the participants a better understanding of research purposes and regulations for using the data during the face-to-face communication. This could help police officers decide whether to join the research. In addition, it is feasible because the frontline police officers were attending training in the university. This makes it possible to adopt this direct and clear way of survey distribution during the breaks between training courses.

This study involves a survey of police officers, so permissions from corresponding institutions are needed beforehand. As mentioned previously, I applied for and obtained permission from the director of Division of Police Training in the police university in China before the start of this survey study.

After permissions had been granted, I contacted supervisors of the trainees and determined the exact time of survey for all six classes with their help. The survey was organized for six times across two weeks. Each round of survey took approximately 30 min, including all the procedures from researcher verbal introduction, handing out, completing, and collecting questionnaires.

The following procedures were followed during the six rounds of survey study.

1. I entered the classroom where officers were trained and briefly introduced myself. Research participants were given an information sheet including the purpose of the study and instructions for completing the questionnaire.
2. I explained the aim and significance of the research project and how the data collected would be used for research. The potential participants were informed that the survey was completely voluntary and anonymous. Participation in this study or not had nothing to do with their training program in the police university.
3. I told the officers that if they would like to participate they should complete the survey in around 20 min and place the anonymously completed questionnaires in a sealed box in front of the classroom. I also introduced how the questionnaire should be completed and answered some related questions raised by the officers.
4. I handed out the questionnaires to the officers and left the classroom to avoid some potential pressure that might influence the decisions of officers about whether to participate or not.
5. I re-entered the classroom, collected the completed questionnaires in the sealed box and the blank questionnaires, and expressed gratitude to all the participants.

6.6 Reliability and Validity

Reliability refers to the extent to which the same results would show under repeated constant conditions when repeat measurements are obtained by any researcher using the research tool (Moser and Kalton 1972). It is a measure of "objectivity, stability, consistency, and precision" of the research instrument (Sarantakos 2005, p. 88). The aim of a good research instrument is to measure variance in the scores that may represent differences between people. If the reliability of a research instrument is low, the variance of scores represents "spurious" instead of "real differences" (Punch 2005, p. 96). Although some degree of error variance exists in all measures, researchers need to take measures to ensure the reliability of their research instruments.

Validity means the extent to which a research tool actually measures the target which it was designed to measure (Punch 2005). It measures the "precision, accuracy and relevance" and reflects the extent to which the results are "in agreement with theoretical or conceptual values" (Sarantakos 2005, p. 83). The variables that researchers intend to investigate are usually latent. Therefore, an inference is involved "between the indicators we can observe and the construct we aim to measure" (Punch 2005, p. 97). If the validity of a research instrument is low, the inferences from indicators to concepts are unreliable.

For this study, the research instrument is designed on the basis of two existing questionnaires that had been designed and used by qualified scholars in the field of policing studies. Before the commencement of the two studies, the research questionnaires went through statistical tests that supported their reliability and validity. All the statements in this survey study were selected from the two existing questionnaires and remained unchanged apart from translation into Chinese. In addition, I invited scholars and practitioners in the field of policing to have an assessment of the content of the research instrument and its applicability among Chinese frontline officers. On the basis of the suggestions from the assessment, some items have been removed due to its low association with Chinese context. For example, some items include concepts that are not available in China have been removed, such as "probable cause" or "participatory management scheme". The combination of scales of two separate survey instruments and the removal of some statements of some scales may influence the reliability and validity of the questionnaire. Therefore, statistical analysis (Cronbach's coefficient alpha) was conducted to test the reliability of the research instrument. There are four common methods for testing the reliability: test-retest, split-half, alternative-form, and internal consistency methods (Sarantakos 2005, p. 89). Carmines and Zeller (1979) made a detailed comparison among the four testing methods for empirical research. Alternative-form and internal consistency are the two methods that were considered suitable ways for empirical research. In addition, the internal consistency approach would be an easy and economical way of testing reliability when compared with the other approaches (Carmines and Zeller 1979). Therefore, this study tested the internal consistency of the research tool by computing Cronbach's coefficient alpha.

Cronbach's alpha is a widely used statistical technique to assess the degree to which the items that make up a scale are internally consistent with each other (Pallant 2005). It is suggested that an alpha value of 0.70 or above is acceptable for a consistent research instrument with high reliability (De Vaus 1995; DeVellis 2003). In addition, it is also suggested that a minimum alpha value of 0.60 could be also accepted for basic research (Nunnally 1978). Therefore, in order to determine the reliability of the dimensions in the research questionnaire, Cronbach's alpha was computed for each scale in the questionnaire and the whole questionnaire. The values are from 0.601 to 0.751. The scores indicate an acceptable level of internal consistency for this measure.

To assess the content validity, item-total correlation coefficients were calculated between the scores of each item and the summed scores of all the items in the corresponding scale (Chen 2013b, pp. 114–115). Before calculations, some items were reversed coded to make sure that higher values on each scale show a higher level of adherence to the specific theme, including Item 13, 17, 18, 22, and 25. The *r* values of all the bivariate correlations range from 0.37 to 0.744, and the *p* values were all below 0.001. This results indicate that the bivariate correlations between scores of each individual item and the summed scores of the items in the corresponding scale are all statistically significant. These correlations are moderate to high (Miller and Whitehead 1996).

6.7 Research Ethics

Ethics is one of the most important parts of a study. All researchers should abide by the ethical standards of conduct during the whole research process. Bayens and Roberson (2011) summarized three ethical guidelines researchers: conducting research in a "neutral and impartial manner", complying with research codes of conduct, and reporting honestly (p. 179). Comparing with experimental or field research designs, survey research usually arouses fewer ethical concerns (Bachman and Schutt 2010, p. 245). One of the main concerns in survey study is the protection of participants (Bachman and Schutt 2010). This study involves a survey among Chinese frontline police officers, and the research plan has been designed with the aim of reducing the potential risk to participants to the minimum.

Contents

The possible risks of this study to the participants were identified and responded to at the stage of planning and preparation. This survey does not include any contents that may lead to negative consequences or arouse stress and emotional trauma of the participants. No question that might inadvertently threaten the interviewees' employment was included in the questionnaire. No additional burden or cost was imposed to the participants during the whole process besides the approximately 30 min time required.

Confidentiality

In addition to the control of sensitive contents, the confidentiality of this study is assured to protect the privacy of the participants. Participation in this survey study is completely voluntary and anonymous. There is no request for any identifiable private information during the whole process of the survey. There is also no linking of any data from the questionnaire to specific individuals. The questionnaires were coded and the collected data would only be used to identify issues instead of identifying individuals. The collected data could only be accessed by the researcher and his supervisors for academic purposes.

Consent and Free Choice

The potential participants were informed of the nature and scope of the study both in the information sheet and verbally. To let the participants have a clear understanding of this study, I also responded to related questions raised by the participants. They were free to choose to participate. In addition, they had the right to withdraw from the research at any time before the anonymous questionnaires were collected. The reason that a signed consent form was not requested from the participants was its potential to nullify the anonymity of the research participants. Completion of the questionnaire implies consent.

Primary Language Not English

Mandarin Chinese was the only language used in the survey to ensure that participants would fully understand the questions and be able to express their opinions clearly. I am Chinese. Therefore, I am familiar with the beliefs, customs and cultural heritage, and laws in China. The research was conducted in line with both the regulations in Australia and China. The questionnaire and information sheet were translated into Chinese. The translation of the questionnaire and information sheet was thoroughly checked to make sure that each question carried similar meaning and therefore would elicit comparable responses. A third party with good command of both languages had been asked to evaluate the questionnaire before the actual survey exercise was carried out.

Data Storage, Analysis, and Reporting

All the research questionnaires are securely stored in my locked cabinets at my university. The electronically generated data are saved in my computer system located on my university's premises and protected through passwords. Research data and questionnaires will be destroyed by shredder or erased from the computer 5 years after completion of the project. Strict procedures and rules were followed during the whole process of data analysis. In order to generate scientific results, I carefully entered data from all valid questionnaires into SPSS for statistical analysis. In the following chapter, I report the results accurately and responsibly because this is the only way to have a scientific reflection of police subculture in China. Only on the basis of these correct results can further discussions and suggestions make sense.

6.8 Data Analysis Plan

The survey data were entered into the statistical analysis software program Statistical Package for the Social Sciences (SPSS) version 22 for Windows. A five-step analysis plan was adopted for this study.

First, preliminary analysis was conducted before the commencement of major calculations in this study. The major tasks in this stage are validity and reliability tests which may ensure that the statistical analysis of data would generate valid and reliable results. Item-total correlation coefficients were calculated to test the content validity of the research questionnaire. Cronbach's coefficient alpha was calculated to determine the internal consistency of each scale in the research questionnaire in order to test the degree of reliability.

Second, descriptive statistics were used to find out whether there is a widespread adherence to the police subculture suggested in the Western literature among a sample of Chinese frontline police officers. Descriptive statistics were calculated for the demographic and work-related variables, and the seven scales of police subculture, to acquire a demographic and attitudinal profile of the sample. This may help to summarise and organise data into a useful form to demonstrate general information about the characteristics of the sample. Descriptive statistical analysis not only helps to answer whether there is a shared adherence among Chinese frontline police officers to police subculture, but also pave the way for further analysis.

Third, MANOVA and chi-square were calculated to determine whether any of the demographic and work-related variables are associated with police perceptions about their subculture. This aims to answer the second research question: "Is there a relationship between some individual and work-related characteristics and adherence to police subculture?" Through MANOVA, the influence of each demographic and work-related variables on the combination of seven subcultural themes is first examined. Univariate procedures are also included to find out the source of the significant associations. The variances between the means of each of the dependent variables and the independent variable are examined to determine if the variance is significant. If the variance is significant, it is suggested that the dependent variable varies as a function of the independent variable. The related assumptions of MANOVA have been taken into consideration and all the requirements have been responded to before the commencement of statistical analysis. In addition, for those themes that were significantly associated with one or several independent variables, Chi-square tests were used to investigate the potential associations between individual items with the corresponding independent variable(s). This aims to examine how the demographic and work-related variables influence each component of the cultural themes, providing further explanations for the MANOVA results.

Fourth, Pearson correlations were conducted to locate any relationships among officers' perceptions on the seven subcultural themes. This step aimed to answer the third research question. Pearson correlation could help to identify the magnitude and direction of the relationship among the scales of police subculture and suggest whether and to what extent any of the variables are correlated with each other. Similar to MANOVA test, the assumptions of Pearson correlation have also been carefully considered and responded to beforehand.

Finally, qualitative data were classified and analysed. In this way, the qualitative data could serve as a remedial measure for the limitations of quantitative research design, because they could "put some flesh on the bones" as further explanations (Fleming and Wakefield 2009, p. 273).

6.9 Summary

To examine police subcultural perceptions in China, a quantitative survey research design was adopted in this study. In order to apply Western-based policing knowledge into Chinese context, I used a research questionnaire that was designed on the basis of two existing questionnaires designed by Western policing researchers. Although a selective sampling design was used due to the availability of participants, the sample to some extent represent the characteristics of Chinese frontline police officers. The survey was conducted among in-service frontline police officers who were training in a national police university in China. The hand-delivered survey may enhance response rate and give the participants a better understanding of research purposes during the face to face communication. In the next chapter, statistical analysis methods used in this study are discussed and a detailed description of results is provided.

Chapter 7
Results

In this chapter I describe the statistical analyses used to answer the research questions, and the results found after the analyses. Section 7.1 examines the descriptive characteristics of the sample in regard to their demographic information and the degree of their police subcultural perceptions through descriptive statistics. This provides the basis to answer the first research question concerning whether there is a monolithic adherence among Chinese frontline police officers to the police subculture suggested in Western literature. Section 7.2 presents the procedures and results of MANOVA and chi-square analyses that used to locate the associations between demographic and work-related factors and the perceptions of police subculture. This section provides the results which help to answer the second research question of this study regarding the potential relationships between dependent and independent variables. Section 7.3 explores the correlations among the seven cultural themes. The results assist in providing answers to the third research question in this study. The last section provides the results from the qualitative data.

There were 500 frontline police officers who were contacted by the researcher for this survey during their training in the police university. A total of 401 questionnaires were completed and returned, representing an 80 % response rate. After the screening the data, 19 questionnaires were eliminated for obvious incorrect answers or containing missing responses for more than 10 % of the questions. Therefore, the final data set for analysis was obtained from 382 respondents. In addition, items that were worded negatively on the scales of police subculture were reverse-coded so that high values corresponded to a high level of adherence to the specific cultural theme. Sixty-two missing responses (0.35 % of all 17,572 responses) in 51 questionnaires were imputed by replacing the missing values with the most frequent values in the variables. Seven new variables were created by summing the scores for all the items within each scale. High values of these variables indicated higher level of adherence to the corresponding theme.

Z. Chen, *Measuring Police Subcultural Perceptions*,
DOI 10.1007/978-981-10-0096-6_7

7.1 Descriptive Analyses

7.1.1 Demographic and Work-Related Variables

Demographic and work-related participant characteristics are provided in Table 7.1. Most of the officers (76.7 %) were under the age of 30, and very few (3 %) were more than 40 years of age. Only a small percentage (11 %) were female. This gender distribution is very close to the gender ratio of Chinese police. According to official statistics in China, the number of female police officers accounts for 13.7 % of all Chinese police officers in 2011 (Jia 2012, p. 118). Nearly 40 % of the respondents completed two-three years college or less; 55.8 % of the respondents completed four year college with bachelor's degrees. These two portions constituted the majority of the sample, representing 95.3 % altogether. Most of the respondents (73.6 %) had 5 years of service or less. This is not surprising because more junior officers who have just come into the police force choose to participate in police training than do their senior counterparts. These young

Table 7.1 Participants' demographic and work-related variables (N — 382)

Variable	N	%
Age in years		
25 or less	121	31.7
26–30	172	45.0
31–35	59	15.4
36–40	20	5.2
41 or more	10	2.6
Gender		
Male	340	89
Female	42	11
Education		
2–3 years college or less	151	39.5
Bachelor's degree	213	55.8
Master's degree or higher	18	4.8
Tenure in police force		
5 years or less	281	73.6
6–10 years	58	15.2
11 years or more	58	15.2
Type of police force		
Provincial	8	2.1
Municipal bureau	63	16.5
Police sub-bureau	185	48.4
Police station	126	33.0
Detective or not		
Yes	227	59.4
No	155	40.6

and well-educated officers are also the main force of Chinese frontline police officers. The largest two portions were officers working in district or county police sub-bureaus and local field stations (81.4 %), with the remainder from municipal departments and provincial departments. This is similar to the percentage of front-line police in China. Most respondents (60 %) were police detectives.

Respondents came from nearly all of the provinces in China and from all seven geographic regions. There were 10 missing responses in provinces of working section. The missing responses were not replaced by modes because this variable was not involved in any bivariate calculations. As shown in Table 7.2, 11 provinces had

Table 7.2 Frequency and percentage distribution for provinces of working

	Frequency	Percent
Beijing	1	0.3
Tianjin	3	0.8
Hebei	7	1.8
Shanxi	2	0.5
Inner Mongolia	7	1.8
Liaoning	10	2.6
Jilin	7	1.8
Heilongjiang	22	5.8
Jiangsu	3	0.8
Zhejiang	5	1.3
Anhui	13	3.4
Fujian	2	0.5
Jiangxi	4	1.0
Shandong	24	6.3
Henan	15	3.9
Hubei	25	6.5
Hunan	28	7.3
Guangdong	11	2.9
Guangxi	22	5.8
Chongqing	2	0.5
Sichuan	8	2.1
Guizhou	3	0.8
Yunnan	7	1.8
Tibet	4	1.0
Shaanxi	5	1.3
Gansu	19	5
Qinghai	5	1.3
Ningxia	4	1.0
Xinjiang	104	27.2
Total	372	97.4
Missing	10	2.6
Total	382	100.0

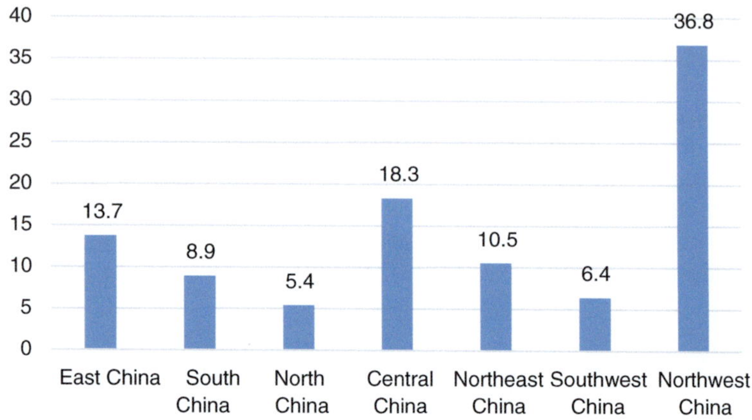

Fig. 7.1 Percentage distribution for geographic regions of working

more than 10 respondents, making up 76.7 % of the sample, and six of them had more than 20 trainees, making up 58.9 % of the sample. The remaining 19 provinces had fewer than 10 trainees. Shanghai and Hainan did not have any representatives among the respondents. Figure 7.1 displays the representativeness of the sample in terms of geographic regions.

7.1.2 Items from Police Subculture Scales

Frequency distributions for the 40 items in the seven subculture scales are displayed in Tables 7.3, 7.4, 7.5, 7.6, 7.7, 7.8 and 7.9. These permit a preliminary overview of police subcultural perceptions.

From the entries in Table 7.3, general support for a crime fighting orientation can be identified. Apart from Item 3, which focuses on the importance of the causes of crime, supporters (who either agreed or strongly agreed) outnumbered non-supporters (who disagreed or strongly disagreed) for all the items. Nearly 70 % of the officers agreed or strongly agreed that law enforcement is the most important task for police (Item 4) and that providing service detracts from their crime control ability (Item 2). Nearly 60 % of the participants supported fewer restrictions on police use of force (Item 6), nearly half of the officers believed that the police should not be involved in non-crime activities (Item 5), and although approximately one third of the officers adopted a neutral stance concerning whether an aggressive policing style was more useful than a friendly courteous one, more than 40 % supported the more aggressive approach (Item 1). It is worthwhile to point out that there are more officers (94 officers) who strongly agreed that police should not be involved in non-crime activities than those who agreed (93 officers). However, on the topic of crime prevention and crime causes (Item 3),

Table 7.3 Percentage distributions of responses on crime control scale

Items ($n = 6$)	Strongly disagree/disagree	Neutral	Agree/strongly agree
1 An aggressive, tough bearing is more useful to a police officer than a friendly, courteous manner	25.9	32.2	41.9
2 If police officers act in a service capacity, it detracts from their ability to fight crime	15.4	15.2	69.3
3 Good law enforcement requires that officers concern themselves with the consequences of crime and not with its root causes	56.2	19.1	24.6
4 Police officers should not forget that enforcing the law is by far their most important responsibility	16.3	14.4	69.3
5 Police officers should not have to handle calls that involve social or personal problems where no crime is involved	33.2	17.8	48.9
6 If police officers in high crime areas had fewer restrictions on their use of force, many of the serious crime problems in these areas would be significantly reduced	25.6	14.7	59.7

Table 7.4 Percentage distributions of responses on service scale

Items ($n = 5$)	Strongly disagree/disagree	Neutral	Agree/strongly agree
1 Police officers should ask citizens what types of services they want. (7)[a]	10.2	20.2	69.6
2 Crimes are only one of several problems about which police officers should be concerned. (8)	19.2	9.7	71.2
3 Assisting citizens in need is just as important as enforcing the law. (9)	22.8	27.2	50.0
4 Lowering citizens' fear of crime should be just as high a priority as cutting the crime rate. (10)	6.8	19.1	74.0
5 Law enforcement should be seen primarily as a service-oriented profession rather than a crime control profession. (11)	82.2	11.8	6.1

[a]Numbers in parentheses refer to the item numbers in the original inventory

in contrast to responses on the other items, only a quarter of the officers (24.6 %) thought that police should concern themselves with the consequences of crime rather than its causes.

Table 7.5 Percentage distributions of responses on traditionalism scale

Items[a] ($n = 5$)	Strongly disagree/disagree	Neutral	Agree/strongly agree
1 To be effective an organization should have clearly defined positions of power/authority among its members/employees. (12)[b]	3.7	7.9	88.5
2 *In law enforcement organizations power should be evenly distributed among its personnel.* (13)	23.8	21.5	54.7
3 Communication works best when it follows clear, established channels from the top down. (14)	19.1	29.8	51.0
4 The quasi-military structure is the most effective organizational type for law enforcement agencies. (15)	26.5	24.9	48.7
5 Subordinates should not be involved in either the setting or the enforcing of policies and procedures within law enforcement agencies. (16)	76.4	16.0	7.6

[a]Items that were later reverse-coded are shown in italics
[b]Numbers in parentheses refer to the item numbers in the original inventory

Table 7.6 Percentage distributions of responses on receptivity to change scale

Items[a] ($n = 5$)	Strongly disagree/disagree	Neutral	Agree/strongly agree
1 *Most changes at work are problematic and ineffective.* (17)[b]	44.7	28.8	26.4
2 *I can usually find some way to get around changes at work.* (18)	53.1	28.3	18.6
3 I often suggest new approaches for doing things at my job. (19)	7.9	22.3	68.9
4 Most changes make my work more efficient (i.e. saves time, effort, money). (20)	6.3	19.1	74.6
5 Most changes make my job more effective (i.e. more arrests, faster response times, crime reduction). (21)	3.2	17.5	79.3

[a]Items that were later reverse-coded are shown in italics
[b]Numbers in parentheses refer to the item numbers in the original inventory

From the entries in Table 7.4, it is evident that most of the officers have a positive attitude toward the role of social service. Four of the five items gained support from at least half of the participants, and three won support from around 70 % of the officers. Interestingly, half of the officers regarded assisting citizens to be just as important as law enforcement (Item 9 on the original inventory), but when asked about whether policing could be seen as a service-oriented profession (Item 11 on the original inventory) a noticeable majority (82.2 %) disagreed or

Table 7.7 Percentage distributions of responses on cynicism scale

Items[a] ($n = 6$)	Strongly disagree/disagree	Neutral	Agree/strongly agree
1 *Most people do not hesitate to go out of their way to help someone in trouble.* (22)[b]	17.3	18.1	64.7
2 Most people are untrustworthy and dishonest. (23)	54.2	28.8	17.0
3 Most people would steal if they knew they would not get caught. (24)	40.9	18.8	40.3
4 *Most people respect the authority of police officers.* (25)	43.8	28.0	28.3
5 Police officers will never trust citizens enough to work together effectively. (26)	40.0	35.9	24.1
6 Citizens will not trust police officers enough to work together effectively. (27)	27.5	36.6	35.8

[a]Items that were later reverse-coded are shown in italics
[b]Numbers in parentheses refer to the item numbers in the original inventory

Table 7.8 Percentage distributions of responses on solidarity scale

Items ($n = 6$)	Strongly disagree/disagree	Neutral	Agree/strongly agree
1 Police officers are careful of how they behave in public. (28)[a]	6.3	16.5	77.2
2 You don't understand what it is to be a police officer until you are a police officer. (29)	4.5	2.4	93.1
3 Police officers have to look out for each other. (30)	0.6	2.4	97.1
4 Members of the public, media and politicians are quick to criticize the police but seldom recognize the good that police officers do. (31)	2.4	6.0	91.6
5 Most members of the public don't really know what is going on 'out there'. (32)	2.1	4.2	93.2
6 To be a police officer is not just another job it is a 'higher calling'. (33)	2.1	10.2	87.7

[a]Numbers in parentheses refer to the item numbers in the original inventory

disagreed strongly, while only 6.1 % agreed or strongly agreed. Taken together, these distributions indicate that, although most of the officers believed providing service to the community to be an important task of the police, they still considered policing to be a crime-oriented profession.

From the entries in Table 7.5 concerning traditionalism, it is difficult to identify clear-cut support or disagreement. The only item that won overwhelming support (88.5 %) from the participants was Item 12 on the original inventory, which stated that there should be clearly defined positions of power among members of an

Table 7.9 Percentage distributions of responses on isolation scale

Items ($n = 5$)	Strongly disagree/disagree	Neutral	Agree/strongly agree
1 I tend to socialize less with my friends outside of the police since I have become a police officer. (34)[a]	43.7	14.9	41.4
2 I don't really talk in-depth to people outside of the police about my work. (35)	17.5	16.0	66.4
3 My husband/wife, boyfriend/girlfriend tends not to understand what being a police officer is all about. (36)	24.4	38.5	37.1
4 Shift work and special duties influence my socializing with friends outside the police. (37)	10.8	13.1	76.1
5 I feel like I belong with my work colleagues more every day, and less with people that I have to police. (38)	30.1	25.9	44.0
6 As a police officer, I am being watched critically by members of the community, even in my social life. (39)	2.9	11.0	86.1
7 I can be more open with my work colleagues than with members of the public. (40)	21.5	33.0	45.5

[a]Numbers in parentheses refer to the item numbers in the original inventory

organisation. Around half of the officers considered a paramilitary organisational structure to be the most effective for police departments (Item 15) and that top-down chains of communication work best (Item 14), but nearly one third of officers were neutral on both of these two items. Though the previous results indicate that officers prefer the paramilitary police organisation structures, it is evident that an evenly distributed power structure (Item 13) and the involvement of subordinates in administrative decision-making (Item 16) gained support from more than half of the officers.

Entries in Table 7.6 concerning receptivity to change indicate that most of the officers were receptive to change at work. The percentage of officers who supported changes was greater than the other two groups on all the five items (Items 17 and 18 were negatively worded). More than 70 % of the officers considered changes at work to be efficient and effective (Items 20 and 21), and nearly 70 % of the officers indicated that they often suggest new approaches for work (Item 19). Only around one fifth of the officers would like to avoid changes at work (Item 18) and about one quarter considered changes to be problematic and ineffective (Item 17), resulting in nearly 30 % of the officers being neutral on those two items—and these items attracting the greatest amount of negativity regarding change.

With regard to cynicism, the most obvious characteristic of the entries in Table 7.7 is that on four of the six items more than 25 % of officers adopted a neutral stance. In particular, 36.8 % chose to be neutral when asked whether citizens would trust the police to work together with them (Item 27), and 35.9 % were neutral concerning the statement that the police would never trust citizens enough to work together effectively (Item 26). Slightly more officers agreed or strongly agreed that citizens would not trust the police to cooperate than those who disagreed or strongly disagreed (35.8 vs. 27.5 %). This echoes the result from Item 25 because 43.8 % of the officers disagreed or strongly disagreed that people respect police authority, while the rest of them either agreed or strongly agreed (28.3 %) or kept neutral (28 %). Although responses on Items 27 and 25 indicate that the respondents did not have a good impression of citizen respect and trust in their work, the other four items suggest that most of them were not cynical. Only 17 % of them considered people to be untrustworthy and dishonest (Item 23); 64.7 % of the participants agreed or strongly agreed that most people do not hesitate to go out of their way to help someone in trouble (Item 22); and only less than a quarter of them believed that the police would never trust citizens enough to work together effectively (Item 26). On Item 24, officers (40.3 %) who agreed or strongly agreed are nearly the same as those (40.9 %) who were against that most people would steal if they knew they would not get caught.

On the topic of solidarity, an overwhelming majority of the participants expressed their support. As can be seen from entries in Table 7.8, four of the six items were endorsed by more than 90 % of the officers, while the other two items gained support from more than 70 % of the participants. On Items 31–33, officers who strongly agreed outnumbered those who agreed—a further indication of the strength of endorsement concerning solidarity.

Entries in Table 7.9 refer to the isolation scale. From those entries it is obvious that officers do feel isolated from the rest of the society because those who agreed or strongly agreed are the highest in number on five of the seven items. 86.1 % of the officers felt that they were watched critically by citizens (Item 39); 66.4 % of them did not talk in-depth to outsiders about police work (Item 35); more than 40 % of them felt that they belonged with colleagues more than with citizens (Item 38) and were more open with colleagues than citizens (Item 40). 76.1 % of them considered shift work and special duties influenced their socialising with non-police friends (Item 37). On the topic of whether their partners tend to understand what being a police officer really means, 38.5 % of them found it hard to answer (kept neutral) and 37.1 % of them agreed or strongly agreed. However, their responses on Item 34 seem to indicate that most of them are indeed not avoiding socialising with non-police friends, because slightly more of them (43.7 vs. 41.4 %) disagreed or strongly disagreed that they tend to socialise less with non-police friends.

7.1.3 Police Subculture Scales

Descriptive analysis of the 40 items in the research instrument gave us a preliminary understanding of police subcultural perceptions. In order to answer the first research question, the descriptive statistics for each of the seven scales of police

Table 7.10 Descriptive statistics for seven subculture scales

Scale (number of items)	Mean	*SD*	Skewness	Kurtosis	Converted mean[a]	Converted *SD*[b]
Crime control (6)	20.36	4.41	−0.242	−0.212	3.39	0.734
Service (5)	16.68	2.97	−0.157	0.013	3.35	0.595
Traditionalism (5)	15.33	2.29	−0.214	0.222	3.06	0.458
Cynicism (6)	17.17	3.55	0.354	0.122	2.86	0.592
Solidarity (6)	25.95	2.66	−0.351	−0.374	4.33	0.442
Isolation (7)	24.65	4.13	0.048	0.196	3.52	0.590
Receptivity to change (5)	18.16	2.87	−0.309	0.220	3.63	0.574

[a]These are obtained by dividing each participants total scale scores by the number of items in the respective scales in order to represent the outcome in terms of the original Likert scale ranging from strong disagreement (1) to strong agreement (5)
[b]These *SD*s are based on data used to calculate the converted means

subculture were examined. These are provided in Table 7.10. Entries in the second and third columns refer to the scores produced by combining all items for each scale but are limited in their meaningfulness because different scales had different numbers of items. Nevertheless, it is obvious from the SDs that none of the scale scores clustered closely around the means. The entries for skewness and kurtosis are all within the bounds of ±1, indicating no significant departures from the normal curve. The converted means indicate that cynicism attracted the least endorsement (at 2.86 lying a little under the neutral position of 3) and that solidarity attracted the most endorsement (at 4.33, moving up from basic agreement toward the "strongly agree" point on the original Likert scale). The means of the remaining five scales lay somewhere between the neutral and agree positions. Traditionalism was close to a neutral position, whether policing should have a crime control or a service focus received a little more, and almost equal, amounts of adherence (at 3.39 and 3.35 respectively), and a sense of isolation and receptivity to change were a little higher still. As with the standard deviations based on the full scale scores, there is obviously a divergence of opinions on all of the scales—although it is interesting that the greatest divergence of opinion concerns whether the focus of policing should be crime control, and the least divergence occurs concerning solidarity.

Frequency distributions for each of the seven scales are shown in Figs. 7.2, 7.3, 7.4, 7.5, 7.6, 7.7 and 7.8. They are characterised by near normality for all but the solidarity scale, which appears to be negatively skewed because of the concentration of high scores.

Summary regarding Research question 1

On the basis of the distributions of individual items in the questionnaire, there is not strong adherence to the subcultural themes of policing identified in Western literature among this sample of Chinese frontline police officers. Endorsement at the level of agree/strongly agree, or disagree/strongly disagree (negatively worded

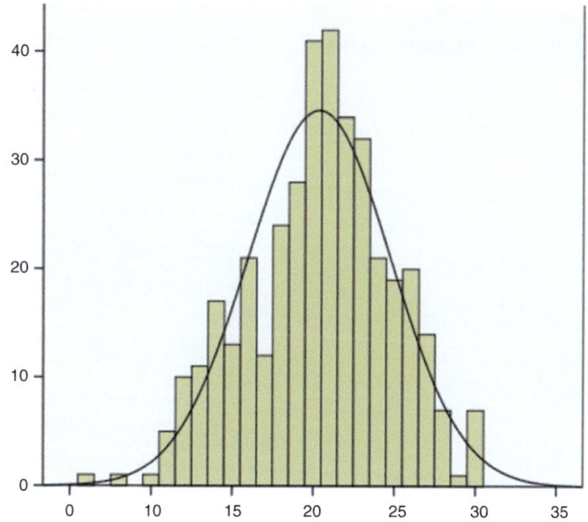

Fig. 7.2 Frequency distribution for crime control scale

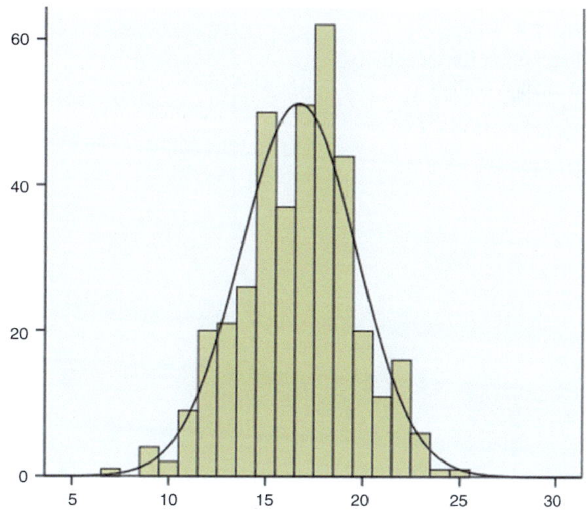

Fig. 7.3 Frequency distribution for service scale

items) was given by 70 % or more of the officers to all six of the items on the solidarity scale but to only nine of 33 items on the remaining six scales.

On six of the seven composite scales, overall adherence might best be described as only moderate given that mean scores were located near the middle of the range of scores and the standard deviations were quite large. However, the solidarity scale had a noticeably high mean score as well as the smallest standard deviation.

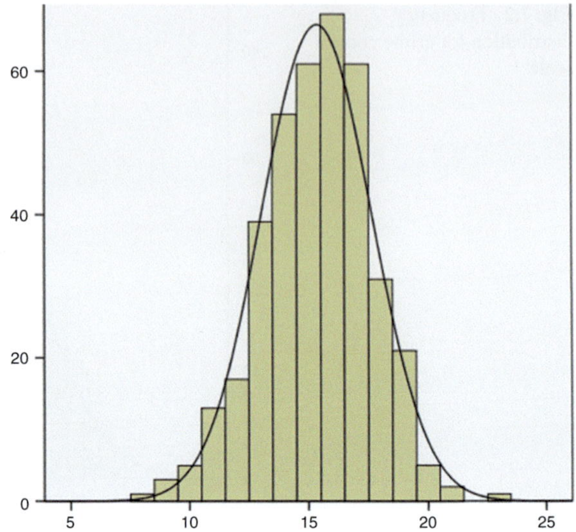

Fig. 7.4 Frequency distribution for traditionalism scale

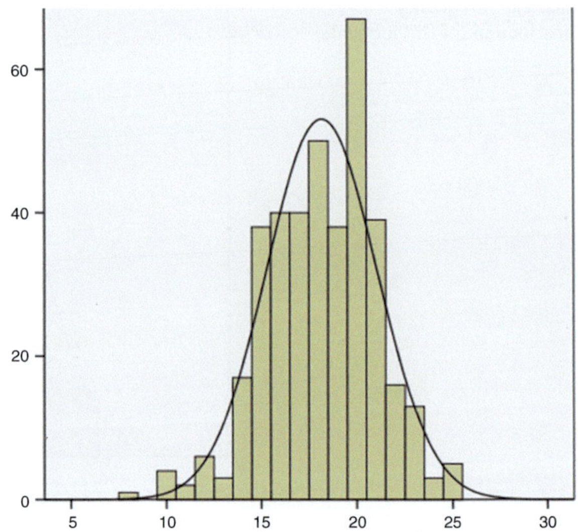

Fig. 7.5 Frequency distribution for receptivity to change scale

7.2 MANOVAs

As well as measuring whether there is a widespread adherence to the police subculture suggested in Western literature among Chinese frontline police officers, this study was designed to explore whether specific demographic and work-related factors are related to police perceptions of the seven key themes in police culture by means of multivariate analysis of variance (MANOVA).

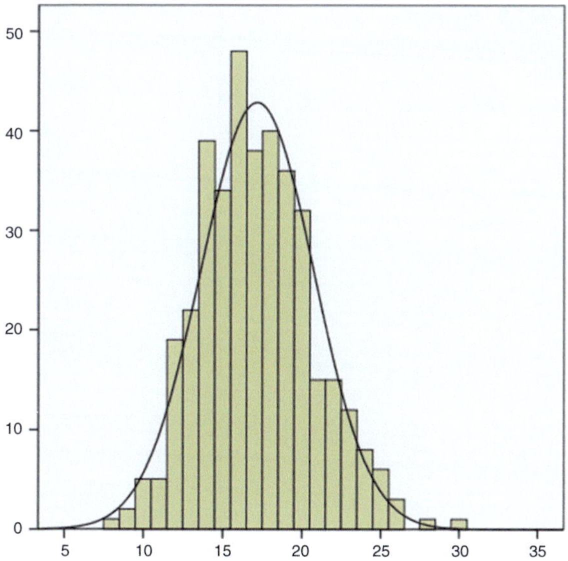

Fig. 7.6 Frequency distribution for cynicism scale

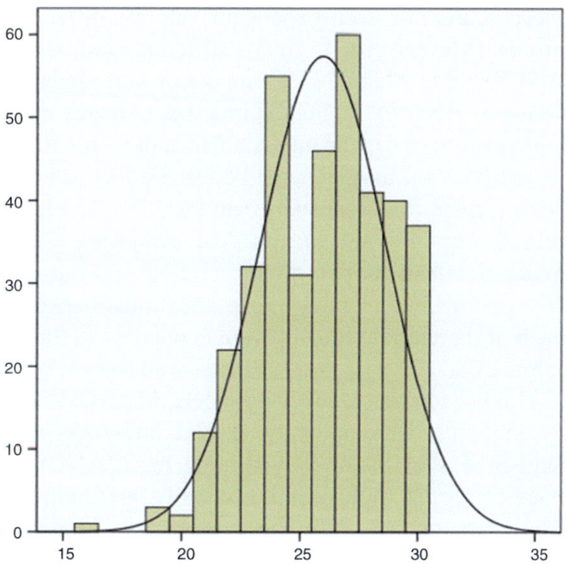

Fig. 7.7 Frequency distribution for solidarity scale

MANOVA is designed to examine outcomes from several dependent variables simultaneously (Field 2013). For MANOVA, the researcher looks at both the multivariate effect and the univariate effects. In the first step, the impact of each of the independent variables upon the combination of the dependent variables is explored. On the basis of the results, univariate tests are conducted to see how the

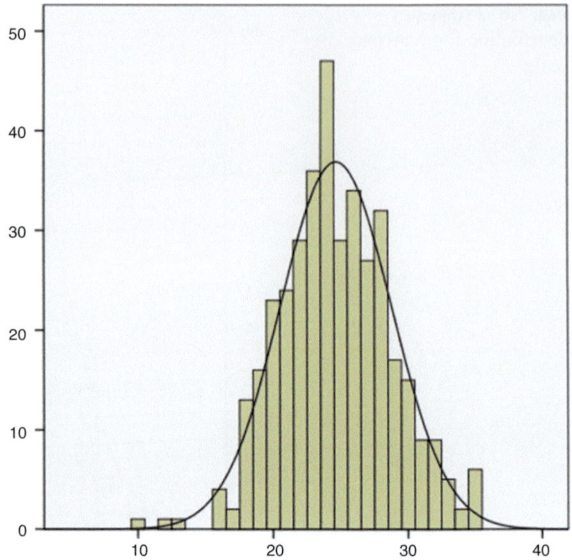

Fig. 7.8 Frequency distribution for isolation scale

mean scores for each dependent variable differ across the independent variable groups (Mayers 2013). This is different from one-way ANOVA in that one-way ANOVA only examines the impact of independent variable upon one dependent. One-way ANOVA cannot explore the influence of an independent variable upon a combination of dependent variables at the same time.

MANOVA was conducted between police subcultural perceptions based on the seven scales (the dependent variables) and each of the demographic and work-related variables (the independent variables). Univariate tests (*t*-tests or Mann–Whitney *U* tests for two-group situations and one-way ANOVAs or Kruskal–Wallis *H* tests for three or more group situations) between the independent variable and each of the cultural themes were conducted to locate where significant differences might exist.

Similar to other statistical models, MANOVA is based on a number of specific assumptions, without which invalid inferences may be generated. Field (2013) suggested four major assumptions for MANOVA: random samples, independence of scores, multivariate normality, and homogeneity of covariance matrices. These assumptions have been taken into consideration before data analysis. I did not adopt a random sampling method in this study due to the availability of research participants and the impossibility to randomly select a sample from all Chinese frontline police officers. As an exploratory study, the main aim is to have a preliminary general idea of police subcultural perceptions in China instead of its generalisability. Therefore, MANOVA test could still be used in this context. Normality of residuals for all seven dependent variables was assessed through the examination of histograms and normal probability plots. Graphical examination of residuals of seven scales suggests that all the seven scales are close to normal distribution. Histograms show that distributions are bell shaped and P-P plots suggest straight diagonal lines. For the homogeneity of covariance matrices, Box's M test has been used to examine this assumption. For all the six independent variables, this assumption is met. For the afterward univariate analyses, tests of homogeneity of variance were conducted. In the presence of heterogeneous variances, the nonparametric Kruskal–Wallis test and Mann–Whitney test—were conducted as a remedial measure (Terrell 2012). All the results of the test of homogeneity of covariance matrices and variance are presented in Appendix B and C.

Research Question 2

Among Chinese frontline police officers, are some demographic and work-related variables associated with police subcultural perceptions?

There are six subquestions (numbered 2.1–2.6) under this research question. For all of these research questions, a $p < 0.05$ level of significance is used. Post hoc comparisons were conducted using the Scheffé method for protection against Type I errors.

Subquestion 2.1

Among Chinese frontline police officers, is age associated with police subcultural perceptions?

Box's *M* test assessing homogeneity of covariance matrices was not significant, $p = 0.114$, indicating that the correlations between the dependent variables can be assumed to be roughly equal. Therefore, a MANOVA was conducted to examine whether age was associated with police cultural perceptions. Entries in Table 7.11 indicate that the first three methods of calculating the F value indicate a nonsignificant multivariate effect for the combined dependent variables of police subcultural perceptions in respect of age. Because Roy's largest root test, the only test that returned a significant finding, should be disregarded in the presence of the three other tests being nonsignificant (Carey 1998), it was disregarded. Therefore, no post hoc tests were conducted between age and the seven scales.

Subquestion 2.2

Among Chinese frontline police officers, is gender associated with police subcultural perceptions?

Box's M test demonstrated homogeneity of covariance matrices, $p = 0.097$. Therefore, a MANOVA was conducted to examine the association of gender with the seven police cultural themes. Entries in Table 7.12 indicate that all four

Table 7.11 MANOVA between age and the seven scales

Effect		Value	F	Hypothesis df	Error df	Sig.	Partial eta squared
Age	Pillai's trace	0.084	1.144	28.000	1496.000	0.276	0.021
	Wilks' lambda	0.918	1.156	28.000	1339.082	0.263	0.021
	Hotelling's trace	0.088	1.167	28.000	1478.000	0.251	0.022
	Roy's largest root	0.068	3.640	7.000	374.000	0.001	0.064

Table 7.12 MANOVA between gender and the seven scales

Effect		Value	F	Hypothesis df	Error df	Sig.	Partial eta squared
Gender	Pillai's trace	0.049	2.774	7.000	374.000	0.008	0.049
	Wilks' Lambda	0.951	2.774	7.000	374.000	0.008	0.049
	Hotelling's trace	0.052	2.774	7.000	374.000	0.008	0.049
	Roy's largest root	0.052	2.774	7.000	374.000	0.008	0.049

methods supported the existence of a significant multivariate effect for the combined dependent variables of police subcultural perceptions in respect of gender. Then a further univariate test was conducted between gender and each of the seven scales to describe the effects of the independent variable against each dependent variable separately.

The assumption of homogeneity of variance was met for all the scales except for receptivity to change ($p = 0.008$) and isolation ($p = 0.035$). Therefore, Mann–Whitney U tests were conducted for these two scales and univariate tests (t test) for the other five scales. Univariate test (Table 7.13) and the Kruskal–Wallis H results reveal that there are significant main effects for gender in respect of crime control: $F(1, 380) = 10.466, p = 0.001$; cynicism: $F(1, 380) = 5.806, p = 0.016$; solidarity: $F(1, 380) = 8.559, p = 0.004$; and isolation: $H(1) = 8.597, p = 0.003$.

With regard to isolation, the Mann–Whitney U test revealed that male officers (median = 25; mean rank = 197.03) scored higher than did female officers (median = 23; mean rank = 144.51), $z = 2.93, p = 0.003$. Group statistics details about the other three scales are provided in Table 7.14. In summary, male officers were more crime-control oriented, more cynical toward the public, more isolated from the community, and they had a greater sense of internal solidarity than their female counterparts.

Subquestion 2.3
Among Chinese frontline police officers, is education associated with police subcultural perceptions?

According to Box's M test, the assumption of homogeneity of covariance matrices was met, $p = 0.429$. As can be seen from the entries in Table 7.15, MANOVA analyses confirmed that there was a significant multivariate effect according to all four methods. Then a further univariate test was conducted between education and each of the seven scales.

The assumption of homogeneity of variance was met for all seven scales. According to Table 7.16, the univariate ANOVA analyses indicated that there were significant differences between officers with different education levels on only three scales: crime control, $F(2, 379) = 4.74, p = 0.009$, solidarity, $F(2, 379) = 5.375$, $p = 0.005$, and isolation, $F(2, 379) = 3.887, p = 0.021$.

Multiple comparisons of officers with different education levels in regard to their perception of crime control, solidarity, and isolation are presented in Table 7.17. Results indicate that officers with bachelor's degree or less tends to think alike in

Table 7.13 Univariate test between gender and five scales

		Sum of squares	df	Mean square	F	Sig.
Crime	Between groups	198.137	1	198.137	10.466	0.001
	Within groups	7193.729	380	18.931		
	Total	7391.866	381			
Service	Between groups	0.071	1	0.071	0.008	0.929
	Within groups	3367.677	380	8.862		
	Total	3367.749	381			
Traditionalism	Between groups	1.696	1	1.696	0.323	0.570
	Within groups	1997.081	380	5.255		
	Total	1998.777	381			
Solidarity	Between groups	59.145	1	59.145	8.559	0.004
	Within groups	2626.007	380	6.911		
	Total	2685.152	381			
Cynicism	Between groups	72.436	1	72.436	5.806	0.016
	Within groups	4740.842	380	12.476		
	Total	4813.277	381			

Table 7.14 Group statistics for gender

			95 % confidence interval	
Scale	Males Mean (*SD*) ($n = 340$)	Females Mean (*SD*) ($n = 42$)	Lower bound	Upper bound
Crime control	20.61 (4.38)	18.31 (4.09)	0.903	3.701
Cynicism	17.32 (3.62)	15.93 (2.73)	0.256	2.528
Solidarity	26.09 (2.67)	24.83 (2.23)	0.412	2.103

Table 7.15 MANOVA between education and the seven scales

Effect		Value	F	Hypothesis df	Error df	Sig.	Partial eta squared
Education	Pillai's trace	0.078	2.165	14.000	748.000	0.008	0.039
	Wilks' lambda	0.923	2.164	14.000	746.000	0.008	0.039
	Hotelling's trace	0.081	2.164	14.000	744.000	0.008	0.039
	Roy's largest root	0.056	2.968	7.000	374.000	0.005	0.053

regard to the crime fighting role orientation. However, officers who have received postgraduate education had significantly different perceptions from the other two groups. Mean differences suggest that postgraduates in this sample expressed less adherence to the traditional crime fighting orientation of policing than officers who have bachelor's degree or below. Furthermore, the lower the education level, the greater the sense of solidarity and sense of isolation from the community.

Table 7.16 Univariate test between education level and seven scales

		Sum of squares	df	Mean square	F	Sig.
Crime	Between groups	180.395	2	90.198	4.740	0.009
	Within groups	7211.471	379	19.028		
	Total	7391.866	381			
Service	Between groups	1.609	2	0.805	0.091	0.913
	Within groups	3366.139	379	8.882		
	Total	3367.749	381			
Traditionalism	Between groups	26.711	2	13.355	2.567	0.078
	Within groups	1972.067	379	5.203		
	Total	1998.777	381			
Change	Between groups	4.705	2	2.352	0.284	0.753
	Within groups	3135.233	379	8.272		
	Total	3139.937	381			
Cynicism	Between groups	15.370	2	7.685	0.607	0.545
	Within groups	4797.907	379	12.659		
	Total	4813.277	381			
Solidarity	Between groups	74.061	2	37.030	5.375	0.005
	Within groups	2611.091	379	6.889		
	Total	2685.152	381			
Isolation	Between groups	130.453	2	65.226	3.887	0.021
	Within groups	6360.542	379	16.782		
	Total	6490.995	381			

Subquestion 2.4

Among Chinese frontline police officers, is tenure associated with police subcultural perceptions?

According to Box's M test, the assumption of homogeneity of covariance matrices was met, $p = 0.072$, so a MANOVA was conducted between tenure and police subcultural perceptions. As can be seen in Table 7.18, there was a significant multivariate effect of tenure on police subcultural perceptions according to all four methods. A further univariate test was then conducted between tenure and each of the seven scales to locate any significant differences.

The assumption of homogeneity of variance was met for all scales except traditionalism, $p = 0.029$ and service, $p = 0.034$. Therefore, Kruskal–Wallis *H* tests were conducted for those two scales, but neither attained significance. Univariate tests (Table 7.19) on the remaining five scales indicated that there was a significant effect on only cynicism, $F(2, 379) = 8.343$, $p < 0.001$. The p value indicates a strong effect of the length of their policing service upon the cynical attitude of police officers.

As presented in Table 7.20, details about the post hoc comparisons indicate that all three tenure groups were significantly different from one another with regard to cynicism. Officers with 6–10 years of service were more cynical than were the other two groups. In addition, officers with 11 years of service or more were the

Table 7.17 Multiple comparisons for education

Dependent variable	(I) Education	(J) Education	Mean difference (I – J)	Std. error	Sig.	95 % confidence interval	
						Lower bound	Upper bound
Crime	2 or 3 year college or less	Bachelor's degree	0.111	0.464	0.972	−1.03	1.25
		Master's degree or above	3.298[a]	1.088	0.011	0.63	5.97
	Bachelor's degree	Master's degree or above	3.187[a]	1.071	0.013	0.56	5.82
Solidarity	2 or 3 year college or less	Bachelor's degree	0.840[a]	0.279	0.011	0.15	1.53
		Master's degree or above	1.317	0.655	0.134	−0.29	2.93
	Bachelor's degree	Master's degree or above	0.477	0.644	0.761	−1.11	2.06
Isolation	2 or 3 year college or less	Bachelor's degree	0.524	0.436	0.487	−0.55	1.59
		Master's degree or above	2.795[a]	1.022	0.025	0.28	5.31
	Bachelor's degree	Master's degree or above	2.272	1.006	0.079	−0.20	4.74

[a]The mean difference is significant at the 0.05 level

Table 7.18 MANOVA between tenure and the seven scales

Effect		Value	F	Hypothesis df	Error df	Sig.	Partial eta squared
Tenure	Pillai's trace	0.094	2.630	14.000	748.000	0.001	0.047
	Wilks' lambda	0.908	2.637	14.000	746.000	0.001	0.047
	Hotelling's trace	0.099	2.643	14.000	744.000	0.001	0.047
	Roy's largest root	0.073	3.883	7.000	374.000	0.000	0.068

least cynical of the three tenure groups. These findings are indicated clearly in the means plots in Fig. 7.9.

Subquestion 2.5

Among Chinese frontline police officers, is type of police associated with police subcultural perceptions?

According to Box's M test, the assumption of homogeneity of covariance matrices was met, $p = 0.239$. A MANOVA indicated that there is a significant multivariate effect according to all four methods. Refer to Table 7.21. Univariate tests (Table 7.22) were therefore conducted between type of police force and each of the seven scales to locate any significant differences.

Table 7.19 Univariate test between tenure and five scales

		Sum of squares	df	Mean square	F	Sig.
Crime	Between groups	53.513	2	26.757	1.382	0.252
	Within groups	7338.353	379	19.362		
	Total	7391.866	381			
Change	Between groups	41.330	2	20.665	2.528	0.081
	Within groups	3098.607	379	8.176		
	Total	3139.937	381			
Cynicism	Between groups	202.980	2	101.490	8.343	0.000
	Within groups	4610.297	379	12.164		
	Total	4813.277	381			
Solidarity	Between groups	32.042	2	16.021	2.289	0.103
	Within groups	2653.110	379	7.000		
	Total	2685.152	381			
Isolation	Between groups	4.310	2	2.155	0.126	0.882
	Within groups	6486.685	379	17.115		
	Total	6490.995	381			

Table 7.20 Multiple comparisons for tenure

Dependent variable: cynicism

(I) Tenure	(J) Tenure	Mean difference (I – J)	Std. error	Sig.	95 % confidence interval	
					Lower bound	Upper bound
5 years or less	6–10 years	−1.327[a]	0.503	0.032	−2.56	−0.09
	More than 11 years	1.534[a]	0.571	0.028	0.13	2.94
6–10 years	5 years or less	1.327[a]	0.503	0.032	0.09	2.56
	More than 11 years	2.861[a]	0.702	0.000	1.14	4.59
More than 11 years	5 years or less	−1.534[a]	0.571	0.028	−2.94	−0.13
	6–10 years	−2.861[a]	0.702	0.000	−4.59	−1.14

[a]The mean difference is significant at the 0.05 level

The assumption of homogeneity of variance was met for all scales except crime control ($p = 0.018$). Therefore, a Kruskal–Wallis *H* test was conducted for this scale. It yielded a significant result, $H(2) = 22.69$, $p < 0.001$. Solidarity and isolation scores were also significantly different between officers from different types of police organisations. For solidarity, $F(2, 379) = 3.40$, $p = 0.034$, and for isolation, $F(2, 379) = 10.58$, $p < 0.001$.

According to the Mann–Whitney *U* tests on the crime control scale, officers from district sub bureaus (median = 21; mean rank = 137.22) were more likely to

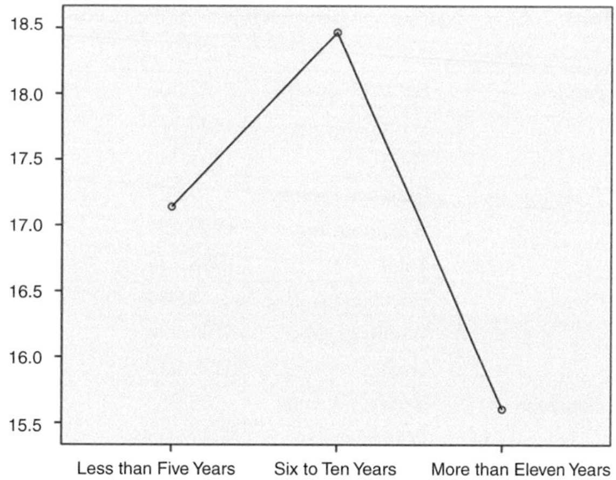

Fig. 7.9 Means plots for cynicism and tenure

Table 7.21 MANOVA between type of police force and seven scales

Effect		Value	F	Hypothesis df	Error df	Sig.	Partial eta squared
Type	Pillai's trace	0.110	3.105	14.000	748.000	0.000	0.055
	Wilks' lambda	0.891	3.176	14.000	746.000	0.000	0.056
	Hotelling's trace	0.122	3.247	14.000	744.000	0.000	0.058
	Roy's largest root	0.117	6.269	7.000	374.000	0.000	0.105

have a crime control orientation than were officers from municipal and higher levels (median = 19; mean rank = 105.77), z = 3.05, $p = 0.002$. In turn, officers from field stations (median = 21; mean rank = 170.67) were more likely to have a crime control orientation than were officers from district sub bureaus (median = 21; mean rank = 146.01), z = 2.38, $p = 0.017$. Not surprisingly, officers from field stations (median = 21; mean rank = 113.54) were more likely to have a crime control orientation than were officers from municipal land higher levels (median = 19; mean rank = 73.19), z = 4.79, $p < 0.001$.

Multiple comparisons of officers with different levels of police force in regard to their perceptions of solidarity and isolation are presented in Table 7.23. In terms of solidarity, multiple comparison test indicates that officers from field stations were in significantly higher levels of solidarity than officers from municipal or provincial police departments. Although differences between field station officers and district sub-bureau officers, and differences between district sub-bureau officers and municipal or provincial officers are not statistically significant, means differences among these three groups do show that the lower the police department level is, the higher degree of police solidarity officers show. Regarding to social isolation, significant differences are identified between municipal or provincial officers and district sub-bureau officers, and between municipal or provincial officers and field station officers in their perceptions. Similar to the previous two

Table 7.22 Univariate test between type of police force and six scales

		Sum of squares	df	Mean square	F	Sig.
Service	Between groups	37.605	2	18.803	2.140	0.119
	Within groups	3330.143	379	8.787		
	Total	3367.749	381			
Traditionalism	Between groups	9.323	2	4.662	0.888	0.412
	Within groups	1989.454	379	5.249		
	Total	1998.777	381			
Change	Between groups	4.984	2	2.492	0.301	0.740
	Within groups	3134.954	379	8.272		
	Total	3139.937	381			
Cynicism	Between groups	65.953	2	32.976	2.633	0.073
	Within groups	4747.325	379	12.526		
	Total	4813.277	381			
Solidarity	Between groups	47.380	2	23.690	3.404	0.034
	Within groups	2637.772	379	6.960		
	Total	2685.152	381			
Isolation	Between groups	343.076	2	171.538	10.575	0.000
	Within groups	6147.918	379	16.221		
	Total	6490.995	381			

Table 7.23 Multiple comparisons for type of police force

Dependent variable	(I) Type	(J) Type	Mean difference (I − J)	Std. error	Sig.	95 % confidence interval	
						Lower bound	Upper bound
Solidarity	Municipal or above	District sub-bureau	−0.757	0.368	0.122	−1.66	0.15
		Field station	−1.008[a]	0.391	0.037	−1.97	−0.05
	District sub-bureau	Field station	−0.251	0.305	0.712	−1.00	0.50
Isolation	Municipal or above	District sub-bureau	−2.174[a]	0.562	0.001	−3.56	−0.79
		Field station	−2.663[a]	0.598	0.000	−4.13	−1.19
	District sub-bureau	Field station	−0.489	0.465	0.576	−1.63	0.65

[a]The mean difference is significant at the 0.05 level

scales, officers from lower levels of police departments were more likely to feel isolated than their counterparts from higher levels of police departments.

In essence, officers from lower levels of police departments were more likely to have a crime control orientation and to feel more solidarity and isolation than did their counterparts from higher levels of police departments.

Subquestion 2.6

Among Chinese frontline police officers, is being detectives or not associated with police subcultural perceptions?

Box's M test indicated that homogeneity of covariance matrices can be assumed, $p = 0.11$. A MANOVA was therefore conducted to examine the association of being detectives or not upon the combination of seven police cultural themes. All four methods supported a significant multivariate effect for the combined dependent variables of police subcultural perceptions in respect of being detectives or not according to all four methods. See Table 7.24. Therefore, univariate tests were conducted between being detectives and non-detectives on each of the seven scales.

Tests of homogeneity of variance indicated that this assumption has been met for all the scales. According to Table 7.25, univariate test result reveals that there

Table 7.24 MANOVA between being detectives or not and seven scales

Effect		Value	F	Hypothesis df	Error df	Sig.	Partial eta squared
Detective/ non-detective	Pillai's trace	0.041	2.267	7.000	374.000	0.029	0.041
	Wilks' lambda	0.959	2.267	7.000	374.000	0.029	0.041
	Hotelling's trace	0.042	2.267	7.000	374.000	0.029	0.041
	Roy's largest root	0.042	2.267	7.000	374.000	0.029	0.041

Table 7.25 Univariate test between being detectives or not and seven scales

		Sum of squares	df	Mean square	F	Sig.
Crime	Between groups	6.041	1	6.041	0.311	0.578
	Within groups	7385.825	380	19.436		
	Total	7391.866	381			
Service	Between groups	41.312	1	41.312	4.719	0.030
	Within groups	3326.437	380	8.754		
	Total	3367.749	381			
Traditionalism	Between groups	1.969	1	1.969	0.375	0.541
	Within groups	1996.808	380	5.255		
	Total	1998.777	381			
Change	Between groups	19.295	1	19.295	2.350	0.126
	Within groups	3120.642	380	8.212		
	Total	3139.937	381			
Cynicism	Between groups	31.696	1	31.696	2.519	0.113
	Within groups	4781.582	380	12.583		
	Total	4813.277	381			
Solidarity	Between groups	44.049	1	44.049	6.338	0.012
	Within groups	2641.103	380	6.950		
	Total	2685.152	381			
Isolation	Between groups	24.628	1	24.628	1.447	0.230
	Within groups	6466.366	380	17.017		
	Total	6490.995	381			

Table 7.26 Group statistics for being detectives or not

				95 % confidence interval	
Scale	Detectives Mean (*SD*) ($n = 227$)	Non-detectives Mean (*SD*) ($n = 155$)	Sig	Lower bound	Upper bound
Service	16.95 (2.98)	16.28 (2.93)	0.030	0.064	1.276
Solidarity	26.23 (2.52)	25.54 (2.79)	0.012	0.151	1.232

are significant main effects on service: $F(1, 380) = 4.719$, $p = 0.03$; and solidarity: $F(1, 380) = 6.338$, $p = 0.012$. According to group statistics shown in Table 7.26, police detectives were found to be more service-oriented in policing, and showing more internal solidarity than their non-detective counterparts.

From the results of MANOVAs, except for age, all independent variables in this study were significantly associated with police subcultural perceptions. In order to provide further explanations, for those scales that were significantly associated with one or several independent variables, Chi-square tests were used to investigate the potential associations between individual items with the corresponding independent variable(s).

7.3 Chi-Square Tests

Chi-square tests were conducted between items in the scale of crime control and gender, education and type of police, between items in service scales and being detectives or not, between items in cynicism scale and tenure, between items in solidarity scale and gender, education, type of police and being detectives or not, between items in isolation scale and gender, education and type of police. Statistically significant associations which were identified are presented below.

Item 1 An aggressive, tough bearing is more useful to a police officer than a friendly, courteous manner.

Chi-square test for the first item showed significant associations with gender, $\chi^2(4) = 11.59$, $p = 0.021$, and type of police force, $\chi^2(8) = 15.753$, $p = 0.046$. As presented in Fig. 7.10, while 44.1 % of the male respondents strongly agreed or agreed with this item, only 23.8 % of the female respondents did. Furthermore, none of the female respondents strongly agreed with it. This shows a clear tendency that male officers were more likely to agree or strongly agree with aggressive styles than their female counterparts. Officers' perceptions of the first item also varied according to their type of police force. As shown in Fig. 7.11, while 50.8 % of the respondents from field stations agreed or strongly agreed, the percentages were 41.6 % for the respondents from district or county police sub-bureaus, and 26.8 % for the respondents from municipal or provincial police departments. Respondents from field stations also constituted the smallest percentage (19.1 %) of those who disagreed or strongly disagreed with this item. The percentages were 25.9 % for the

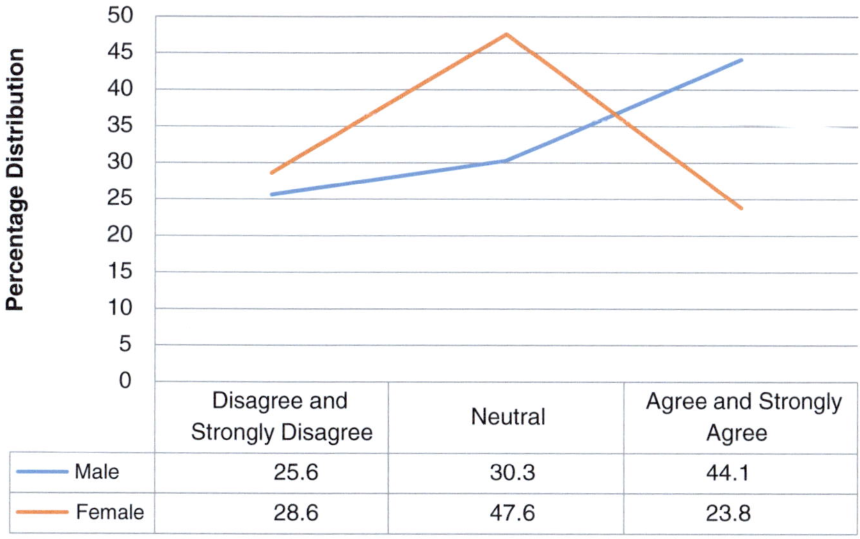

	Disagree and Strongly Disagree	Neutral	Agree and Strongly Agree
Male	25.6	30.3	44.1
Female	28.6	47.6	23.8

Fig. 7.10 Percentage distribution within gender for Item 1

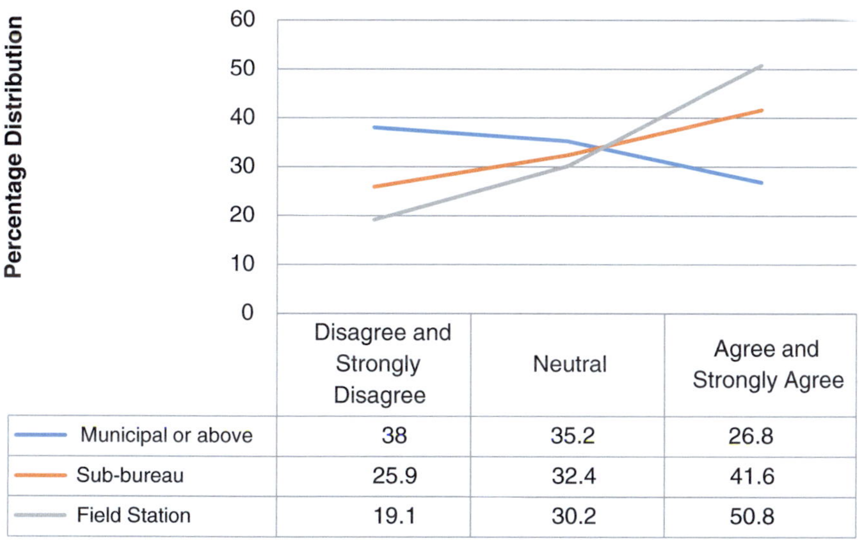

	Disagree and Strongly Disagree	Neutral	Agree and Strongly Agree
Municipal or above	38	35.2	26.8
Sub-bureau	25.9	32.4	41.6
Field Station	19.1	30.2	50.8

Fig. 7.11 Percentage distribution within type of police force for Item 1

respondents from district or county police sub-bureaus, and 38 % for the respondents from municipal or provincial police departments. This suggests that officers from lower-level police departments are more likely to prefer aggressive policing style than their counterparts from higher-level departments.

Item 3 Good law enforcement requires that officers concern themselves with the consequences of crime and not with its root causes.

Gender was the only factor that significantly influenced officers' perceptions on the third item, $\chi^2(4) = 11.384$, $p = 0.023$. As illustrated in Fig. 7.12, while 12.4 % of male respondents strongly disagreed with this item, the percentages were 28.6 % for female respondents. On the other hand, 9.4 % of male respondents strongly agreed with this item; only 2.4 % of female respondents strongly agreed with it. According to these findings, female respondents are more likely to concern about the causes of crime than their male counterparts.

Item 5 Police officers should not have to handle calls that involve social or personal problems where no crime is involved.

Chi-square for the fifth item showed significant relationships with education level, $\chi^2(8) = 22.305$, $p = 0.004$, and type of police force, $\chi^2(8) = 25.647$, $p = 0.001$. In regard to education level, the percentages of the respondents who strongly disagreed or disagreed with this item were as follows: 26.4 % of high school or 2–3 year college graduates, 34.7 % of bachelor's graduates, and 72.2 % of postgraduates. The percentages of respondents who agreed or strongly agreed with this item were: 51.7 % of high school or 2–3 year college graduates, 48.8 % of bachelor's graduates, and 27.8 % of postgraduates. As seen in Fig. 7.13, this distribution shows that officers who received more education were more likely to accept police involvement in non-crime activities. Officers' perceptions of the first item also varied according to their type of police force. As shown in Fig. 7.14, while 58.8 % of the respondents from field stations agreed or strongly agreed, the percentages were 49.7 % for the respondents from district or county police sub-bureaus, and 22.4 % for the respondents from municipal or

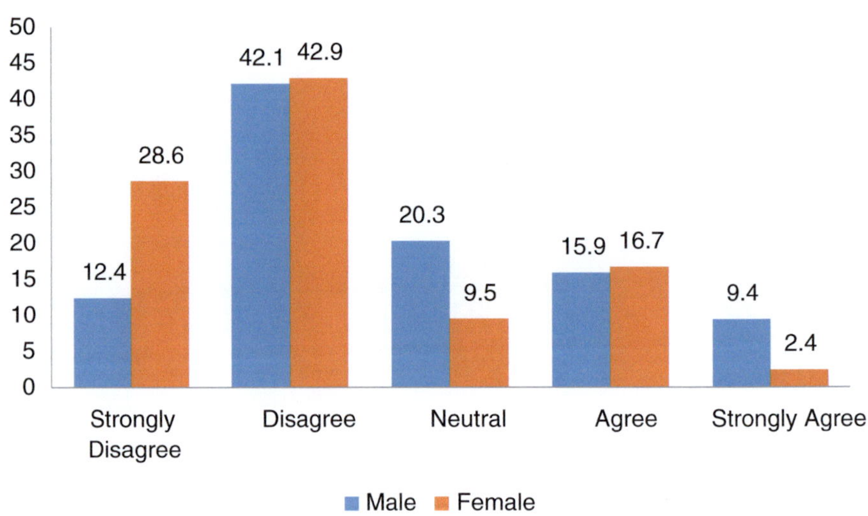

Fig. 7.12 Percentage distribution within gender for Item 3

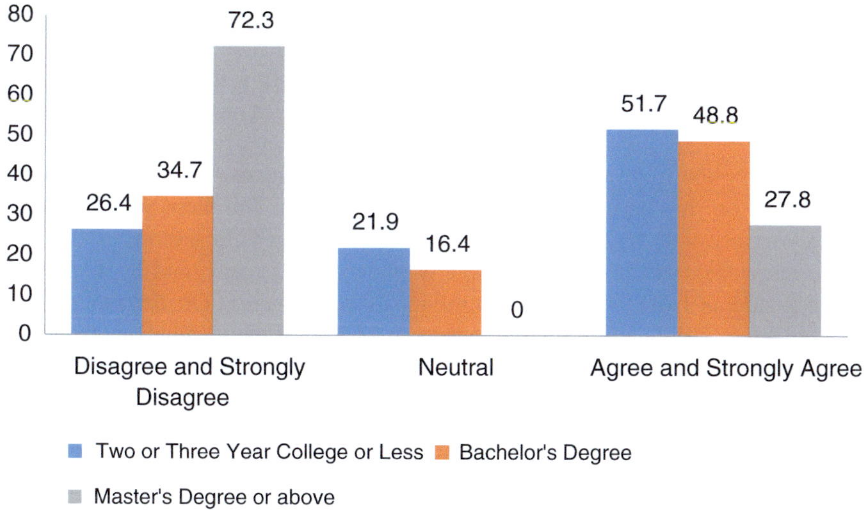

Fig. 7.13 Percentage distribution within education level for Item 5

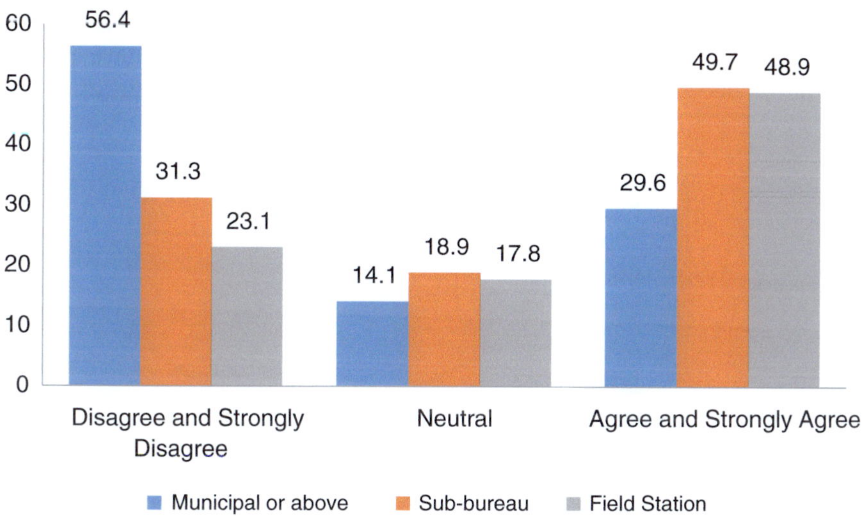

Fig. 7.14 Percentage distribution within type of police force for Item 5

provincial police departments. Respondents from field stations also constituted the smallest percentage (23.1 %) of those who disagreed or strongly disagreed with this item. The percentages were 31.3 % for the respondents from district or county police sub-bureaus, and 56.4 % for the respondents from municipal or provincial police departments. This suggests that officers from higher-level police departments are more likely to accept police involvement in non-crime activities than their counterparts from lower-level departments.

Item 6 If police officers in high crime areas had fewer restrictions on their use of force, many of the serious crime problems in these areas would be significantly reduced.

Type of police force was the only factor that significantly influenced officers' perceptions on this item, $\chi^2(8) = 16.061$, $p = 0.042$. This item was agreed or strongly agreed with by 70.7 % of the respondents from field stations, by 56.8 % of the respondents from district or county police sub-bureaus, and by 47.9 % of the respondents from municipal or provincial departments. On the other hand, 15.1 % of the respondents from field stations, 27.5 % of the respondents from district or county police sub-bureaus, and 39.5 % of the respondents from municipal or provincial departments either disagreed or strongly disagreed with this item. According to these findings, officers from lower-level police departments are more likely to accept police use of force than their counterparts from higher-level departments. This is best represented in Fig. 7.15.

Item 25 Most people respect the authority of police officers.

Tenure was found to be significantly related to police perceptions on this item, $\chi^2(8) = 17.251$, $p = 0.028$. While 51.2 % of respondents with 11 years of service or more agreed or strongly agreed with this item, 17.2 % of respondents with 6–10 years of service and 27 % of respondents with 5 years of service or less agreed or strongly agreed with it. On the other hand, there were similar proportions of respondents with 5 years of service or less and with 6–10 years of service

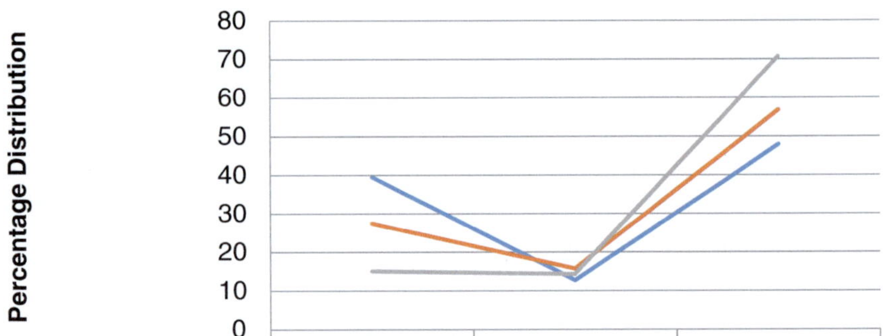

	Disagree and Strongly Disagree	Neutral	Agree and Strongly Agree
Municipal or above	39.5	12.7	47.9
Sub-bureau	27.5	15.7	56.8
Field Station	15.1	14.3	70.7

Fig. 7.15 Percentage distribution within type of police force for Item 6

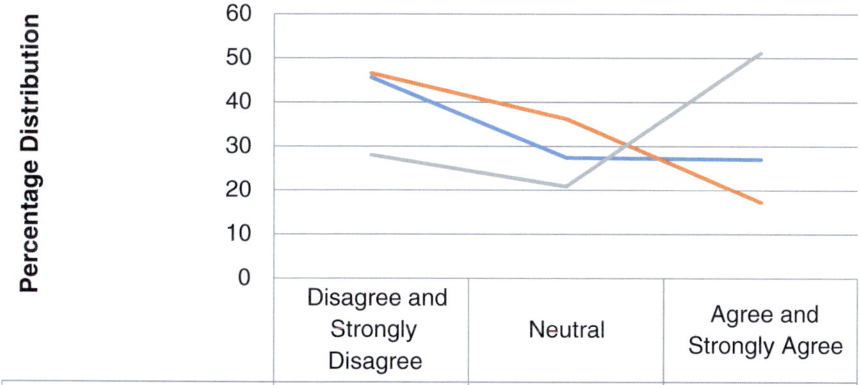

	Disagree and Strongly Disagree	Neutral	Agree and Strongly Agree
Less than five years	45.6	27.4	27
Six to Ten Years	46.5	36.2	17.2
More than Eleven Years	28	20.9	51.2

Fig. 7.16 Percentage distribution within tenure for Item 25

who disagreed or strongly disagreed with this item, representing 45.6 and 46.5 % separately. Only 28 % of officers with 11 years of service or more either disagreed or strongly disagreed with it. This distribution suggested in Fig. 7.16 indicates that respondents with 11 years of service or more were more likely to acknowledge people's respect for police authority than less experienced officers in this sample.

Item 28 Police officers are careful of how they behave in public.

Chi-square analysis of this item indicated significant relationships with gender, $\chi^2(4) = 31.836$, $p < 0.001$, education level, $\chi^2(8) = 44.14$, $p < 0.001$, and type of police force, $\chi^2(8) = 16.759$, $p = 0.033$. 80 % of male respondents and 54.7 % of female respondents agreed or strongly agreed with this item, while 4.2 % of male respondents and 23.8 % of female respondents disagreed or strongly disagreed with it. As indicated in Fig. 7.17, although both male and female respondents showed their support for this item, female respondents were more balanced in percentages than their male counterparts. Officers' education levels also influenced their perceptions on this item. While 86.7 % of 2 or 3 year college graduates and high school graduates agreed or strongly agreed with this item, the same percentages were 71.4 and 66.6 % for bachelor's graduates and postgraduates. On the other hand, 3.3 % of 2 or 3 year college graduates and high school graduates, 6.6 % of bachelor's graduates, and 27.8 % of postgraduates disagreed or strongly disagreed with this item. This distribution shown in Fig. 7.18 indicates a clear pattern that the lower the education level is, the stronger the support is shown for this item. Type of police force was also identified to be influential to police perceptions on this item. The percentages of respondents who agreed or strongly agreed with this item were 63.4 % among municipal or provincial officers, 77.3 % among sub-bureau officers, and 84.9 % among field station officers. In addition, the percentages of respondents who

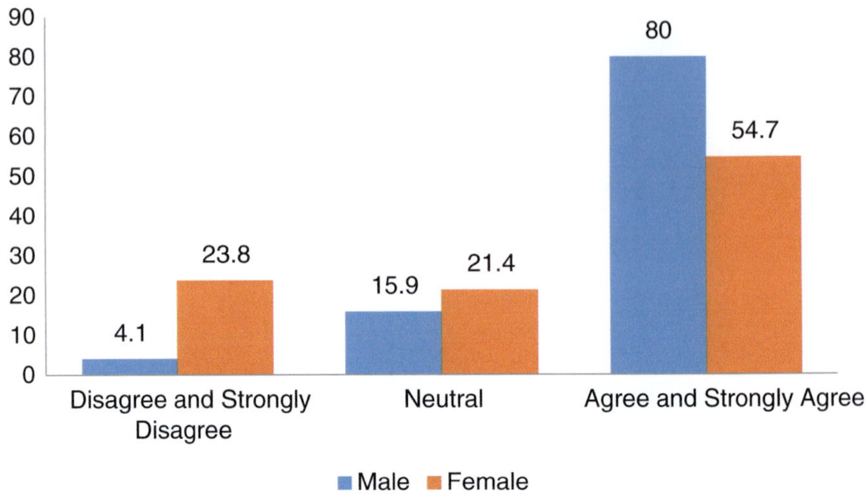

Fig. 7.17 Percentage distribution within gender for Item 28

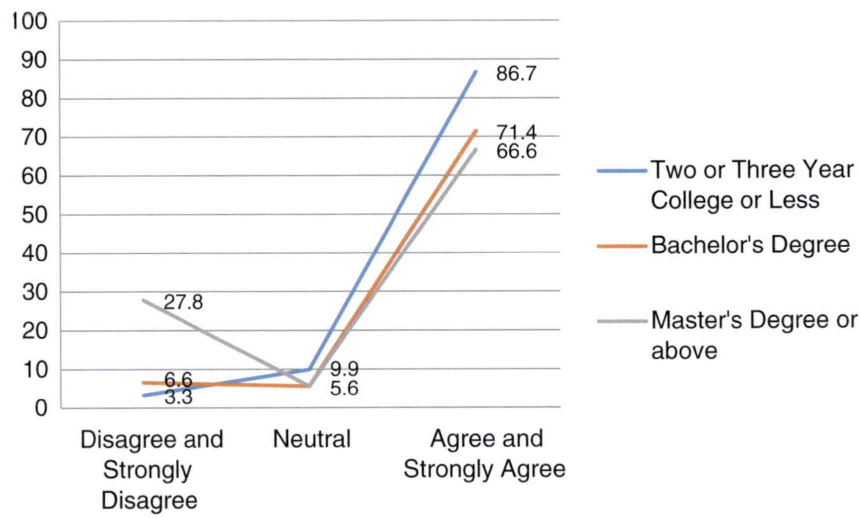

Fig. 7.18 Percentage distribution within education level for Item 28

disagreed or strongly disagreed with this item were 12.7 % among municipal or provincial officers, 5.4 % among sub-bureau officers, and 4 % among field station officers. As presented in Fig. 7.19, this suggests that the lower the level of organisation is, the stronger the support is shown for this item.

Item 34 I tend to socialise less with my friends outside of the police since I have become a police officer.

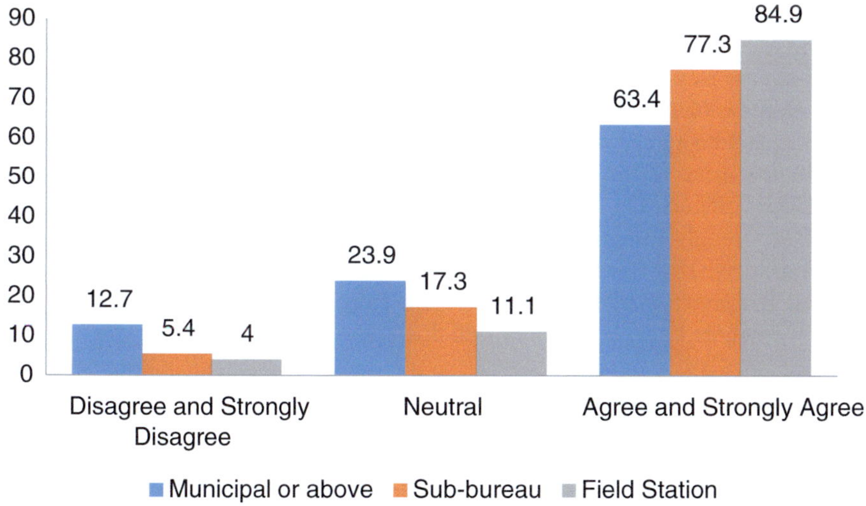

Fig. 7.19 Percentage distribution within type of police force for Item 28

Gender was found to be a factor influencing perceptions on this item, $\chi^2(4) = 20.45$, $p < 0.001$. 44.7 % of male respondents agreed or strongly agreed with this item, while only 14.3 % female respondents agreed or strongly agreed with it. On the other hand, it was disagreed or strongly disagreed by 42.4 % of male respondents and by 54.8 % of female respondents. As suggested in Fig. 7.20, the results suggest that male officers are more likely to socialise less with outsiders than their female counterparts in this sample.

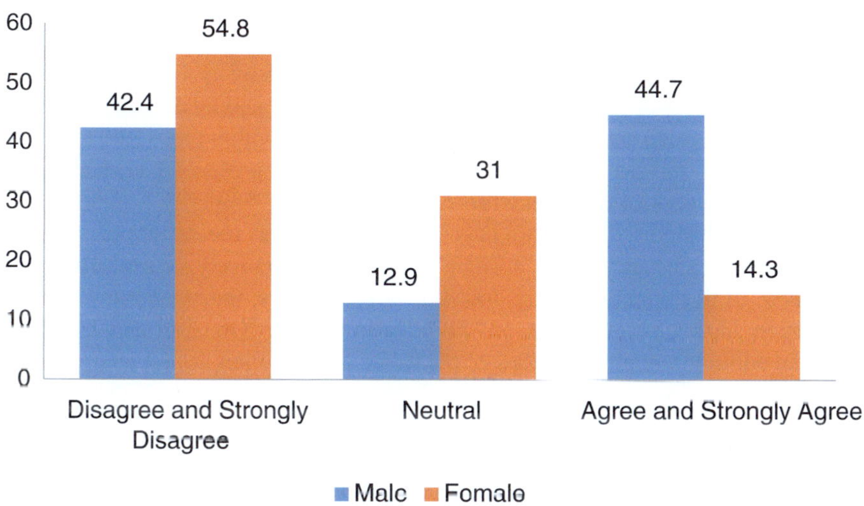

Fig. 7.20 Percentage distribution within type of police force for Item 34

Item 40 I can be more open with my work colleagues than with members of the public.

Chi-square results show that perceptions on this item were significantly influenced by type of police force, $\chi^2(8) = 15.723$, $p = 0.047$. The percentages for respondents who agreed or strongly agreed with this item were 33.8 % of municipal and provincial officers, 47.5 % of district sub-bureau officers, and 49.2 % of field station officers. On the other hand, the percentages for respondents who disagreed or strongly disagreed with this item were 28.2 % of municipal and provincial officers, 18.9 % of district sub-bureau officers, and 21.5 % of field station officers. The results suggest that respondents from municipal or provincial departments were more likely to disagree with this item.

7.4 Pearson Correlations

MANOVA and chi-square analysis results provide an overall understanding of the relationships that demographic and work-related variables have with the seven scales of police subculture. These addressed the second research question. Pearson correlation was also conducted to find out whether there were any bivariate correlations among the seven cultural themes. This is to answer the third research question in this study.

Similar to MANOVA, Pearson's correlation are based on several assumptions, including normally distributed data, a linear relationship, and interval or ratio data (Cunningham and Aldrich 2012; Miller and Whitehead 1996). Normality of scores on all seven scales was assessed through the examination of histograms, stem-and-leaf plots, box plots, and normal probability plots. Graphical examination of the scores of seven scales suggests that all the seven scales are very close to normal distribution. Histograms show that distributions are bell shaped and Q-Q plots suggest straight diagonal lines. M-estimators results indicate that values are very close to the means although some values are slightly above or below the means. Finally, the z-scores of skewness and kurtosis were calculated by dividing values of skewness and kurtosis by the stand error. The values are within the $+1.96$ to -1.96 range for crime, service, traditionalism, and isolation, representing normal distribution. The z-scores of skewness for cynicism (2.832), solidarity (-2.808), and receptivity to change (-2.472) are beyond that range. This means that perceptions on these three scales are slightly positively skewed or negatively skewed. However, the sample in this study is nearly 400. For large samples, the standard of normal distribution should be changed to ± 2.58 or even broader (Ghasemi and Zahediasl 2012). In addition, minor violations of the normal distribution do not tend to cause major problems for large samples (Field 2013; Ghasemi and Zahediasl 2012). Mayers (2013, p. 53) suggested ± 1.96 for samples smaller than 50, ± 2.58 for samples from 51 to 100, and ± 3.29 for samples larger than 100 as cut-off points when used in conjunction with the examination of graphs. Another simplified method for normality suggests that if the value of skewness is within the range between ±1, an approximate normal distribution of the data can be assumed (Leech et al. 2005). For this study, the values of skewness of all seven scales of police subculture are within ±0.4, so no major violations of normal distribution are present. For the level of measurement in this study, it may be assumed that the data obtained from Likert scales are interval in order to locate the exact quantities and distances and add "values and variability to the data" for parametric analysis (Allen and Seaman 2007, p. 65). Although Likert scales data are intrinsically ordinal, many scholars regard them as being equal interval data, because "for many statistical tests, rather severe departures (from intervalness) do not seem to affect Type I and Type II errors dramatically" especially if a 5 or 7 point scale is used (Jaccard and Wan 1996, p. 4). For linearity, scatter plots were examined before the calculation of Pearson correlation for all the scales.

Research Question 3

For Chinese frontline police officers, are there significant relationships among the seven police subcultural themes suggested in Western literature?

The third research question comprised three subquestions (numbered 3.1–3.3), each of which is presented below followed by the relevant results. All correlations are presented in Table 7.27.

Subquestion 3.1

Are there any significant correlations between a crime control orientation and the other six subcultural themes?

One of the key components of police subculture perceptions in this study is police role orientation towards crime control and community service. The existing literature also suggests that the crime-fighting role orientation is closely associated with other themes of police culture, such as solidarity, cynicism, isolation, and traditionalism (Packer 1968; Sparrow et al. 1990). It is one of the main aims of this study to identify the possible correlations through statistical analysis on the basis of empirical data.

Results indicate that there are significant relationships between crime control orientation and all other six subcultural themes. Crime control orientation is significantly correlated with service orientation, $r = -0.205$, $p < 0.001$, traditionalism, $r = 0.132$, $p = 0.01$, receptivity to change, $r = -0.203$, $p < 0.001$, solidarity, $r = 0.213$, $p < 0.001$, cynicism, $r = 0.306$, $p < 0.001$, and isolation, $r = 0.31$, $p < 0.001$.

Entries in Table 7.27 indicate that a crime control orientation is positively correlated with traditionalism, solidarity, cynicism, and isolation and negatively correlated with service orientation and receptivity to change. However, although the correlation values are all significant they are not high, varying from ±0.1 to ±0.4, which could be regarded as low to moderate (Miller and Whitehead 1996, p. 322). In essence, therefore, as the level of crime control orientation increases, the levels of cynicism, traditionalism, solidarity, and isolation also tend to increase and vice

Table 7.27 Pearson's correlations (r) between subcultural themes (N = 382)[a]

		Traditionalism	Cynicism	Solidarity	Isolation	Service	Change
Crime control	*r*	0.132	0.306	0.213	0.310	−0.205	−0.203
	p	0.010	0.000	0.000	0.000	0.000	0.000
Traditionalism	*r*		−0.083	0.102	0.026	0.067	−0.033
	p		0.106	0.047	0.617	0.193	0.526
Cynicism	*r*			0.078	0.219	−0.210	−0.258
	p			0.126	0.000	0.000	0.000
Solidarity	*r*				0.309	0.091	0.111
	p				0.000	0.077	0.030
Isolation	*r*					0.002	−0.107
	p					0.975	0.036
Service	*r*						0.095
	p						0.064

[a]Probability levels are based on 2-tailed tests

versa. Conversely, as the level of crime control orientation increases, the levels of service orientation and receptivity to change tend to decrease and vice versa.

Subquestion 3.2

Are there any significant correlations between a service role orientation and the other subcultural themes?

Community service is one of the most important police functions under the framework of community policing. Entries in Table 7.27 indicate that, apart from the already-acknowledged negative correlation with a crime control orientation, the only other significant correlation with service orientation is a negative one with cynicism, $r = -0.21$, $p < 0.001$. It is a low correlation, indicating that higher levels of service orientation tend to be associated with lower levels of cynicism and vice versa.

Subquestion 3.3

Are there any significant correlations among traditionalism, receptivity to change, cynicism, solidarity, and isolation?

According to entries in Table 7.27, there are a number of significant correlations among these variables, but they are all relatively low or moderate. There are positive correlations of isolation with cynicism, $r = 0.219$, $p < 0.001$, and solidarity, $r = 0.309$, $p < 0.001$. These results suggest that as the level of police isolation increases, the degree of solidarity and cynicism also increase and vice versa. However, there is an inverse correlation between isolation and receptivity to change, $r = -0.107$, $p = 0.036$, indicating that the more officers feel isolated, the less they are receptive to change at work and vice versa. Receptivity to change was significantly correlated with cynicism, $r = -0.258$, $p < 0.001$ and solidarity, $r = 0.111$, $p = 0.03$. The negative correlation between receptivity to change and cynicism shows that the more cynical officers are, the less receptive to change they are; the positive correlation between receptivity to change and solidarity suggest that as the level of solidarity increases, the degree of receptivity to change also increases and vice versa. In addition, the degree of solidarity was also found to be significantly related to police traditionalism, $r = 0.102$, $p = 0.047$. This correlation suggests that as the level of solidarity increases, the degree of traditionalism also increases and vice versa.

7.5 Qualitative Data Analysis

Unlike quantitative data analysis, qualitative data analysis deals with verbal accounts rather than numbers. The researcher needs to adopt a more flexible and complex way to make sense of themes and meanings because all these generated themes and meanings need to be comprehended within their original contexts (Richards 2005, pp. 34–36). There are mainly four ways to guide data analysis: narrative analysis, thematic analysis, grounded theory analysis, and discourse analysis (Minichiello et al. 2008, pp. 275–293). Thematic analysis is used as the main method of qualitative data analysis for this study. The focus of thematic analysis is to "identify themes emerging from the transcripts recorded" by "a systematic examination and re-examination of the data line by line in order to obtain meaningful categories that can be grouped to form a theme or a series of themes" (Minichiello et al. 2008, p. 280). In this study, research participants' responses to the open-ended questions have already been organised by the seven cultural themes. Therefore, I subclassified the responses into smaller themes under each cultural theme to identify some underlying reasons and additional information to further interpret the results of quantitative data analysis.

Crime and Service

Aggressive manner and use of force

Reasons to **agree**

1. The police should use an aggressive manner and force because they are the state apparatus with coercive power. (frequency = 8)
2. The police are now usually in a passive position under attack. (frequency = 8)
3. The police should not be of low status and without dignity. (frequency = 3)
4. Lack use of force will threaten personal safety of officers. (frequency = 4)
5. Restrictions on use of force will bind one's hands and feet and officers cannot combat crimes effectively. (frequency = 4)
6. Restrictions on use of force temper the enthusiasm of crime control. (frequency = 1)
7. The police should "govern the country with severe law during the trouble times" (an old saying in China, which is similar to the deterrence theory in the West) (frequency = 1)
8. Without enough right to use force, officers are unable to protect civilians. (frequency = 1)

Reasons to **disagree**

1. Laws should be enforced in a standard, fair and civil manner. (frequency = 3)
2. against extorting confessions by torture (frequency = 1)
3. Use of force only treats symptoms. (frequency = 1)
4. Use of force is ineffective and increases contradictions. (frequency = 4)

Reasons to be **neutral**

1. flexible responses to deal with situations (frequency = 3)
2. different policing styles in different regions (frequency = 1)
3. Use of force should be under supervision. (frequency = 1)
4. reasonable use of force, not infringing upon civil rights (frequency = 2)

Reasons for crime-fighting oriented policing

1. Crime control is the premise for providing service. (frequency = 2)
2. Service increases workloads and pressures. (frequency = 8)
3. The main job of policing is crime control; other corresponding government departments should provide service. (frequency = 29)
4. police forces shortage (frequency = 1)
5. As a result of service-oriented policing, citizens are not afraid of police officers and being uncooperative and unreasonable. (frequency = 3)
6. Service makes the police role more complex. (frequency = 3)

Reasons for service-oriented policing

1. people-oriented (frequency = 1)
2. window units (departments that provide service for citizens need to show enough enthusiasm, professionalism, friendliness etc. to make people satisfied) (frequency = 1)

Against involvement in non-crime activities

1. a waste of police manpower (frequency = 1)
2. reduce efficiency of policing (frequency = 3)
3. The police should work within the functions and authorities regulated by the laws. (frequency = 5)
4. The police are not "omnipotent", "bodyguards", "babysitters", or "the God". (frequency = 9)
5. Non-crime activities affect police image, such as forced evictions and demolition, and stopping petitioners. (frequency = 3)

Crime prevention

The main responsibility of policing is crime control; crime prevention is the responsibility of the whole society. (frequency = 1)

Fear of crime

As long as crime rate is reduced, citizens' fear of crime is automatically reduced. (frequency = 1)

From the above statistics of comments with regard to their role orientations of crime fighting and service, many officers had opinions or suggestions to express on this topic. This section has attracted the most comments among all of the cultural themes. One hundred and seventeen comments were made by the participants of the survey for these two scales. Among these comments, 46 provided reasons for a crime-fighting-oriented policing, while only two stated why they thought policing should be service-oriented. The main reason that officers provided is that they believe themselves to be crime fighters and service functions should be taken over by other related government departments. Other concerns including increasing workloads and threatening police authority were also mentioned once and again. In addition, 46 comments discussed about aggressive policing styles and police use of force. While 30 officers expressed support for a more aggressive policing style and less limitation on use of force, nine officers were against it and another seven officers kept neutral. The most frequently mentioned reasons for aggressive policing and use of force is the Marxist conceptualisation of police as the coercive state apparatus and the bad policing environment of Chinese officers which make officers feel unsafe and of low dignity. Another topic that attracted much attention is police involvement in non-crime activities. Twenty-one comments expressed different reasons against non-crime activities. Nine officers used terms such as "omnipotent", "bodyguards", "babysitters" or even "the God" to describe how they considered non-crime activities as the work that should not fall into their scope of responsibility. Some of the officers stated that their work should be consistent with their legitimate functions regulated by the Police Law and some of the non-crime activities are certainly not involved. Officers also worried that non-crime work would reduce their work efficiency and affect police image. On the topics of crime prevention and fear of crime, few officers made any comments. The open-ended question is not compulsory, so officer comments are unbalanced. This may also indicate their willingness to discuss. The qualitative results are generally consistent with the statistical findings from responses to the close-ended questions.

Traditionalism

Clearly defined positions of power

Effective and efficient (frequency = 2)

Evenly distributed power

This shows respect for each individual. (frequency = 1)

Against quasi-military structure

Over-centralised power (frequency = 2)

Sub-ordinates involved in the setting and the enforcing of policies and procedures

1. Frontline officers are in charge of law enforcement activities, so they have right of speech. (frequency = 5)
2. happy law enforcement (frequency = 1)
3. respect (frequency = 5)

Change

Reasons to **support**

1. "Innovate or die" (frequency = 1)
2. We should move with the times; the trend is irreversible. (frequency = 2)
3. Innovation may intensify the police by technology and innovation. (frequency = 2)
4. This is the only method to improve police work. (frequency = 3)

Reasons to **disagree**

1. Most changes serve for political achievements without deep consideration. (frequency = 3)
2. Changes bring trouble. (frequency = 1)
3. Supervisors don't allow changes or don't attach importance to changes. (frequency = 3)
4. Changes break through the standard, so they are uneasy to be justified. (frequency = 1)
5. Changes will finally be rigidified, so it is not worth doing because the costs and benefits are not positively correlated. (frequency = 1)
6. problematic (frequency = 1)

Reasons to be **neutral**

1. Changes cannot be unrealistic and aimless. (frequency = 5)
2. Consequences should be taken into consideration. (frequency = 1)
3. Feasibility should be taken into consideration. (frequency = 1)

From the comments in regard to traditionalism and receptivity to change, it is indicated that these two topics did not attract many comments from the officers participated in this study. There were 16 and 25 comments for these two scales respectively. For the theme of traditionalism, more comments were provided for whether sub-ordinates should be involved in the process of policy making and enforcement. Eleven officers expressed their support for more decentralised authority toward sub-ordinate frontline officers because they are more familiar with first line police work and they deserve respect to work happily. For the theme of receptivity to change, officers provided relatively balanced comments in regard to "agree" (eight comments), "disagree" (10 comments), and "keep neutral" (seven comments). Although many officers considered changes to be good for work improvement, they also had many realistic concerns.

Cynicism

Citizens will not trust police and work together
Reasons to **support**

1. Officers need to improve their qualities. (frequency = 6)
2. Citizens need to improve their qualities. (frequency = 1)
3. Citizens don't understand officers. (frequency = 1)
4. Citizens are ignorant of law. (frequency = 1)

5. The police are in lack of positive propaganda; negative events attract public attentions. (frequency = 1)
6. Chinese social environment (frequency = 3)
7. bad law enforcement environment (frequency = 1)
8. Service-related activities reduce police authority. (frequency = 2)
9. Low government credibility makes citizens not trust police. (frequency = 5)

Reasons to be **neutral**

It depends on whether it is related with citizens' own interests. (frequency = 3)

From officer comments in regard to cynicism, many officers provided their opinions on the reasons that citizens do not trust the police and do not want to cooperate. Among the 21 responses that acknowledged the lack of trust and cooperation between police and citizens, nine officers considered police-related problems lead to this situation, while nine officers attributed it to the outer influence and three officers believed that citizens' faults are the main cause.

Solidarity

The public and media often criticize police.

1. lack of positive propaganda (frequency = 2)
2. Officers need to improve their own qualities. (frequency = 2)
3. bad police-citizen relationship; a bad image of police in eyes of citizens (frequency = 1)
4. State organ with authority attract attacks. (frequency = 1)
5. Media needs eye-catching reports. (frequency = 2)
6. public mindless attack (frequency = 1)

Police work is a higher calling.

Reasons to **support**

We have a sense of mission. (frequency = 2)

Reasons to **disagree**

1. Police work should not be deified. (frequency = 3)
2. unbalanced pay and gain (frequency = 2)
3. We are making a living without sense of recognition. (frequency = 1)
4. lack of honour (frequency = 1)

Reasons to be **neutral**

Senior officers make a living; police recruits consider it to be a higher calling. (frequency = 1)

Citizens don't understand police officers.

1. hard work (frequency = 1)
2. low income (frequency = 1)
3. high pressure (frequency = 1)

4. high risks (frequency = 2)
5. no private space (frequency = 1)

From police comments in regard to solidarity, indications are that officers have a lot to grumble about, such as media and public criticism, hard work, low income, high risks, and no sense of recognition. All these reasons reinforce the "us versus them" view that has been formed through the occupational socialisation.

Isolation

Reasons to **support**

1. no time to make and maintain non-police friends (frequency = 4)
2. no time for family (frequency = 4)
3. bad police-citizen relations (frequency = 1)
4. lack of understanding from the public (frequency = 3)
5. lack of communication with the citizens (frequency = 3)
6. irregular work time, long work hours, high pressure (frequency = 5)

Reasons to be **neutral**

Socialising is unrelated with occupations (frequency = 1)

Among the officers who addressed on the topic of police isolation, two main types of reasons were mentioned. The first reason is the work characteristics of police, namely, irregular working time, long working time, and high pressure. The second cause is the lack of understanding and communication between police and citizens.

From the above thematic analysis, it is clearly indicated that some of the topics, such as role orientation and police-citizen relationship, are of great interest among officers. These qualitative data may help us interpret some of the statistical results. In particular, some of the results mirror western police subcultural characteristics, but the underlying causes may differ significantly.

7.6 Summary

In this chapter, the findings for this study were presented in order to answer the three research questions.

First of all, descriptive statistics were performed to find out whether and to what extent the sample of Chinese frontline police officers adhere to the police subculture suggested in Western literature. On six of the seven composite scales, overall adherence might best be described as only moderate given that mean scores were located near the middle of the range of scores and the standard deviations were quite large. However, the solidarity scale had a noticeably high mean score as well as the smallest standard deviation.

Second, MANOVAs and chi-square tests were conducted to locate the relationships between demographic and work-related variables and police subcultural perceptions. Except for age, all of the remaining demographic and work-related variables were found to be significantly correlated with some of the cultural themes of the police subculture. Female officers show less cynicism, solidarity, isolation, and crime control orientations than do their male counterparts. Education level and type of police force were inversely correlated with cultural themes of crime control, solidarity, and isolation. The higher education levels and the higher levels of police departments are, the lower levels of crime control orientations, solidarity, and isolation. Police detectives and non-detectives were found to bear significantly different perceptions on service orientation and solidarity. Police detectives have higher level of solidarity than non-detectives. In addition, the results suggest that police detectives are more service-oriented in policing than their non-detective counterparts. A significant correlation was also discovered between tenure and cynicism. Results indicate that officers with 6–10 years of service experience were more cynical than their counterparts with 5 years of service or less and 11 years of service or more. Besides the above findings, chi-square tests were conducted to locate how the demographic and work-related variables influence each of the items in the cultural themes.

Third, Pearson correlations were calculated among the seven cultural themes in this study. For the crime-fighting role orientation, results support significant correlations between crime-fighting orientation and all other six cultural themes. Positive correlations were identified between crime-fighting orientation and traditionalism, cynicism, isolation, and solidarity, while negative correlations were discovered between crime-fighting orientation and service orientation and receptivity to change. For the service role orientation, the results only support a significant negative correlation between service role orientation and cynicism. In addition, isolation was found to be significantly related to the level of cynicism, solidarity, and receptivity to change. There are positive correlations with cynicism and solidarity, and negative correlation with receptivity to change. Meanwhile, receptivity to change was found to be significantly correlated with cynicism negatively and with solidarity positively. In addition, the degree of solidarity was also found to be significantly related to police traditionalism in a positive way. All of the correlations above were statistically significant, but relatively low or moderate.

Finally, qualitative thematic analysis was performed to the data obtained from the open-ended questions in the research questionnaire. Responses in each scale were coded and sub-classified into smaller themes in order to provide further interpretation to the quantitative data.

In the next chapter, these results will be discussed in detail.

Chapter 8
Discussion

As an occupational group, police officers possess a specific subculture that includes values, norms, and behaviours that are formed through the process of occupational socialisation and shared by police officers. Scholars in the West have long noticed the influence of police subculture on their perceptions and behaviour and have conducted sizable studies to examine the intangible myth. However, policing studies in China is still in a preliminary stage with few empirical studies conducted, let alone police cultural studies. Most studies on police culture in China are characterised by a prescriptive account of idealised cultural norms and regulations that officers ought to abide by or a theoretical analysis of police cultural studies as a discipline.

Therefore, I conducted a quantitative survey study among a sample of Chinese frontline police officers to have a preliminary look at the police subcultural perceptions in Chinese context. Statistical analyses have been conducted to investigate to what extent officers in China adhere to the Western police subculture, the influence of demographic and work-related characteristics upon police perceptions, and the potential bivariate correlations between the cultural themes in this study. Results of data analysis have been reported in previous chapter. In this chapter, detailed discussions of results of each research question are rendered.

8.1 Research Question One

- Is there a widespread adherence to the police subculture suggested in the Western literature among Chinese frontline police officers?

The first research question in this study set out to investigate whether the sample of Chinese frontline police officers adhere to the Western police subculture. Descriptive statistics indicate that there is not a widespread adherence to the police subculture suggested in the Western literature. On six of the seven composite scales, overall adherence might best be described as only moderate, but a high level of solidarity was evidenced.

Z. Chen, *Measuring Police Subcultural Perceptions*,
DOI 10.1007/978-981-10-0096-6_8

8.1.1 Role Orientations of Crime Control and Service

Frequency distributions suggest that although there is not widespread adherence to the crime fighting orientation, a group of the frontline officers are indeed very supportive of the crime fighter image. In this scale, there are six items, representing six main components of crime control orientation, namely, aggressive manner, service distraction, crime prevention and control, high preference to law enforcement, non-crime service, and use of force. From frequency distributions of police perceptions on the six items, it could be concluded that officer responses on the three items in regard to the importance of law enforcement, community service detracting from police ability of crime control, and the restrictions on police use of force, are supportive of a crime-fighting oriented policing. Nearly 70 % of the officers supported law enforcement as being the most important responsibility of policing and service activities detract their crime fighting function; nearly 60 % of the officers agreed that fewer restrictions on police use of force would reduce serious crimes. Different from these three items, more than half of the Chinese frontline police officers in this sample considered both crime consequences and causes should receive attention from the police. On the issues of policing manner and non-crime service, officers expressed restrained support. For aggressiveness in policing, more than 40 % of the officers supported and more than 30 % kept neutral. For non-crime service, while nearly one third of the respondents supported police involvement in non-crime activities, nearly half of them disagreed or strongly disagreed. Officers who expressed strong disagreement amount to nearly a quarter of the total.

Therefore, it could be concluded that many Chinese frontline officers are generally crime control oriented. This conclusion is also supported by the qualitative data obtained from the open-ended section of the questionnaire. Whether law enforcement is the most important responsibility of policing and whether service functions detract from their crime fighting ability attracted the greatest attention of all the thematic points in the open-ended part of the questionnaire. Twenty-nine respondents expressed their support for these two items because they think that the main job of policing is crime control and other corresponding governments should provide service. One officer commented: "The central part of police work is to combat crimes and reduce crimes. Providing a social service is unrealistic and will impede law enforcement." Another officer stated: "A clear division of labour is the trend of social development. The police should know that their main responsibility is crime control and prevention; social service function should be handed over to other related government departments." Eight officers proposed that service activities would increase workloads and pressures and make their role more complex. An officer provided the following comment: "Nowadays a majority of policing activities are related with providing service to citizens, which makes police work miscellaneous and trivial. This greatly increases the difficulty and pressure of police work. In addition, this detracts police from crime control." It was also mentioned three times that community service may reduce the authority of the police.

As a result of this, citizens would be more uncooperative because they are not "afraid" of police officers. An officer stated: "Now police officers have become private security guards, and people are not 'afraid' of the police and not cooperative during police law enforcement."

This crime-fighting image has long been documented by scholars in the West (Klockars 1985b; Paoline 2003, 2004; Paoline et al. 2000; Rumbaut and Egon 1979; Sparrow et al. 1990; Walker and Katz 2005; Westley 1970; Wilson 1968). According to this role orientation of crime fighting, police officers should not waste their time and effort doing social service tasks because they are not social workers (Harrison 1998). Instead, they should take part in the "war against crime" (Reiner 1985, p. 112), which is considered to be the only real police work (Terrill et al. 2003). These perceptions of police role have been passed on to police officers from their training in police academies and reinforced through their real police work and interactions with their senior peers (Chappell and Lanza-Kaduce 2010; Ford 2003). However, it has been continually pointed out by both scholars and practitioners that criminal law enforcement occupies only a small part of police work (McLaughlin 2007, p. 52; Miller et al. 2014, p. 33). Sociologists in the West persist in exploring police role perceptions through empirical studies and the preference for crime fighting has been evidenced by different research methods in different time periods (Loftus 2010; Paoline et al. 2000; Perrott and Taylor 1995). Similar to the results of this study, the study conducted by Cochran and Bromley (2003) in America suggested that 64.2 % of the surveyed officers considered law enforcement to be the most important police work, and nearly half of the officers believed that officers spent too much time in non-crime service. According to a recent study (Paoline and Terrill 2014, p. 145), officers who agreed that law enforcement is the most important responsibility for patrol officers account for 65.6–82.1 % of the surveyed officers across seven American police agencies; 58.2–78.4 % of officers agreed that officers spent too much time dealing with non-crime calls.

Although the crime-fighting image is also supported in the context of Chinese frontline police, the underlying reasons may be different from their counterparts from Western societies. First, the Chinese government adopted a Marxist conceptualisation of police as the guideline for police work since the founding of the PRC. According to Marxism, the police are "an armed force which represents the interest of the ruling party and maintain national security and public order on the basis of violent, coercive, and special manners" (Yuan 2007, pp. 130–131). This classical explanation of police was maintained as the only acceptable understanding of police functions for a long time. This principle served "political goals such as suppressing counterrevolutionaries, and safeguarding and facilitating political movements with legal means" in the early years of the PRC (Dai 2001, p. 151). For the early period during the founding of the new China, the main function of the Chinese police was to consolidate the communist control of the country on the basis of coercive power from the state sovereignty (Yuan 2007). Along with the social development and the legalisation of China, we are now in a society where there is no need to maintain state control through class struggle and crackdowns.

Police officers have been made aware that their authority comes from the law and that their main task is to enforce the law in a professional manner. However, the traditional understanding of policing still remains the guiding principle of police work in the minds of many Chinese police officers. Second, the series of strike-hard campaigns from 1978 to 2002 influenced police role orientations. During that time, providing social service gave way to cracking down on serious crimes. The performance of police officers was also assessed via the statistics concerning successful arrests or other forms of punishment in the campaigns (Wang and Wong 2012). This also enhanced their crime-fighting role orientation (Dutton 2000; Wang and Wong 2012). In addition, many officers believe that non-crime activities reduce police authority and dignity. According to the qualitative data in this study, some respondents argued that citizens will not be afraid of the police if they are more of service providers instead of law enforcers. This demonstrates that some officers regard citizens as the policed, not the protected. Finally, the shortage of police manpower is also a fact that cannot be neglected in China. Although there is not an official police population ratio in China, Professor Dawei Wang from China People's Public Security University estimated that the ratio is 11:10,000, which is much lower than the ratio of 35:10,000 in Western countries on average (Luo and Ruiz 2012). Therefore, providing service is frequently considered to be additional work that increases the already heavy burden on the shoulders of the police.

On the topic of non-crime service, nearly half of the officers were opposed to it and nearly one third of them endorsed it (see percentage distribution offered in Sect. 7.1.2 in regard to Item 5). This frequency distribution does not indicate a clear-cut negative attitude against service function of police. This suggests the interaction between different ideologies and their influence upon policing strategies. Mao's mass-line principle, which advocates mutual support between the police and the community, does have a great influence upon Chinese policing styles and police role orientations (Jiao 2001b). Under the mass-line principle, the police were required to serve the people whenever possible and maintain a close relationship like that between fish and water. The emphasis of collective interests in traditional Chinese culture also requires officers to place the safety and well-being of people before one's own interest. The Confucian ideology that emphasises ethics and morality was also integrated in the social control in China. Police officers were expected to be role models and public educators instead of law enforcers. Their decisions and behaviours were also expected to represent the interests of the community. In addition, the communist ideological commitment of "serving the people wholeheartedly" has always been officially upheld by the Chinese police force (Wang and Wong 2012, p. 35). Although these ideologies have tended to fade with the dramatic socioeconomic changes in China, their influence has not totally disappeared. However, since the promulgation of the new police law in 1995, the professionalisation and legalisation of Chinese police force has been greatly enhanced (Jiao 2001b). Officers are more inclined to operate within the functions regulated by the police law. This is evidenced by the responses of five officers in this study. An officer commented: "The police should perform law enforcement according to the responsibilities and authority regulated in the law. The police should not be involved in other activities. The police are not omnipotent." Many kinds of non-crime work, such as participating in forced evictions and demolition, and stopping petitioners, obviously do not fall into the scope of police duties regulated by the police law. Although scholars and practitioners in the West also mentioned that police work is very broad in nature (Millie 2014), Chinese police officers are actually handling more. There are mainly two reasons. Firstly, the both centralised and decentralised system determine that police departments are not only under the guidance of MPS, but also under the control of local governments (Dai 2008; Sun et al. 2010; Wong 2009a). Local governments frequently assign administrative tasks, such as controlling petitioners, to the police because the police have coercive law enforcement authority (Wang 2011). It is clearly seen from the qualitative part of the survey that officers perceive these activities to ruin police-citizen relationships and affect the positive image of police. In addition, in order to uphold the principle of "serving the people wholeheartedly", police departments use some slogans like "turn to the police if you need help" and "the police should handle any crime-related problems you have, help with any difficulties you have, save you from any dangers you have, and meet any needs you have" (Gong 1999). These slogans greatly increase the police workload of social service, such as opening doors when keys are locked inside (Wang 2011). This contributes to the suggestion that the police are "the most overworked civil servants in China" (Wang et al. 2014, p. 2). This is evidenced by the responses like "the police are not omnipotent", "the police are not bodyguards", "the police are not babysitters", and "the police are not the God" by nine officers in this study.

With regard to policing styles, nearly 60 % of the officers supported fewer restrictions on police use of force to deal with serious crimes; more than 40 % of the officers supported aggressive policing. According to the survey, the Marxist doctrine, which defines the police as a coercive and violent state apparatus, is the main reason that officers support aggressive policing. Eight officers stated that the police are now usually in a passive position under attack and three officers mentioned that the police should not be of low status and without dignity. An officer commented: "In the process of law enforcement, the police usually become the weak group because they cannot fight back when they are under physical assault or coarse language. Frontline officers should have enough authority." These comments indicate that officers would like to use aggressive manners to safeguard their authority and dignity during law enforcement. The main reasons for police use of force turn out to be protecting personal safety of officers and combating crimes effectively. Some officers mentioned that they dare not use force even when their personal safety was threatened because they would be severely punished if they raised complaints from citizens. An officer stated: "There is too much limitation on police use of force. Therefore, the police even cannot protect themselves from attacks of criminals, let alone to protect citizens." However, some other officers suggested that laws should be enforced in a standard, fair and civil manner and use of force is ineffective and increases contradictions. An officer commented: "Force cannot eradicate crime because crime is a social problem. Force will only lead to more conflict. Civilised law enforcement is the best choice." Therefore, at least from the comments from officers in this sample, it could be seen that officers tend to use an aggressive approach and force as self-protecting solutions but not for its own sake. The lack of trust from the public makes it difficult for the police to perform their duty when there is disagreement between the police and the people. The conflict between the police and the community members may easily attract the attention of other people and grow out of control. Some of the cases do threaten the safety of both officers and people if they are not dealt with appropriately as quickly as possible. This has been vividly illustrated by an example provided by Chen (2013), the head of a municipal police bureau: "Anyone shouting that an officer hit people may immediately attract many people's attention and criticism without asking about the details" (p. 38). This is supported by the following analysis by Wong (2012), the leading expert of Chinese policing:

> People are becoming less civil and less likely to follow police instructions, which leads to the police using force; offenders have very little respect for either the law or the police. People resent the police for carrying out legitimate policing activities, such as traffic code enforcement, but they are quick to take advantage of a police officer who demonstrates tolerance. To the public, the police appear to be weak and irresolute when in fact they are working on being "civilized". The police try to avoid problematic encounters and troublesome offenders, which only encourages strongheaded offenders and emboldens recalcitrant violators (p. 159).

From the frequency distribution on the scale of service, there appear to be more positive attitudes about community service than negative ones among this sample of Chinese officers. Descriptive statistics of each item in the scale also provide evidence for this tendency. Nearly 70 % of the respondents agreed or strongly agreed that "crimes are only one of several problems about which police officers should be concerned", "police officers should ask citizens what types of services they want", and "lowering citizens' fear of crime should be just as high a priority as cutting the crime rate". Even on the topic of "assisting citizens in need is just as important as enforcing the law", half of the respondents expressed support. However, more than 80 % of the officers disagreed or strongly disagreed that law enforcement is service-oriented rather than crime-fighting-oriented. The above results clearly show that Chinese frontline officers believe that the main responsibility of policing is crime control, but officers should also devote themselves to providing service to citizens according to their needs. The paramilitary organisation structure of police departments that limits the effectiveness of police performance has also reduced the energy and power of frontline officers especially in regard to their social service (Wang 2014b). It has been found that the extent to which officers are given structural and psychological support from their work (i.e. opportunities, resources, self-determination, power, etc.) is significantly associated with their role strain level (Wang 2014b). The evidence collected in this study clearly suggests that social service is considered to be an important but secondary task compared with crime control. This opinion, which has been held by officers and police administrators, may lead to a lesser sense of achievement for the role of social service and more role strain.

A clear picture of the role orientations of Chinese frontline police officers can be identified. Similar to the findings of Western literature, Chinese frontline police embody a strong orientation toward crime fighting. However, they also attach great importance to social service. Both of these two police functions have their roots in traditional Chinese culture, communist ideology, and Chinese socioeconomic background. The specific centralised and decentralised structures lead to many extra burdens and tasks for officers in China. The lack of clear regulations and boundaries regarding police functions and inappropriate slogans such as "meet any needs you have" have reduced police enthusiasm for social service.

One of the main requirements of community policing is a broad police function and community focus (Kappeler and Gaines 2009). Therefore, some entrenched opinions that have been evidenced through this study do contradict the essence of community policing, such as the ideological conceptualisation of the police as the state apparatus with coercive power and the opinion that the primary responsibility of the police is crime control and service functions should be handled by other government departments. Indeed, the crime-fighting role orientation is the cause of other perspectives, such as emphasising aggressiveness and coercion in policing. For a successful transfer from traditional policing to community policing, it is crucial to let officers accept the expansion of the police mandate and shift the focus of their attention and willingness from "responding to random crime calls to proactively addressing community concerns" (Kappeler and Gaines 2009, p. 5). What needs to be noticed is that Chinese officers do not repel community service in their heart due to the resemblance between the principle of community policing and the mass-line policing in China. It is necessary to let officers reaccept the traditional perspective that values community participation and police-citizen partnership.

8.1.2 Traditionalism

Police departments are characterised by paramilitary and bureaucratised structures with fixed lines of command and communication, a specialised division of labour, and extensive rule systems (Chappell and Lanza-Kaduce 2010; Cochran and Bromley 2003). Police officers are socialised to accept the culture of traditionalism from when they enter police academies (Chappell and Lanza-Kaduce 2010; Ford 2003). Descriptive statistics of the responses on the scale of traditionalism suggest that there is not a strong adherence to traditionalism among the sample of Chinese officers. A detailed look at each of the items in this scale provides further explanations. A majority of the officers (88.5 %) believe that clearly defined positions of power promote effectiveness. In addition, the top-down communication channels and the paramilitary structure are both considered to be effective by around half of the respondents, though around a quarter to one third of the respondents were neutral on these two topics. From the statistics and the comments by officers, it seems that Chinese frontline officers have taken this traditional police organisational structure for granted and have acknowledged its effectiveness because few officers left any comments on this topic. One officer mentioned: "Only if there are clearly defined positions of power and smooth top-down communications, police departments may function well as the state control instrument." This indicates that the Marxist definition of the police role as state coercive control organ is deeply rooted among some officers. Therefore, they are inclined to accept the traditional structure of police organisations, and unwilling to reconsider whether the structure is still an effective and efficient one for the contemporary policing in China. In addition, many frontline officers have been accustomed to the fact that subordinates could only listen to what their supervisors say; they may consider the organisational structure issue as a topic irrelevant to them. Just as one officer commented: "I do not have any idea on this topic because I have never thought about it before."

However, most of them are quite concerned about their authority as frontline police. To be in detail, more than half of the respondents (54.7 %) supported for evenly distributed power among officers in police departments; 76.4 % of them advocated that subordinates should be involved in the setting or the enforcing of policies and procedures within police departments. The fact is that the paramilitary police organisations grant little authority of decision-making to frontline officers. Frontline officers are restricted by detailed rules of police departments and heavy supervision from their supervisors. An officer commented: "Frontline officers do not have any decision-making power; all we need to do is to carry out orders from our directors." Five officers mentioned that frontline officers should be involved in policy setting because they are the backbone of law enforcement and they know more than others about whether policies or procedures are effective or not in practice. Therefore, the limit of authority of frontline officers greatly neglects and devalues their expertise and enthusiasm. Officers also consider the right to be involved in policy setting as a form of equality and respect. An officer commented: "Allowing frontline officers to be involved in policy making will give them a sense of happiness and respect." Otherwise, the traditional authoritarian style cannot provide enough job satisfaction and motivate work enthusiasm (Walker and Katz 2005). The strict control of decision-making power of frontline officers may make "most of their abilities, creativity, and intelligence" "inactive" and quickly erode their motivation (Reiter 1999, p. 9). To some extent, there are contradictory opinions among these Chinese officers. On one hand, they consider the traditional paramilitary organisational structure to be effective for police work; on the other hand, they would like to have more decision-making power to improve police work and to gain more respect and satisfaction. A decentralised police command structure is one of the characteristics of community policing, which aims to enhance the effectiveness and efficiency of police departments and provide frontline officers more power in their problem-solving and service work (Palmiotto 2011). Frontline officers who are granted authority in solving problems for the community may feel accountable and become more responsible for the community (COPS 2009). In fact, some Chinese police agencies have begun to flatten their organisations through debureaucration (Zhang 2010a, pp. 276–279). Police departments in Liaoyuan (a city in Jilin Province), Daqing (a city in Heilongjiang

Province), and Henan Province, have attempted to change the original three-level organisation (municipal bureau–sub-bureau–field station) to a two-level structure (municipal bureau–sub-bureau or field station) from the beginning of the 21st century (Xiao and Liu 2012). These reforms are aimed at decentralising the organisational structure and redistributing police power to grass-roots work units.

8.1.3 Receptivity to Change

The successful shift from traditional policing to community policing relies on practitioners who understand and accept the change (Cochran et al. 2002; Lurigio and Skogan 1994). The traditional police subculture may create a cynical attitude to resist potential reforms and changes of policing philosophy (Lurigio and Skogan 1994). However, the data collected in this study do not seem to support a strong resistance to change among Chinese frontline police officers. Instead, frequency distributions indicate that most of the surveyed Chinese officers accept the importance of changes and innovations at work. 70 % of the respondents indicated that they "often suggest new approaches for doing things"; more than 70 % of the respondents agreed or strongly agreed that "most changes make my job more efficient" (74.6 %) and "effective" (79.3 %). In addition, 44.7 % of the respondents disagreed or strongly disagreed the idea that "most changes at work are problematic and ineffective"; 53.1 % of the respondents disagreed or strongly disagreed that they would usually avoid changes. The findings are quite different from police perceptions obtained from their American counterparts. According to the study conducted by Cochran and Bromley (2003), only 27.6 % of the surveyed officers believed that changes make police work more efficient; only 21.5 % of the officers considered changes to be effective for police work.

The qualitative responses provide further insight into the respondents' attitudes on this point. For instance, one officer wrote: "We should move with the times and the trend is irreversible"; another noted: "Changes are the only way to improve police work". One interesting finding is that three officers stated that they would like to avoid change because most change serves political ends, or their supervisors don't allow changes. One officer commented: "Changes should be based on large-scale investigations. We should not make innovations only for political achievements and that will greatly increase costs of law enforcement and work difficulties." Another officer wrote: "Police chiefs only like those who comply with their command without hesitations; they don't like sub-ordinates who frequently initiate changes." Officers who kept neutral on this topic also explained that they only accept feasible and realistic changes based on careful considerations. From the above discussions, it is clear that most Chinese officers are receptive to feasible changes because they believe that it is the way that police work could be improved. Western analysts have suggested that the traditional police organisation and police cynical attitudes both contribute to resistance to change among police officers (Buerger 2007; Lingamneni 1979; Roberg et al. 2009).

This study to some extent supports this link because on average the respondents were not as traditional and cynical as Western literature suggests, while they also do not embody a negative attitude toward change and innovation at police work. Supervisors' perceptions seem to be an important factor that influences their attitudes toward changes at work. For instance, some police leaders would like to take the advantage of changes and reforms to have more political achievements but those changes usually cannot endure practical tests. Some other police chiefs feel reluctant to initiate changes because they want to avoid the problems that change may bring. An officer made the following comment: "Innovation means breaking standards, so it is hard to make evaluations." Another officer stated: "Changes bring troubles; it is better to keep on the rails." These opinions are quite similar to the obstacles of changes summarised by Geller (1997), such as considerations of changes to be impractical and temporary, and to be bad for discipline of frontline officers. It is necessary for officers to be open to changes at work in this era of philosophical shift towards a community-oriented policing style both in China and the world. The police need their perceptions and actions to conform with the requirements of contemporary policing in the changing society.

8.1.4 Cynicism

Sizable literature has depicted a cynical attitude of police as one of the main characteristics of traditional police subculture (Buerger 2007; Burke and Mikkelsen 2005; Cockcroft 2013; Crank 2004; Crank et al. 1987; Graves 1996; Lotz and Regoli 1977; Niederhoffer 1967; Poole and Regoli 1979; Reiner 2010). The nature of police work, namely, a mixture of embedded danger, a learned craft of suspicion, and the pursuit of efficiency, can lead police to regard all citizens as problematic (Buerger 2007; Cochran and Bromley 2003; Cockcroft 2013). In addition, the idea that outsiders have no idea of the real police work reinforces the cynical attitude when police officers find that their work is critically appraised by members of the public who know nothing (Caplan 2003). However, just as the question raised by Kääriäinen and Sirén (2012, p. 280), more empirical studies are needed to find out whether officers are "really as suspicious, isolated or cynical as suggested by studies of police culture" in contemporary policing. Data collected in this study do not support a very strong cynical attitude among Chinese frontline police officers. On average, Chinese frontline police are not as cynical as indicated by studies in the West. Of course, there are some very cynical officers, many in the middle, and some who are not cynical at all.

A detailed look at the items in this scale shows that most officers do not have a "contemptuous distrust of human nature and motives" (Behrend 1980, p. 1) because more than 60 % of them agreed or strongly agreed that "most people do not hesitate to go out of their way to help someone in trouble" and more than half of them disagreed or strongly disagreed that "most people are untrustworthy and dishonest". The relatively negative attitude toward citizens comes from their judgement of respect for police authority from citizens: 43.8 % of them disagreed or strongly disagreed with the statement that "most people respect the authority" of police officers. For mutual trust between citizens and the police, more than one third of the officers kept neutral. In addition, relatively more officers (40 % vs. 24.1 %) believe that they will trust citizens to cooperate, but more officers (35.8 % vs. 27.5 %) do not think that citizens will trust the police enough to cooperate. This indicates that most of the officers do not feel enough respect and trust from citizens. It was found that 47.2 % (28.3 % of Chinese officers in this study) of the surveyed American officers agreed or strongly agreed that most people respect police authority and only 12.9 % (35.8 % in this study) of the officers believed that citizens would not trust the police to work together (Cochran and Bromley 2003). This finding is also supported by a comparative study that indicated that Chinese police receive less trust from citizens than do their American counterparts (Wu and Sun 2009). However, there seems to be no evidence that Chinese officers have strong negative attitudes toward human nature. According to a recent empirical survey of American police officers, the percentages of officers who believed that police officers have reason to be distrustful of most citizens are from 33.1 to 60.7 % across seven police agencies (Paoline and Terrill 2014). In this study, only 17 % of the surveyed officers agreed or strongly agreed that most people are untrustworthy and dishonest.

The above findings indicate that the support, respect, and trust that Chinese frontline police feel from the public are far from sufficient. The expectation of support and trust from the people and the contrasting reality may lead to a negative and cynical view (Bennett and Schmitt 2002). In addition to the findings in this study, the lack of trust and authority for the police in China has been evidenced by another recent survey study of 31 Chinese police officers (Scoggins and O'Brien 2015). A young officer felt much less trust and authority than expected: "I can tell someone on the street to stop, but they don't care. They just start arguing with me" (Scoggins and O'Brien 2015, p. 13). The reasons that Chinese citizens' trust towards the police decrease are complicated. First of all, along with the socioeconomic development, different social strata are clearer in contemporary Chinese society. This is embodied in different forms of social inequality, such as the rich and the poor, and those who possess political power and those who do not. Many of the rich have become rich due to their connections with government officials; others gained political positions with the help of their money (Wu and Sun 2009). This is vividly represented in the recent study that demonstrates how illicit businesses have benefited through protection from corrupt government officials and police officers through connections or *guanxi* ("a Chinese version of personal connections, networks or social capital") networks (Wang 2014a, p. 809). Due to the protection for those who have money and power, it is very easy for the citizens to oppose the police (Zhao 2012). Secondly, police could not gain public trust because of the low credibility of local governments. An officer made the following comment in the questionnaire: "People's unsatisfactory feelings are indeed toward the local government; the police are scapegoats." The police are "the most visible manifestation of power and authority in society", so "attitudes toward the police are influenced by people's attitudes toward the political system generally" (Walker and Katz 2005, p. 13). The lack of trust of police has led to obstruction and resistance of police operations, even resulting in mass incidents and police injuries (Wong 2012). Thirdly, police misconduct and corruption may also contribute to the lack of public trust in police. Various forms of police misconduct and even police corruption have been documented by sociological observers who are interested in Chinese policing, such as minor corruption, abuse of power, excessive use of force or fines, torture etc. (Du 1997; Wei and Tom Vander 2010; Wong 1998; Wu and Sun 2009). Finally, lack of communication channels hinders the build-up of trust.

Jiao (2001a) stated more than a decade ago that Chinese officers are less cynical than their American counterparts because of the influence of collective interests in traditional Chinese culture. Although this study does not help from a comparative perspective, the negative attitudes from some of the officers could be explained from their real experiences and social background. The data do not seem to support a strong cynical attitude toward citizens purely due to their police socialisation as described in Western literature (Buerger 2007). However, the results do suggest that officers feel that they cannot get enough trust, support, and respect from citizens. While this is different from the cynical attitude that considers citizens to be totally unsupportive and distrustful, it is still inconsistent with the level of police-citizen cooperation required by community policing. Building mutual trust with citizens is one of the most important requirements of community policing philosophy (Kappeler and Gaines 2009). Community support is vital for the successful implementation of community policing, so the police need to communicate more with community members, and gain the trust from the community back through heartfelt concern and qualified service for citizens.

8.1.5 Solidarity

Solidarity is considered to be one of the pivotal features of police subculture (Banks 2009; Cockcroft 2013; Kappeler et al. 1998; Reiner 2010; Shernock 2007). Group loyalty is important for teamwork, especially for police work that is characterised by danger and uncertainty. However, what attracts even more attention is the link between police solidarity and police misconduct, because the strong sense of brotherhood may lead to cover-ups of violations or even complicity with misconduct (Lester and Brink 1985; Loftus 2010; Reiner 2010; Shernock 2007). In contrast to other cultural themes, descriptive statistics in this scale suggest an overwhelming endorsement among this sample of Chinese frontline police officers. All of the six items won support from more than 70 % of the officers, four by more than 90 % of the total. Police solidarity was also evidenced in an American study: Around 99 % of the surveyed officers agreed that protecting their work partners is one of their highest priorities, and more than 80 % of the officers agreed that outsiders would not understand the police camaraderie (Paoline and Terrill 2014).

As discussed by Loftus (2010), some characteristics of police culture remain untouched in the developments of policing. It is not surprising that a great majority of officers believe that loyalty to colleagues is essential and unquestionable. Solidarity is important for building up self-esteem and confidence especially for practitioners in a profession with embedded danger and uncertainties. Protecting work partners from outside attacks is also one of the basic skills that are trained in police academies. From another perspective, the high level of agreement in solidarity among peers indicates that frontline officers in China feel less confident in their interactions with people. A strong support for the argument that the public do not understand police and police work also reveals that there is a big psychological gap between the police and non-police due to the lack of mutual support and understanding. Many officers supported the saying of "to be a police officer is not just another job, it is a 'higher calling'", because they feel "a sense of mission". Others also stated that they consider the police job as only a means of making a living because they do not feel "a sense of recognition" and they have "unbalanced pay and gain". An officer noted: "Policing is just an occupation. Maybe for police cadets in police academies, it is a career; for us who have been officers for many years, it is just a way to make a living." Another officer commented: "The value of the police is only understood by officers themselves."

The idea that only police officers know about police work, while outsiders know nothing about the police, is closely connected with the crime fighter image and the corresponding traditional and paternalistic attitude that crime control is so complicated that only trained officers know how to deal with it (Kappeler and Gaines 2009, p. 23). This to great extent contradicts with the requirement of community policing that the police should encourage citizens to work together with them for solving community problems. In addition, according to the theoretical framework of community policing provided by Kappeler and Gaines (2009), three important requirements of community policing philosophy are closely connected with the needs of community members: sharing power, creativity, and neighbourhood variation. The police should provide qualified service according to the needs of the community and make corresponding change depending on citizens' requirements in different local communities. It is difficult to imagine that officers who believe that members of the community know nothing about police work may put the needs of people into consideration in their work. Therefore, a transfer of police perception from traditional policing to community oriented policing is vital.

8.1.6 Isolation

Closely related to solidarity is another key theme of police subculture: isolation (Clark 1965; Meyer and Steyn 2009; Reiner 2010; Skolnick 1986; Swanton 1981; Westley 1953, 1970). The more that officers are mutually supportive, the more they are likely to feel a sense of belonging to their peers; at the same time, a sense of social isolation promotes group loyalty (Cockcroft 2013; Kappeler et al. 1998;

Reiner 2010). Although unlike the widespread support of solidarity, a large proportion of officers in this sample do feel rather isolated from the public. Interesting findings from a detailed examination of the seven items in this scale are that the most supported three items which explain the causes of isolation are "being watched critically by members of the public" (86.1 %), "shift work and special duties" (76.1 %), and unwillingness to have in-depth talk to outsiders about police work (66.4 %). This is evidenced in Western studies of isolation sources: intrinsic determinants such as police self-protection against potential threats (outsiders) and special work structures, and the hostility or the resentment from citizens (Kappeler et al. 1998; Reiner 2010). Hostility or discrimination toward police officers and even their family members have long been documented by Western scholars (Banton 1964; Swanton 1981). Both the irregular and long working hours, and the hostility experienced by officers and their family members in their social communications, have been associated with socialising difficulties and psychological suffering (Swanton 1981). Swanton proposed four types of determinants of police isolation initiated by the public (Swanton 1981, p. 18). The sense of isolation was vividly expressed in the interview of a Scottish police officer by Banton:

> If someone asks my wife "What does your husband do?", I've told her to say "He's a clerk", and that's the way it went well because she found that being a policeman's wife … a sort of invisible wall was up for conversation purposes when a policeman was there (Banton 1964, p. 198).

Comments provided by the officers in this study suggest that the top two causes of social isolation are no time for socials, and lack of understandings and communications with outsiders. An officer mentioned: "Wives of police officers often have a lot to grumble about because of the difficulties they face due to marrying a police officer." Another officer commented: "Since I became a police officer, I have gradually lost contact with my friends and eventually lost my wife because she could not stand frequently being alone." On the willingness of socialising with non-police friends, a slightly larger group of officers (43.7 %) are actually not avoiding communications with outsiders than officers (41.4 %) who are not willing to. In addition, although slightly more officers suggest that they (44 %) belong with colleagues more than citizens, and that they (45.5 %) tend to be more open with colleagues than citizens, the percentages are not high. These feelings are understandable for members of an organisation or an occupation with relatively strong shared subcultural values. In fact, it is very easy for police officers to keep themselves away from the outsiders because the existence of the integrated set of shared assumptions may make it more comfortable for them to be with their peers and uncomfortable to encounter different assumptions (Schein 2004). Therefore, it is not surprising that respondents in this study consider outside hostility and the irregular nature of police work are the main reasons for police isolation. On the topic of private socialisation, American officers expressed more willingness than did respondents in this study to socialise with non-police friends: 46.4–69.5 % of surveyed officers across seven police agencies would like to socialise with non-police friends than police friends when off duty (Paoline and Terrill 2014, p. 151).

Though facing the difficulties such as irregular work hours and lack of trust from the public, the police should make use of various social organisations and activities to build partnerships with community members. It should be clear to both the police and the community that the ultimate aim of policing is to solve problems for the community, and this could only be fulfilled with the involvement of the community members. Alienation of the police from the public will only ruin the attempts for the aim.

In conclusion, the data collected from Chinese frontline police officers do indicate adherence to some cultural themes suggested in the Western literature, such as solidarity and isolation. However, that is far from a widespread adherence. Different from what is described in Western literature, Chinese frontline police officers tend to be receptive to changes at work. In addition, they are oriented to crime-fighting, but they also attach importance to the functions of service.

8.2 Research Question Two

- Among Chinese frontline police officers, are some demographic and work-related variables associated with police subcultural perceptions?

Subquestion 2.1

Among Chinese frontline police officers, is age associated with police subcultural perceptions?

Similar to existing findings, the results do not support a significant association of age with police subcultural perceptions in China (Britz 1997; Cochran et al. 2002; Scripture 1997). Few researchers have reported associations between age and police perceptions, such as cynicism (Burke and Mikkelsen 2005). According to a study conducted by Britz (1997, p. 140) in the USA, there was a significant but weak correlation indicating that younger officers (20–25 years old) were more likely to agree that they were "one of the gang" than were older ones. Another study suggested that police constables in the early career stage (less than 34 years old) were less cynical than were those in later career stages (Burke and Mikkelsen 2005). In this study, while the results do support a significant correlation between cynicism and tenure, there is no sign of any relationship between cynicism and age.

Subquestion 2.2

Among Chinese frontline police officers, is gender associated with police subcultural perceptions?

While it is reasonable to expect less adherence among policewomen to the traditional masculine police subculture, most empirical studies in the West did not find significant differences in police perceptions between male and female officers (Brooks et al. 1993; Paoline et al. 2000; Worden 1993, 1990). However, the results of this study indicate significant associations between gender and police perceptions in the scales of crime control, cynicism, solidarity, and isolation. Female officers among respondents in this study were found to be significantly less adherent to a crime-fighting role, a cynical attitude toward citizens, group solidarity among peers, and social isolation from the public than their male counterparts. Chi-square tests between male and female officers on Item 1 and Item 3, indicate that female officers express significantly less support for aggressive policing and more preventive instead of punitive attitudes than did male officers. Although gender is not evidenced as a significant determinant of police behaviour and attitudes, some studies of police behaviour do indicate that female officers tend to use less physically controlling behaviour (Rabe-Hemp 2008), and to obey legal restrictions in situations that involve weapons (Eterno 2006). However, this study did not provide evidence of significant gender differences on the role orientations of community service, while a broader role orientation has been identified among female officers in the USA (Sun 2003). While there is an overwhelming support for solidarity among the officers surveyed, female officers were found to express less support that "officers are careful of how they behave in public". In addition, a significantly less proportion of female officers (14.3 %) agreed or strongly agreed that they socialised less with non-police friends since they became officers than their male counterparts (44.7 %). This finding actually echoes with the findings of Britz (1997) because he found that female officers were less likely to indicate that their old friends felt uncomfortable after they became officers. All of these findings indicate that female respondents in the present study are less socialised into the masculine police subculture. There are several possible explanations for this. First, due to the physical differences between genders, female officers are more likely to be assigned to office work rather than field operations. Their work orientations also tend to be alike. According to a survey of the female police officers in a municipal police bureau in China, only 14.75 % of female officers would like to be in the department of field work, while others were more willing to do office work (25.22 %), administration (31.14 %), or secretarial work (27.86 %) (Ling and Liu 2002, p. 53). Therefore, they are less likely to engage in aggressive police coercion and also less likely to have unpleasant interactions with citizens. It is also likely that they tend to be less adherent to the crime fighter image and find it easier to have good associations with the public. In addition, female officers are born with some feminine traits that may help them take advantage of communication skills to solve problems less aggressively than do their male counterparts (Miller 1998; Rabe-Hemp 2008; Rong 2013). These communication skills make them less isolated with the community than are male officers. Miller (1998) summarised the styles female officers may bring to policing:

> peacemaker, naive and caring styles, negotiator, cooperative style, informal style of interaction; values empathy and strong communication skills; emphasizes connections among relationships, family, and community; problem solver; tenacious interest in knowing history of problem and causes; reform minded (long term) (p. 164).

In an era of strategic transition from traditional policing to community policing, it is likely that some of the "softer" roles that used to be regarded as not "real" police work, should now be promoted to establish a better police-citizen relationship (Miller and Bonistall 2012). These styles may serve the philosophy of community policing better than the traditional masculine style of policing in that mutual trust and understanding might be built upon these "softer" strategies.

Subquestion 2.3
Among Chinese frontline police officers, is education associated with police subcultural perceptions?

As more and more college graduates enter police forces, many scholars have tried to examine the potential influence of tertiary education on the career of policing which has been traditionally described as "generally being smart and savvy in a peculiarly police way" (Punch 2007, p. 106; Rydberg and Terrill 2010; Scott et al. 2009; Shernock 1992). Education levels were found to be significantly correlated with officers' role orientations of crime-fighting, solidarity, and isolation in this study. With regard to a crime-fighting role orientation, perceptions of officers with master's degree or above are significantly less inclined toward a crime-fighter orientation than are officers with less education. Chi-square tests between education and police responses on the items in this scale indicate that officers with more education were more likely to accept police involvement in non-crime activities. In contrast, not many studies in the West indicated an association between education levels and police role orientations. While studies found mixed results (Paoline et al. 2000) or no significant relations (Shernock 1992) on the issue of role orientations, less aggressiveness in policing styles (Paoline et al. 2000) and less use of force (Rydberg and Terrill 2010) have been evidenced. In addition, results in this study indicate that officers with higher levels of education are also found to show less solidarity and isolation than their counterparts with less education experience. It is reasonable to assume that more educational experience would equip officers with more skills and knowledge to deal with human-related problems (Eskridge 1989; Worden 1990). With these advanced abilities, highly educated officers may employ some non-traditional solutions other than aggressive coercion, and therefore maintain better relations with the public. This analysis is evidenced by a study of police behaviour conducted by Wilson (1999) in that officers with higher education level were found to have fewer citizen complaints and attract higher citizen satisfaction. Meanwhile, this study does not find any significant associations between education background and levels of cynicism, although in other research cynicism was higher among officers who had more college education (Paoline et al. 2000; Regoli 1976; Scott et al. 2009). In conclusion, there is some evidence that Chinese frontline officers with more education tend to be less linked with the traditional police subculture and more receptive to community service and police-citizen communications. This is in line with the comments by Punch (2007) that higher education may help change the existing police culture toward a more positive one. However, the validity of this finding should be considered carefully because of the small number of officers with a master's degree or above (18 of the total 382 officers) compared with others in the sample.

Subquestion 2.4

Among Chinese frontline police officers, is tenure associated with police subcultural perceptions?

One of the interesting findings related with length of police service is its correlation with the levels of cynicism that has been documented by a couple of empirical studies (Britz 1997; Burke and Mikkelsen 2005; Niederhoffer 1967; Paoline et al. 2000). In this study, a significant curvilinear relationship is evidenced between cynicism and tenure. Officers with 6–10 years of service had higher levels of cynicism, while officers with 5 years or less or 11 years of service or more were less cynical. Police responses on the 25th item clearly illustrate the finding: while 51.2 % of respondents with 11 years of service or more agreed or strongly agreed that most people respect the authority of police officers, the percentages for officers with 6–10 years of service and officers with 5 years of service or less are 17.2 and 27 % respectively. This finding strongly supports the classical discovery of Niederhoffer (1967) that police cynicism reaches its peak between 7 and 10 years of service before declining. Later, similar findings were generated from the study of Cooper (1982). However, a more recent study conducted in Norway identified a linear relationship between tenure and cynicism among police constables in that the level of cynicism increased with thc length of service (Burke and Mikkelsen 2005). Reasonable explanation for this could be that senior constables are more cynical due to the fact that they did not receive promotion as they expected (Burke and Mikkelsen 2005). However, mixed results have been generated by different studies. Both regarded as being negatively influenced by cynicism, attitudes toward citizen cooperation and willingness to socialise with citizens have seen different associations with tenure. For instance, more experienced officers are more positive toward citizen cooperation (Paoline et al. 2000) and more experienced officers are less likely to socialise with members of the community (Britz 1997). In this study, although tenure was not significantly associated with police perception of citizen cooperation indicated by Item 26, percentage distribution within tenure does show that officers with 6–10 years of service tend to have relatively more negative expectation of citizen cooperation while officers with 11 years of service or more tend to be more positive (Fig. 8.1). Similarly, with regard to socialising with non-police friends, cross-tabulation results of Item 34 suggest that the group with medium years of service tend to gradually stop socialising with non-police friends more than other groups despite that the correlation is not statistically significant (Fig. 8.2). These results all evidence the curvilinear relationship between tenure and police perceptions of citizen-related aspects, including citizen cooperation, respect for police authority, socialising with community members etc. As explained by previous studies, this finding may be explained through promotion of senior officers. Officers with 11 years of service or more may have more opportunities to have been promoted than less tenured officers, so it is reasonable to expect that they are the least cynical among all police officers. It is also not difficult to understand that officers with 5 years of service or less are less cynical than their counterparts with 6–10 years

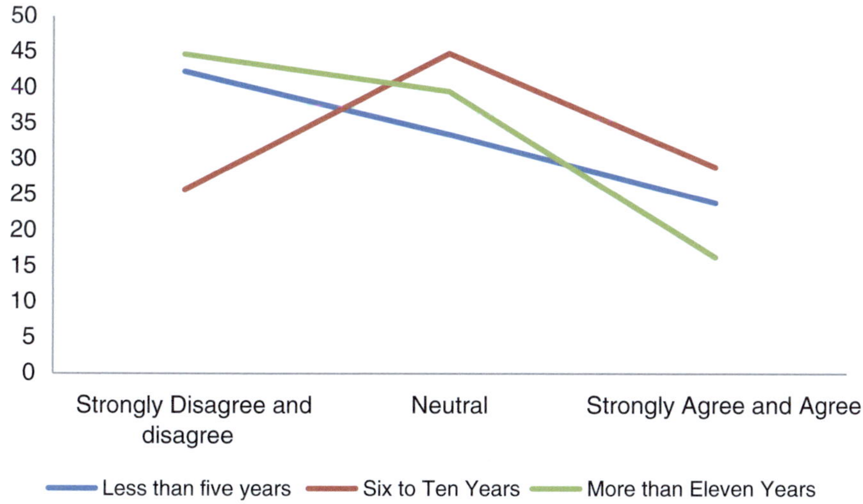

Fig. 8.1 Percentage distribution within tenure for Item 26 (Police officers will never trust citizens enough to work together effectively)

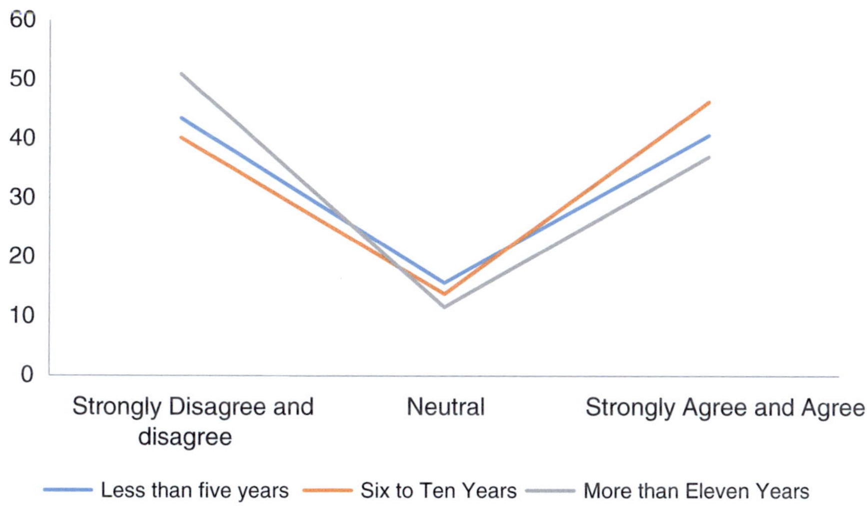

Fig. 8.2 Percentage distribution within tenure for Item 34 (I tend to socialise less with my friends outside of the police since I have become a police officer)

of service because occupational socialisation is gradually completed along with engaging in the profession. The limitation of findings lies in the fact that more than 70 % of the respondents in this study have 5 years' service experience or less in the police force.

Subquestion 2.5
Among Chinese frontline police officers, is type of police associated with police subcultural perceptions?

Frontline officers from different types of police forces are responsible for different kinds of assignments, so it is reasonable to expect differences of subcultural perceptions due to levels of police force. Responses in this study indicate that there are significant associations between police perceptions of crime-fighting role, solidarity, and isolation, and the types of police force they work in. In regard to their role orientations, the results clearly show that officers from lower-level police departments are more likely to stick to the crime fighting image. In detail, chi-square tests between police perceptions on the items in the scale of crime control and type of police force indicate that the lower-level departments officers work in, the more likely they prefer an aggressive policing style, and dislike non-crime activities and restrictions on use of force. The interpretation may be that field station officers need to handle the majority of street tasks, while officers from police sub-bureaus deal with fewer but more complicated or serious cases that are handed over by field stations. Because officers from municipal and provincial police departments are involved in frontline work when serious crimes occur, but most of the time they are responsible for coordination and direction for police operations, officers from lower-level departments are more socialised into the frontline police subculture which is formed on the basis of uncertainties and risks of frontline policing. Although there is an overwhelming support of solidarity among the officers in the present study, type of police force was found to be one of the factors that significantly influence police perceptions of solidarity. Specifically, officers from municipal or provincial departments have significantly different perceptions from their counterparts from field stations. According to chi-square results, officers from lower-level departments are more likely to think that "officers are careful of how they behave in public". In addition, officers from municipal or provincial departments were found to feel less isolated from the public than were other officers. This is best represented by their responses on the 40th item. Officers who work in municipal or provincial departments were significantly less likely to think that they are more open with peers than with community members than were officers from lower-level departments. Both of these two items are related with police-community relations. Officers from higher-level departments tend to be more critical about police public behaviour and to establish better relations with the public through communication. However, they do not have many chances to face citizens in their daily work. Similarly, they are more receptive to non-crime service but they are not usually involved in the various kinds of non-crime tasks as field officers are. This is just like the saying "absence makes the heart grow fonder".

Subquestion 2.6
Among Chinese frontline police officers, is being detectives or not associated with police subcultural perceptions?

Both Western and Chinese studies have pointed out the work and cultural differences between police detectives and uniformed police (Yang 2011; Young 1991), but few empirical studies have been conducted to examine the differences of their perceptions. Results in this study suggest that Chinese police detectives are more receptive to service functions and are relatively more socialised into group solidarity than are non-detectives. However, these differences are substantively small (albeit statistically significant). These findings are surprising because uniform police officers are more involved in social service and citizen-related interactions than police detectives and police detectives are mainly responsible for criminal investigations and bringing criminals to justice rather than assisting people. However, the finding in this study suggests that police detectives are more inclined to the service role and having more trust in citizens than non-detectives. The explanation could be that the cynical attitude and dislike about community service come from and become reinforced through the continuous service work and deteriorating police-citizen relations for uniformed police officers. On the other hand, the low rate of crime detection makes police detectives more like being engaged in some "paper exercise of statistical detections" (Young 1991, p. 83). In spite of their efforts, they see "no hope of breaking out of an endless cycle of the world becoming worse by the day, with more and more crimes and worsening criminals" (Wong 2012, p. 106). It seems that these results are in line with the findings of the previous section because again officers (detectives) who have relatively less contact with citizens are less cynical and those who do less service work are more receptive to it.

In summary, except for age, the demographic and work-related variables were found to be significantly correlated with some cultural themes of the police subculture. Gender, education level, and type of police force are more influential than are other factors upon police subculture. In addition, most of the findings support the existing Western studies and our expectations. For instance, female officers and officers with more educational qualifications are relatively less adherent to the traditional police subculture. These findings suggest that some key characteristics of police subculture are embodied by law enforcement practitioners across social and cultural borders.

8.3 Research Question Three

- For Chinese frontline police officers, are there significant relationships among the seven police subcultural themes suggested in Western literature?

Subquestion 3.1
Are there any significant correlations between a crime control orientation and the other subcultural themes?

The crime fighting orientation is one of the key components of police subculture (Klockars 1985b; Paoline 2003, 2004; Paoline et al. 2000; Rumbaut and Egon 1979; Sparrow et al. 1990; Walker and Katz 2005; Westley 1970; Wilson 1968). The Pearson's correlations indicate that police perceptions of crime fighting role orientation are significantly correlated with all other six cultural themes in this study. There are moderate positive but significant correlations of a crime-fighting orientation with cynicism, isolation, and solidarity. This means that the more that officers are crime-fighting oriented, the more they tend to be cynical toward the public, to be isolated from the rest of the society, and to have internal solidarity. Not surprisingly, there were moderate negative correlations of crime-fighting orientation with a service role orientation and receptivity to change. That is to say, the more officers are crime-fighting oriented, the less they tend to accept police service functions and changes at work. In addition, traditionalism was found to be significantly correlated with role orientation of crime fighting, though the correlation value was very weak. This weak correlation indicates that crime-oriented officers tend to stick to the traditional organisational structures of police departments.

These findings confirm the role that the crime fighter mentality plays in the police subculture. Officers consider themselves to be "the only real crime fighters", but not social workers (Sparrow et al. 1990, p. 52). There is an obvious paradox in the police role perceptions. The function of crime control in policing is highly valued despite statistics showing that only one third of frontline police work is related to law enforcement (Walker and Katz 2005, pp. 5–6). The functions of community service and order maintenance are undervalued; officers cannot get a sense of accomplishment from social service due to the evaluation system that emphasises only the crime detection rate. However, the actual crime detention rate is rather low (Walker and Katz 2005, p. 6). In addition, officers tend to establish and maintain their occupational expertise of crime fighting which can only be grasped by them (Manning 1997). Therefore, the need to keep this "dishonest" impression of crimes and arrests, and the specialised expertise of crime control by the police, fosters the internal solidarity among peers. In addition, it also isolates the police from the public–the potential co-producer of a community's security. The crime fighter image also includes a pragmatic action-oriented attitude with which officers tend to justify their actions by the noble cause (Loyens 2009). Officers are inclined to support the use of force and aggressive approaches in policing, while legal restrictions are regarded as "handcuffing the police" (Cochran and Bromley 2003, p. 89). This "tough" inclination and the corresponding negligence of legal restrictions could foster power abuse and social isolation. The crime-fighting orientation also leads to a mentality that officers treat people as potential offenders, namely, those who are policed instead of those who are protected by the police. This is best represented by a popular saying in China: to supervise people for social security or to maintain social security for people. This mentality, together with the trained "craft of suspicion" reinforces the cynical attitude toward citizens. The significant correlations between a crime-fighting orientation and cynicism, solidarity, and isolation provide evidence for the Western findings in the context of Chinese policing. However, the correlations are moderate, indicating the complexity of sources of subcultural themes and their interactions.

The two cultural themes that are negatively correlated with the role orientation of crime fighting are service orientation and receptivity to change. Not surprisingly, officers who are crime-oriented are less likely to support the service function of policing, because one of the main characteristics of crime fighter image is not to deem social service as real police work (Chan 1996; Terrill et al. 2003). In this study, many officers recommended that non-crime service should be handled by corresponding social welfare departments of the government. However, the value of significance actually echoes with previous descriptive statistics in this study. The significant correlations are low. Descriptive statistics also suggest that most of the officers in this study are both crime- and service-oriented. Although most of them consider law enforcement to be the primary function of policing, a majority of them also believe that they should provide assistance when people are in need. The problem seems to be a clearer definition of their service functions so that many local government-allocated administrative tasks and non-emergency citizen calls could be dealt with by other government departments. Officers who are crime-oriented are also less likely to accept changes at work. This finding is in accordance with the results of Cochran et al. (2002). However, the negative correlation is still not strong. The positive correlation between crime-fighting orientation and traditionalism is the weakest one of all the correlations. Nevertheless, it indicates that officers who are crime-oriented are more likely to adhere to the traditional paramilitary structure and the strict chain of command. The crime fighter image is nourished by the paramilitary structure of police departments that is based on strict chains of command and authoritarianism (Walker and Katz 2005). The paramilitary style also fosters a "war on crime" attitude that emphasises the function of crime control (Walker and Katz 2005).

Subquestion 3.2

Are there any significant correlations between a service role orientation and the other subcultural themes?

Besides the role orientation of crime fighting, the role orientation of service is correlated only with police cynicism according to the Pearson's correlations. This is a moderate negative but significant correlation. It suggests that the more officers are service-oriented, the less likely they are to be cynical toward the public. Cynicism is considered to be an attitude that includes distrust about people, society, and even human nature (Niederhoffer 1967). Intuitively, it is difficult to image that an officer who is cynical toward citizens would regard providing service to the public as a major function of policing. Other cultural themes such as isolation, solidarity, traditionalism, and receptivity to change are not significantly correlated with service orientation. One of the reasons could be that the police service function includes many administrative tasks assigned by local governments, such as forced evictions and demolition, activities related with birth control policy, stopping petitioners, and safeguarding commercial entertainment activities (Wang 2011). These activities are not included in the service function regulated in the People's Police Law of 1995 (Cao 2003; Gong 2004; Wang 2011). There is a widely-accepted agreement among policing practitioners that these activities should not be assigned to the police (Wang 2011). This could also be represented by police responses in this study in that many officers stated that local governments were making use of their coercive power in these administrative activities that should fall into the scope of other government departments. It is the more complex definition of "service" in the context of Chinese policing that has influenced the correlations.

Subquestion 3.3
Are there any significant correlations among traditionalism, receptivity to change, cynicism, solidarity, and isolation?

Besides role orientations of crime fighting and service, the Pearson's correlations indicate that there are a small number of significant bivariate correlations among the rest of the subcultural themes, namely, traditionalism, receptivity to change, cynicism, solidarity, and isolation. The level of police isolation from the public was found to be positively correlated with solidarity and cynicism. It is not difficult to understand that the more officers feel isolated from the rest of the society, the more they stand closely with their fellow officers. In addition, the protective bond or brotherhood keeps reminding officers that they could only rely on other officers instead of members of the public who know little or nothing about the real police work (Scaramella et al. 2011). Police solidarity reinforces the isolation from the public because it is "loyalty to colleagues rather than loyalty to the community" (Shernock 2007, p. 995). The cynical attitude also facilitates alienating the police from the community, because this negative attitude toward almost everything may be considered socially unattractive or even offensive to citizens (Swanton 1981). In addition, social isolation can also become a determinant of police cynicism in that the more an officer perceives alienation from the community, he is more subject to the protective subculture that characterises the public as hostile and untrustworthy.

Police social isolation and cynicism were negatively, albeit only weakly, correlated with receptivity to change at work: The more officers feel isolated and are cynical, the less they be accepting of changes, and vice versa. Police officers' resistance to organisational change has been widely documented by sociological researchers (Cochran et al. 2002; Lingamneni 1979; Roberg et al. 2009). The police subcultural values have been considered to be a main reason to keep the traditional ways of behaving and thinking, and to refuse any change (Lingamneni 1979; Roberg et al. 2009). The strong adherence to a cynical attitude toward the public and the alienation from the rest of the society may reinforce the resistance to any organisational change; it is also reasonable that officers who are more receptive to change may become less vulnerable to the subcultural themes like cynicism and isolation, and accept the philosophical change toward a community-oriented policing style. The negative correlation between receptivity to change and cynicism was also evidenced in an American study conducted by Cochran et al. (2002).

Besides isolation, police solidarity was also found to be positively correlated with traditionalism and receptivity to change. It is within expectation that officers who prefer the traditional organisational structure of police departments also adhere more to the protective loyalty among peers. However, the positive correlation between receptivity to change and solidarity is a little bit surprising. The correlation is very weak but significant. These findings indicate that officers who adhere more to police solidarity also find organisational change more acceptable.

8.4 Summary

In this chapter, results of the research questions were discussed together with the existing literature and the qualitative responses in this study. Some findings support Western studies, while other results can be interpreted on the basis of specific Chinese situations. Therefore, it could be concluded that police occupational subculture is influenced by both the police work that shares many common characteristics across borders and the specific social context that shapes the perceptions and behaviour of people within its territory. In the following chapter, the key findings will be summarised, and implications, limitations, and recommendations for further studies will be discussed. There are some useful implications in regard to police training and policy making for police administrators and police instructors in China. These implications may assist in a successful philosophical and strategic transmission from traditional policing to community policing. However, there are also some methodological limitations in this study, such as a selective sampling technique and the imbalance of the sample in some demographic aspects. For further studies, methodological improvements should be considered to enhance the generalisability of research findings.

Chapter 9
Conclusion

The concept of culture was first discussed by early anthropologists as a human-specific construct that is generated along with human behaviours and provides interpretations for them (Geertz 1973; Jenks 2005). Sociologists moved forward to suggest that everything in a society that is learned through social life and shared by members of the society should fall into the scope of culture (Chalfant and LaBeff 1988). Although culture is not a concept that could be seen as some concrete codes of conduct, nobody could deny that all the members in a society live under the influence of a powerful intangible cultural web. However, under the social culture, there are also subcultures that are formed during the socialisation of some specific groups of people due to their unique occupational or organisational characteristics. An occupational subculture is developed among people in a particular vocation in the course of doing similar tasks. A set of accepted norms and values are socialised through occupational interactions in order to protect members in the occupation from outside risks and uncertainties (Manning 2007b; Trice and Beyer 1993). As a cohesive occupational group, police officers have considerable impetus for forming a strong and rich police subculture, such as the imbedded nature of danger, the special skills, the formal and painstaking training process, and the rich material culture (uniforms, etc.). Police subculture is learned by newcomers through both formal and informal occupational socialisation. In formal lessons at a police academy, they are equipped with necessary skills and knowledge about police work; the newcomers also need to become real insiders after they become acquainted with the informal rules in the field (Van Maanen and Schein 1979). Meanwhile, the more officers are socialised into police subculture, the more they know how to defend internal interests and move away from their previous roles.

The police subculture has attracted sizable research due to its widespread influence upon police behaviour and perceptions. A number of cultural themes have been proposed by academics and practitioners to describe the complicated and mysterious "working personality", such as solidarity, isolation, traditionalism, a crime-fighting mentality, masculinity, cynicism, suspicion, and the use of force (Crank 2004; Reiner 2010; Skolnick 1986). It is the working environment that is

Z. Chen, *Measuring Police Subcultural Perceptions*,
DOI 10.1007/978-981-10-0096-6_9

featured with imbedded danger, together with the police role with authority and coercion, which creates the informal rules of the police world. Some scholars have discussed the beneficial effects of the police subculture. For instance, solidarity is extremely important for police teamwork and effectiveness, and even isolation and cynicism could be regarded as protective mechanisms against outside risks and hostility (Harrison 1998; Reiner 2010; Skolnick 1986). However, most analyses of police culture focus on its potential negative effects (Loyens 2009). An adherence to the police subculture may foster negative and cynical attitudes toward citizens and even the legal system (Cochran and Bromley 2003), and may reinforce peer loyalty so that police misconduct is undetected because of the wall of silence (Mollen et al. 1994; Wood 1997).

As more sociologists delve into studying police subculture, it seems that discussions are moving toward greater variation in opinions rather than reaching agreement. Some researchers question the traditional depiction of a monolithic police subculture by presenting cultural variations (Paoline 2001, 2003, 2004). It has also been pointed out that most of the theorising and research about police subcultural themes are based on studies in the 20th century (Loyens 2009). There are new developments in policing and society that have brought new trends to the culture of policing. These include more female officers and college-educated officers in the police team. As Chan (1996) pointed out in her study, the traditional depictions failed to take the changing nature of police culture into account. In addition, the traditionally depicted police subculture has been questioned because many early researches were considered "impressionistic" and "imprecise" (Walker and Katz 2005, p. 157). However, at the same time, some recent studies have indicated that many core components of traditional police subculture still function in contemporary policing because uncertainties and pressures of police work remain the same as the past (Corsianos 2012; Loftus 2010; Skolnick 2008).

There is another reason that more studies are needed in the field of police subculture beside the much-debated negative effects and the lack of agreement among academics. As Loyens (2009, p. 481) stated, more research is needed in the context of non-Anglo-Saxon countries. In China, very few empirical policing studies could be found. One of the main reasons is that Chinese scholars tend to draw conclusions on the basis of their own experiences or opinions instead of conducting empirical research (Bao 2002; Lian 2002; Lv 2012). In addition, the adoption of community policing in China requires a good police-citizen relationship, a service role orientation, and more accountability in a police team. However, some police subcultural themes contain contradictory ideas from community policing. These include cynicism, a crime-fighting image, and the us versus them mentality. Empirical inquiries of police subcultural perceptions among Chinese police officers not only add to the existing knowledge by investigating police subculture in the context of China, but also pave the way for the successful implementation of community policing from the perspective of subcultural influences.

This study was designed to investigate police subcultural perceptions among a sample of Chinese frontline officers. More specifically, it examined whether and to what extent the sample of Chinese frontline police officers adhere to some core themes of the police subculture described in the Western literature. In addition, the study was designed to discover associations between police subcultural perceptions and some demographic and work-related variables. Finally, this study was designed to explore the relationships among the subcultural themes.

9.1 Key Findings

Based on the results of quantitative analyses and qualitative thematic analyses, the following are the main findings.

First, there is not a widespread adherence to the police subculture suggested in Western literature among Chinese frontline police officers. However, police perceptions on some cultural themes, such as internal solidarity and social isolation, are somewhat consistent with the existing findings in the West. Solidarity, however, is the only theme that attracted overwhelming support by the Chinese police officers in this sample. This indicates that solidarity is a universal attribute of policing. Some Chinese frontline police officers in this sample do show a high level of social isolation, although adherence is far from being uniform. Similar to existing findings, the main interpretations for their isolation are outside hostility and the irregular nature of police work. With regard to role orientations, although many frontline officers consider crime fighting to be their primary responsibility and consider policing to be a crime-fighting oriented occupation, they also regard a service function as an important component of police work. To some extent, they are both crime and service oriented. This is the result of the interactive influence of different policing strategies, the communist doctrine, and the complex social and law enforcement environment in China. Unlike Western descriptions, Chinese officers do not show a strong adherence to cultural themes of traditionalism, unreceptivity to change, and cynicism. On the scales of traditionalism and cynicism, their perceptions are almost normally distributed. In addition, they are actually quite receptive to changes at work because they consider changes to be very useful to improve police work. Meanwhile, officers did express a need of more authority for frontline officers and a lack of trust and respect from the public.

Second, apart from age, all other factors have been found to have significant influence upon police perceptions. Unsurprisingly, female officers had significantly lower levels of cynicism, isolation, solidarity, and crime control role orientations than did their male counterparts. Officers with higher levels of education were less likely to have a crime control role orientation and senses of internal solidarity and social isolation. Police tenure was found to be significantly associated with the level of cynicism. Officers with 6 to 10 years of service had higher levels of cynicism than did officers with 11 years of service or more and officers with 5 years of service or less, and officers with 11 years of service or more were the least cynical. Officers from lower levels of police departments are more likely to have a crime-fighting orientation and to have higher solidarity than did their counterparts from higher levels of police departments. Police detectives were more receptive to service functions and were relatively more socialised into group solidarity than were non-detectives.

Finally, some significant associations were located among the seven subcultural themes. There were moderate but significant positive correlations of a crime-fighting role orientation with cynicism, isolation, and solidarity. The more officers were crime-fighting-oriented, the higher levels of cynicism, isolation, and solidarity they had. There were moderate but significant negative correlations of a crime-fighting role orientation with a service role orientation and receptivity to change. The more officers are crime-fighting-oriented, the more they are unreceptive to service functions and changes at work. There was a moderate but significant negative correlation between a service role orientation and cynicism. The more officers are service-oriented, the less they are cynical. The level of police isolation from the public was found to be positively correlated with solidarity and cynicism. Police social isolation and cynicism were found to be negatively correlated with receptivity to change at work. Police solidarity was also found to be positively correlated with traditionalism and receptivity to change.

9.2 Implications

As one of the first empirical quantitative studies in police perceptions in China, this study is exploratory in nature in that it provides an overall insight into how Chinese frontline police officers perceive the widely discussed components of police subculture in the West. In addition, this study aims to be interpretive and instructive. To be interpretive means that I intend to provide explanations for the results obtained in this study and the open-ended comments by some respondents, through the analysis of the background of Chinese policing and social culture, and by considering the associations between variables in this study. On the basis of the interpretations, some implications can be generated and be of interest to police administrators, police practitioners, police educators, and police researchers in China.

The findings of this study have important implications for police training in China. As discussed in previous chapters, the crime-fighter image was discovered among many Chinese frontline police officers. Combating crime is considered to be their primary task, while community service detracts from their crime fighting efforts. Aggressive policing and fewer restrictions on police use of force were supported by many officers because these elements were considered to be effective in crime control and to be helpful to protect police authority and safety. Many officers in this study felt the lack of trust and support from citizens, which further isolates police from the public and makes police work harder. Some of the problems addressed above could be improved through appropriate police training and education. It is necessary for police universities, police academies, and police departments to provide regular training programs that emphasise interpersonal skills, problem solving, ethical standards, community culture, and essential social service skills, such as emergency aid and dispute resolution. Regular in-service training may help frontline police officers grasp necessary updated community-oriented knowledge and skills for the implementation of community policing in China. Officers would be equipped with a proactive philosophy of policing that emphasises crime prevention and problem solving. The interpersonal communication and social service skills may help officers fulfil the above policing philosophy by improving police–citizen relations and providing qualified community service for community members. Meanwhile, special training courses of skills and philosophies of community policing for police supervisors should also be designed and conducted, because the priorities of police supervisors may greatly influence the attitudes and behaviour of frontline officers (Engel and Worden 2003). These first-line police supervisors may play an important role in passing the philosophical guidelines of police administrators to frontline practitioners (Vito et al. 2005). Therefore, whether these police supervisors embrace the philosophy of community policing and require the acceptance of the new perspective in the daily work of frontline officers would be crucial for the implementation of community policing to be a success (Peak et al. 2010).

In addition, the correlation analysis between role orientation and other themes of police subculture clearly indicates that the crime fighter image remains in the centre of the police subculture because it has moderate significant correlations with all the other themes. It is positively correlated with solidarity, traditionalism, cynicism, and isolation; it is negatively correlated with service orientation and receptivity to change. Although these findings conform to expectations, it is important to have them supported empirically. The correlation network to some extent explains why the crime fighter image is not easily replaced by a service-oriented one. However, regular training and education sessions with an emphasis on a proactive service-oriented strategy may gradually change the whole police subculture toward the requirements of community policing.

Some management implications have also been proposed here on the basis of both quantitative and qualitative findings in this study. First, it is necessary and urgent to implement clearer delimitations and regulations about police service functions. Officers expressed strong dislike about service activities in which no crimes are involved. Nearly half of them said that officers should not handle those problems. In their comments, many of them suggested that non-crime service should be provided by government departments. In a variety of ways they expressed strong feelings that police should not handle more because their work is already over-loaded, such as "the police are not omnipotent", "the police are not bodyguards", "the police are not babysitters", and even "the police are not the God". They also stated that some of the non-crime activities, such as forced evictions and demolition, and stopping petitioners affected the police image. The negative feelings against some specific kinds of activities have affected their overall orientations toward service. Therefore, it is necessary for police administrators to delimit the contents and responsibilities for police service functions and establish specified regulations and guidelines for frontline officers. In essence, frontline police work needs to be narrowed and police workloads need to be decreased (Millie 2014; Wang and Wong 2012). Police departments should negotiate with local governments to reduce administrative tasks assigned by them. In addition, the police should rely on multi-agency cooperation in administration tasks. The police should maintain public order and keep social security, while administrative law enforcement should be conducted by corresponding government departments. Finally, police departments should also use realistic slogans instead of the broad ones such as "help with any difficulties you have". These slogans tend to over-load police work and cause dissatisfaction and reduce police credibility when citizens find that the police cannot solve all their problems (Gong 2004).

Findings in this study indicate that many frontline officers in China feel that they do not receive sufficient trust and respect from the public. They even feel that their authority of law enforcement is challenged due to the lack of understanding from and even misunderstanding of the public. Most of the respondents believe that people do not really understand police work. Therefore, officers tend to socialise with their colleagues rather than with non-police friends. The irregular work hours further isolate police officers from members of the public. This wall of isolation not only keeps police away from the rest of the society, but also generates barriers for the effectiveness and efficiency of police work. Therefore, it is necessary for police administrators to establish more communication channels for police and citizens. This has been repeatedly suggested in the comments left by officers in this study. Besides traditional channels of communication such as visiting communities, schools, enterprises, and households, the police should be encouraged to develop various activities to create more opportunities for communication. For instance, the police may set some regular "open days" for citizens to visit police departments; the police may also encourage citizens to select their "favourite police officers" and hold corresponding celebration activities; some policing related exhibitions such as traffic safety or anti-narcotics knowledge exhibitions can be held by police departments for both education and communication purposes. In addition, the Internet and mass media could be used to facilitate police-citizen communication.

Quantitative results in this study suggest that demographics such as gender, education, and tenure are significantly associated with police subcultural perceptions. Female officers were found to be significantly less cynical, less isolated, and less crime-fighting oriented than were their male counterparts. Education also has positive effects on police subcultural perceptions. Officers with higher education qualifications tended to have a lower level of social isolation and adhere less to the crime fighter mentality than did those with less education experience. Therefore, it is reasonable to recommend police administrators to recruit more female and more people with higher education qualifications into police force. In particular, the increased proportion of policewomen will have "a fundamental impact on dominant, take-for-granted work practices" which form the cultural barriers for successful police reform (Dick et al. 2014, p. 135). Their greater abilities in conflict resolution and their greater patience may function in daily patrol and criminal interrogation, and especially in investigation of sexual assault. However, when we think about how to make use of the feminine traits to better achieve goals in community policing, it is also reasonable to take further steps to reduce the entrenched bias of these softer police roles and feminine traits so that female officers may feel more comfortable and will not be afraid that feminine skills and traits may cause more questioning about their credibility as efficient crime fighters (Miller and Bonistall 2012).

In addition, efforts to encourage in-service police officers to have further education are beneficial for fostering community-oriented traits among police teams. It was also found that officers with 11 years of service or more are the least cynical among all officers. Therefore, it is likely to be advantageous if female officers, highly educated officers, and experienced officers played more important roles in police teams. Different length of service was found to be significantly correlated with the level of police cynicism, so it is worthwhile for police administrators to consider arranging officers with different length of service to work together and cooperate. This would be helpful for fostering a more positive working atmosphere, especially while dealing with mass incidents when police cynicism and citizen dissatisfaction are more easily brewed.

Another finding is that most Chinese frontline officers consider that changes at work will improve police work by enhancing effectiveness and efficiency. However, some officers suggest that attitudes of police chiefs may negatively influence their enthusiasm for new work approaches. Officers' perceptions and behaviour are easily influenced by the styles of police chiefs. The leader of an organisation imposes "his or her beliefs, values, and assumptions" to the organisation (Schein 2004, p. 225). Therefore, there are some important implications for police administrators. It is very important for police chiefs to receive some training and improve their knowledge about management. They should equip themselves with updated knowledge and a positive attitude toward change, and influence others positively. In addition, the standards of achievement evaluation should be reframed to take both actions and outcomes into consideration so that innovations should be put into effect only subsequent to thorough investigations.

This study also contributes to the existing literature by adding empirical studies about police subculture in the context of Chinese policing. Some subcultural themes suggested in Western literature are evidenced among frontline officers in China. However, there are also some characteristics of Chinese police subculture that are different from what has been described in the existing Western literature. These embody the influence of the entire social culture of China upon its members and the influence of the specific history, structure, and strategies of Chinese policing on Chinese police themselves. This study provides implications for academics in the field of policing that the police subculture should be investigated on the basis of both the characteristics of police occupational socialisation and the impact of the specific sociocultural background.

9.3 Limitations

As with any study, some limitations are inherent in this study. First, the sample group used was not randomly selected. Due to the availability of participants, a nonprobability sampling design was used. A more random sample would have permitted greater generalisability of the findings. However, it is almost impossible to conduct a random sampling with all the frontline police officers in China as the population. Therefore, I selected the in-service frontline officers training in a national police university as the sample, because this university receives trainees from nearly all the provinces in China annually. It is one of the only two national police universities in China that train officers across the country. Therefore, officers training there to some extent represent the characteristics of frontline police officers across China. In addition, this study is exploratory because few empirical studies inquiring subcultural perceptions among Chinese officers have been conducted. It is more important to have an initial investigation into the facts on the basis of feasible conditions.

Second, although the sample of officers who are training in the national police university are of great demographic diversity, there were some limitations in regard to some variables. For instance, certain groups of officers were still quite small in number compared with other groups. These were female officers, senior officers, officers with a long period of service, and officers with postgraduate qualifications. The lack of an adequate number of individuals from these groups may limit the generalisability of this study and create some limitations to the correlation analysis of demographic and work-related variables with subcultural perceptions. However, some of the features realistically represent the characteristics of Chinese police officers in that there are fewer female officers and officers with postgraduate qualifications in the police force. With regard to age and tenure, it is surely a limitation of this sample, because relatively fewer senior and highly experienced frontline officers are assigned to receive training in police universities. These limitations have been taken into consideration when discussing the results.

In addition, the sensitive nature of the topic may limit the extent to which the participants would be honest in their answers. Therefore, this study was designed to ensure the anonymity of participants as the best way to overcome this threat.

Finally, as there are few empirical inquiries related with Chinese police subcultural perceptions (Sun and Wu 2010), the existing literature on the subject in China provided very little foundational information for this study. Therefore, the framework of this study is mainly based on theoretical inquiries in Western literature. This study serves as an exploratory investigation that may provide useful insights for the establishment of scientific studies on Chinese police subculture.

9.4 Recommendations

This study has revealed a number of areas where future research would be valuable. First, generalisation beyond the respondents of this study warrants further attempts to replicate the findings by using different samples. A random sample from some regions or across China may provide additional insights into police cultural perceptions in China.

Second, although I explored the associations between some demographic and work-related variables and police cultural perceptions, there are still some meaningful variables that need attention in future studies. These include race, unit of assignment, and area of assignment. Future research could be used to explore whether these factors are associated with police subcultural differences. In addition, this study focuses on police subculture among frontline officers. It could be worthwhile to explore whether there are subcultural differences between frontline officers and command officers. Meanwhile, because there were small numbers in some groups of officers in this study further research could be focused on these groups through stratified samples to guarantee an adequate number of participants. This will provide a better understanding of the influence of these variables.

In addition, because this study was primarily quantitative in nature, with only a small amount of qualitative data, future studies may employ more extensive qualitative methods, such as in-depth interviews, to look at the subtleties of perceptions that are not easily investigated by quantitative means.

Finally, to seek interpretations of the findings on the basis of quantitative and qualitative data together with Chinese social cultural background, the main aim of this study was to provide an exploratory overall understanding of police perceptions in China. Therefore, future studies are needed to focus on explanatory studies and causal relationships. It would be most effective if longitudinal studies were conducted that followed police officers throughout the socialisation process. This would allow researchers to measure the differences in perspectives that officers had from the time they entered the police force until they were fully socialised. In addition, empirical studies could be conducted to find out the potential relationships between police subcultural perceptions and the actual behaviour of police, including their misconduct. This would add value to police subculture studies in China and generate more useful implications for Chinese policing.

Appendix A
Research Questionnaire

RESEARCH QUESTIONNAIRE

Thank you for participating in this survey study. This questionnaire is designed to measure attitudes and perceptions of police subculture among Chinese frontline police officers. It will help us to have a better understanding of the extent to which Chinese frontline police officers adhere to police subculture and the similarities and variations between Chinese police officers and their counterparts in the west. Further research and suggestions will be generated on a basis of this study for improvements in police training and education in regards to positive police culture.

If you decide to take part in this study, you are asked to complete this questionnaire and to be as honest with your responses as you can be. A code will be used so you will not be individually named. There is also no linking of any data from the questionnaire to specific individuals. The collected data will only be used to identify issues instead of identifying individuals. The results will be only used for academic purposes by the researcher.

It is expected that this questionnaire will take approximately 20 minutes to complete. We thank you in advance for your willingness to take part in this study.

INSTRUCTIONS FOR COMPLETING THE QUESTIONNAIRE

Please answer the following questions as honest as possible. There is no right or wrong answer. Please choose the answer which represents your opinion.

Z. Chen, *Measuring Police Subcultural Perceptions*,
DOI 10.1007/978-981-10-0096-6

Section 1: Demographic Information

---

1. What is your age?

☐ 25 or less ☐ 26-30 ☐ 31-35 ☐ 36-40 ☐ 41 or greater

2. What is your gender?

☐ Female ☐ Male

3. What is the highest level of education you have completed?

☐ 2-3 years college or less
☐ Bachelor's degree
☐ Master's degree or above

4. How long have you been working in the police force?

☐ 5 years or less
☐ 6 to 10 years
☐ more than 11 years

5. What type of police force are you in?

☐ Provincial department
☐ Municipal bureau
☐ Police sub-bureau
☐ Police station

6. Are you a police detective or not?

☐ Yes, I am.
☐ No, I am not.

7. Which province are you working in?

____

Section 2: Police Subcultural Perceptions

Please answer the following questions as honestly as possible from 1 to 5 where 1 represents that you "strongly disagree" with the statement and 5 represents that you "strongly agree" with the statement. Nominate the answer that most closely fits with your view. Please circle the appropriate response.

1. Crime Control	Strongly Disagree	Disagree	Neutral	Agree	Strongly Agree
1. An aggressive, tough bearing is more useful to a police officer than a friendly, courteous manner.	1	2	3	4	5
2. If police officers act in a service capacity, it detracts from their ability to fight crime.	1	2	3	4	5
3. Good law enforcement requires that officers concern themselves with the consequences of crime and not with its root causes.	1	2	3	4	5
4. Police officers should not forget that enforcing the law is by far their most important responsibility.	1	2	3	4	5
5. Police officers should not have to handle calls that involve social or personal problems where no crime is involved.	1	2	3	4	5
6. If police officers in high crime areas had fewer restrictions on their use of force, many of the serious crime problems in these areas would be significantly reduced.	1	2	3	4	5

Please provide additional comments if you wish:

____

____

____

2. Service	Strongly Disagree	Disagree	Neutral	Agree	Strongly Agree
7. Police officers should ask citizens what types of services they want.	1	2	3	4	5
8. Crimes are only one of several problems about which police officers should be concerned.	1	2	3	4	5
9. Assisting citizens in need is just as important as enforcing the law.	1	2	3	4	5
10. Lowering citizens' fear of crime should be just as high a priority as cutting the crime rate.	1	2	3	4	5
11. Law enforcement should be seen primarily as a service-oriented profession rather than a crime control profession.	1	2	3	4	5

Please provide additional comments if you wish:

____
____
____
____
____

3. Traditionalism					
	Strongly Disagree	Disagree	Neutral	Agree	Strongly Agree
12. To be effective an organization should have clearly defined positions of power/authority among its members/employees.	1	2	3	4	5
13. In law enforcement organizations power should be evenly distributed among its personnel.	1	2	3	4	5
14. Communication works best when it follows clear, established channels from the top down.	1	2	3	4	5
15. The quasi-military structure is the most effective organizational type for law enforcement agencies.	1	2	3	4	5
16. Subordinates should not be involved in either the setting or the enforcing of policies and procedures within law enforcement agencies.	1	2	3	4	5

Please provide additional comments if you wish:

____
____
____
____
____

4. Receptivity to Change					
	Strongly Disagree	Disagree	Neutral	Agree	Strongly Agree
17. Most changes at work are problematic and ineffective.	1	2	3	4	5
18. I can usually find some way to get around changes at work.	1	2	3	4	5
19. I often suggest new approaches for doing things at my job.	1	2	3	4	5
20. Most changes make my work more efficient (i.e. saves time, effort, money).	1	2	3	4	5
21. Most changes make my job more effective (i.e. more arrests, faster response times, crime reduction).	1	2	3	4	5

Please provide additional comments if you wish:

____
____
____
____
____

5. Cynicism					
	Strongly Disagree	Disagree	Neutral	Agree	Strongly Agree
22. Most people do not hesitate to go out of their way to help someone in trouble.	1	2	3	4	5
23. Most people are untrustworthy and dishonest.	1	2	3	4	5
24. Most people would steal if they knew they would not get caught.	1	2	3	4	5
25. Most people respect the authority of police officers.	1	2	3	4	5
26. Police officers will never trust citizens enough to work together effectively.	1	2	3	4	5
27. Citizens will not trust police officers enough to work together effectively.	1	2	3	4	5

Please provide additional comments if you wish:

____
____
____
____
____

6. Solidarity					
	Strongly Disagree	Disagree	Neutral	Agree	Strongly Agree
28. Police officers are careful of how they behave in public.	1	2	3	4	5
29. You don't understand what it is to be a police officer until you are a police officer.	1	2	3	4	5
30. Police officers have to look out for each other.	1	2	3	4	5
31. Members of the public, media and politicians are quick to criticize the police but seldom recognize the good that police officers do.	1	2	3	4	5
32. Most members of the public don't really know what is going on 'out there'.	1	2	3	4	5
33. To be a police officer is not just another job it is a 'higher calling.'	1	2	3	4	5

Please provide additional comments if you wish:

____
____
____
____
____

7. Isolation	Strongly Disagree	Disagree	Neutral	Agree	Strongly Agree
34. I tend to socialize less with my friends outside of the police since I have become a police officer.	1	2	3	4	5
35. I don't really talk in-depth to people outside of the police about my work.	1	2	3	4	5
36. My husband/wife, boyfriend/girlfriend tends not to understand what being a police officer is all about.	1	2	3	4	5
37. Shift work and special duties influence my socializing with friends outside the police.	1	2	3	4	5
38. I feel like I belong with my work colleagues more every day, and less with people that I have to police.	1	2	3	4	5
39. As a police officer, I am being watched critically by members of the community, even in my social life.	1	2	3	4	5
40. I can be more open with my work colleagues than with members of the public.	1	2	3	4	5

Please provide additional comments if you wish:

____
____
____
____

You have reached the end of this questionnaire. Thank you for participating in this important research project.

Appendix B
Test of Equality of Covariance Matrices

Age

Box's test of equality of covariance matrices

Box's M	151.592
F	1.166
df1	112
df2	5455.016
Sig.	0.114

Gender

Box's test of equality of covariance matrices

Box's M	40.591
F	1.359
df1	28
df2	17,853.095
Sig.	0.097

Education

Box's test of equality of covariance matrices

Box's M	63.028
F	1.022
df1	56
df2	6486.312
Sig.	0.429

Z. Chen, *Measuring Police Subcultural Perceptions*,
DOI 10.1007/978-981-10-0096-6

Tenure

Box's test of equality of covariance matrices

Box's M	76.234
F	1.289
df1	56
df2	46,012.248
Sig.	0.072

Type of Police Force

Box's test of equality of covariance matrices

Box's M	65.153
F	1.127
df1	56
df2	162,251.048
Sig.	.239

Detective or Non-detective

Box's test of equality of covariance matrices

Box's M	38.183
F	1.336
df1	28
df2	382,778.453
Sig.	.110

Appendix C
Test of Homogeneity of Variance

Age

Test of Homogeneity of Variances

	Levene statistic	df1	df2	Sig.
Crime	1.132	4	377	0.341
Service	4.258	4	377	0.002
Traditionalism	1.235	4	377	0.296
Change	1.690	4	377	0.152
Cynicism	1.080	4	377	0.366
Solidarity	0.920	4	377	0.452
Isolation	0.983	4	377	0.417

Gender

Test of homogeneity of variances

	Levene statistic	df1	df2	Sig.
Crime	0.017	1	380	0.895
Service	0.139	1	380	0.709
Traditionalism	1.446	1	380	0.230
Change	7.219	1	380	0.008
Cynicism	3.757	1	380	0.053
Solidarity	2.354	1	380	0.126
Isolation	4.480	1	380	0.035

Education

Test of homogeneity of variances

	Levene statistic	df1	df2	Sig.
Crime	0.202	2	379	0.817
Service	0.157	2	379	0.855
Traditionalism	0.619	2	379	0.539

Z. Chen, *Measuring Police Subcultural Perceptions*,
DOI 10.1007/978-981-10-0096-6

	Levene statistic	df1	df2	Sig.
Change	0.233	2	379	0.793
Cynicism	0.446	2	379	0.641
Solidarity	1.024	2	379	0.360
Isolation	0.558	2	379	0.573

Tenure

Test of homogeneity of variances

	Levene statistic	df1	df2	Sig.
Crime	2.066	2	379	0.128
Service	3.400	2	379	0.034
Traditionalism	3.588	2	379	0.029
Change	1.295	2	379	0.275
Cynicism	0.958	2	379	0.385
Solidarity	1.314	2	379	0.270
Isolation	2.475	2	379	0.085

Type of Police Force

Test of homogeneity of variances

	Levene statistic	df1	df2	Sig.
Crime	4.037	2	379	0.018
Service	0.672	2	379	0.511
Traditionalism	0.652	2	379	0.522
Change	0.423	2	379	0.656
Cynicism	2.678	2	379	0.070
Solidarity	1.542	2	379	0.215
Isolation	2.236	2	379	0.108

Detective or Non-detective

Test of homogeneity of variances

	Levene statistic	df1	df2	Sig.
Crime	0.241	1	380	0.624
Service	0.000	1	380	0.995
Traditionalism	1.893	1	380	0.170
Change	0.268	1	380	0.605
Cynicism	1.650	1	380	0.200
Solidarity	3.013	1	380	0.083
Isolation	0.485	1	380	0.487

References

Allen IE, Seaman CA (2007) Likert scales and data analyses. Qual Prog 40(7):64–65

Alpert GP, Dunham RG (1997) Policing urban America. Waveland Press, Prospect Heights

Archbold CA (ed) (2013) Policing: a text/reader. Sage, Thousand Oaks

Armacost, B. E. (2003). Organizational culture and police misconduct. George Washington Law Rev 72

Bachman R, Schutt RK (2010) The practice of research in criminology and criminal justice, 4th edn. Sage, Thousand Oaks

Bacon M (2014) Police culture and the new policing context. In Brown JM (ed) The future of policing. Routledge, Abingdon, pp 103–119

Banks C (2009) Criminal justice ethics: theory and practice. Sage, Thousand Oaks

Banton M (1964) The policeman in the community. Basic Books, New York

Bao J (2002) Dongxifang kexuechuantong he siweifangshi bijiao (A comparative study on scientific tradition and thinking mode between the East and the West). J Zhejiang Univ Technol (Socia Science Edition) *30*(3)

Barley SR (1983) Semiotics and the study of occupational and organizational cultures. Adm Sci Q 28(3):393–413

Bayens GJ, Roberson C (2011) Criminal justice research methods: theory and practice, 2nd edn. CRC Press, Boca Racon

Behrend KR (1980) Police cynicism: a cancer in law enforcement. FBI Law Enforcement Bull 49(8):1–4

Belknap J (2007) The invisible woman: Gender, crime, and justice, 3rd edn. Wadsworth, Belmont

Bennett RR, Schmitt EL (2002) The effect of work environment on levels of police cynicism: a comparative study. Police Q 5(4):493–522

Bittner E (1974) Florence Nightingale in pursuit of Willie Sutton. In: Bittner E (ed) Aspects of police work. Northeastern University Press, Boston

Bourdieu P (1990) In other words: essays toward a reflexive sociology. Stanford University Press, Stanford

Brecher JA (2009) Generation and the occupational culture of policing (D.P.A. 3353965), University of Illinois at Springfield, United States—Illinois. Retrieved from http://search.proquest.com/docview/305168934?accountid=10344 ProQuest Dissertations & Theses (PQDT) database

Brinkerhoff DB, White LK (1988) Sociology. West Publishing Company, St Paul

Britz M (1997) The police subculture and occupational socialization: Exploring individual and demographic characteristics. Am J Crim Justice 21(2):127–146

Broderick JJ (1987) Police in a time of change, 2nd edn. Waveland Press, Prospect Heights

Z. Chen, *Measuring Police Subcultural Perceptions*,
DOI 10.1007/978-981-10-0096-6

Brooks L, Piquero A, Cronin J (1993) Police officer attitudes concerning their communities and their roles: comparison of two suburban police departments. Am J Police 12(3):115–139

Brown B (2014) Community policing. In: Albanese JS (ed) The encyclopedia of criminology and criminal justice. Wiley, New York

Brown MK (1981) Working the street: police discretion and the dilemmas of reform. Russell Sage Foundation, New York

Buerger ME (2007) Cynicism, police. In: Greene JR (ed) The encyclopedia of police science, 3rd edn. Routledge, New York

Burke RJ, Mikkelsen A (2005) Career stage and police cynicism. Psychologica Rep 96(3c):989–992

Cai J, Liu Y (2011) Luelun zhongguochuantongwenhua de jiazhiquxiang dui jingchawenhua-jianshe de yingxiang yi hunanjingchaxueyuan zhongzhenzhiyong xiaoxun weili (On the influence of the value orientation of traditional Chinese culture on the culture construction of police organ–with the example of academic slogan of human police academy). J Hunan Police Acad 23(6):129–131

Cain M (1973) Society and the policeman's role. Routledge, London

Calhoun CJ, Light D, Keller SI (1994) Sociology, 6th edn. McGraw-Hill, New York

Cancino JM, Enriquez R (2004) A qualitative analysis of officer peer retaliation: preserving the police culture. Policing: Int J Police Strat Manage 27(3):320–340

Cao C (2003) Shequjingwuzhanluezhong feijingwuhuodongde ezhiduice [On countermeasures of non-policing activities in the strategy of community policing]. J Guizhou Police Officer Vocat Coll 15(5):81–85

Cao L, Hou C (2001) A comparison of confidence in the police in China and in the United States. J Crim Justice 29(2):87–99

Caplan J (2003) Police cynicism: police survival tool? Police J 76(4):304–313

Carey G (1998) Multivariate analysis of variance (MANOVA): I. Theory. From http://ibgwww.colorado.edu/~carey/p7291dir/handouts/manova1.pdf

Carmines EG, Zeller RA (1979) Reliability and validity assessment. Sage, Thousand Oaks

Carter DL, Sapp AD (1990) The evolution of higher education in law enforcement: preliminary findings from a national study. J Crim Justice Educ 1(1):59–85

Chalfant HP, LaBeff E (1988) Understanding people and social life: Introduction to sociology. West Publications Co., St. Paul

Chan J (1996) Changing police culture. Br J Criminol 36(1):109–134

Chan J (1997) Changing police culture: policing in a multicultural society. Cambridge University Press, Cambridge

Chan J (2000) Backstage punishment: police violence, occupational culture and criminal justice. In: Coady T (ed) Violence and police culture. Melbourne University Press, Carlton South

Chan J, Devery C, Doran S (2003) Fair cop: learning the art of policing. University of Toronto Press, Toronto

Chappell AT (2009) The philosophical versus actual adoption of community policing: a case study. Crim Justice Rev 34(1):5–28

Chappell AT, Lanza-Kaduce L (2010) Police academy socialization: understanding the lessons learned in a paramilitary-bureaucratic organization. J Contemp Ethnography 39(2):187–214

Chen W (2013) Duizuohao xinshiqi gonganqunzhonggongzuo goujianhexiejingminguanxi de fansiyutanxi (Thoughts on establishing a harmonious police-citizen relationship). Pub Secur Sci J—J Zhejiang Police Coll 6:37–41

Chen X (2002) Community and policing strategies: a Chinese approach to crime control. Policing Soc 12(1):1–13

Chen Y (2013) Social science research methods. Chien Hua Learning Resources Network, New Taipei

Chu DC, Tsao C-C (2014) Attitudes toward women in policing; an empirical inquiry into the gender views of police cadets in Taiwan. Policing: Int J Police Strat Manage 37(2):324–339

Clark JP (1965) Isolation of the police: a comparison of the British and American situations. J Crim Law Criminol Police Sci 56(3):307–319

Cochran JK, Bromley ML (2003) The myth (?) of the police sub-culture. Policing: Int J Police Strat Manage 26(1):88–117
Cochran JK, Bromley ML, Swando MJ (2002) Sheriff's deputies' receptivity to organizational change. Policing: Int J Police Strat Manage 25(3):507–529
Cockcroft T (2013) Police culture: themes and concepts. Taylor & Francis, London
Cooper WH (1982) Police officers over career stages. Can Police Coll J 6(2):93–112
COPS (2009) Community policing defined. Department of Justice Office of Community Oriented Policing Services, Washington D.C., U.S
Corsianos M (2012) The complexities of police corruption. Rowman and Littlefield Publishings Inc., Lanham
CPPSU (2015) Enrollment guide of CPPSU 2015. from http://www.cppsu.edu.cn/download/2015zsjz.pdf
Crank JP (2004) Understanding police culture, 2nd edn. Anderson Publications, Cincinnati
Crank JP, Culbertson RG, Poole ED, Regoli RM (1987) The measurement of cynicism among police chiefs. J Crim Justice 15(1):37–48
Creswell JW (2003) Research design: qualitative, quantitative, and mixed method approaches. Sage, Thousand Oaks
Cullen FT, Link BG, Travis LFI, Lemming T (1983) Paradox in policing: a note on perceptions of danger. J Police Sci Adm 11(4):457–462
Cunningham JB, Aldrich JO (2012) Using SPSS: an interactive hands-on approach. Sage, Thousand Oaks
Dai M (2008) Policing in the People's Republic of China: a review of recent literature. Crime Law Soc Change 50(3):211–227
Dai Y (2001) New directions of Chinese policing in the reform era. In: Messner SF, Liu JF, Zhang L (eds) Crime and social control in a changing China. Greenwood Press, Westport, pp 151–157
De Vaus DA (1995) Surveys in social research, 4th edn. Allen & Unwin, St Leonards
Dejong C (2004) Gender differences in officer attitude and behavior. Women Crim Justice 15(3–4):1–32
Dempsey JS, Forst LS (2012) An introduction to policing, 6th edn. Delmar Cengage Learning, New York
DeVellis RF (2003) Scale development: theory and applications. Sage, Thousand Oaks
Dick P, Silvestri M, Westmarland L (2014) Women police: Potential and possibilities for police reform. In: Brown JM (ed) The future of policing. Routledge, Abingdon, pp 134–148
Ding L (2011) Senior Chinese leader stresses cultivation of police culture. Xinhua News.
Du J (1997) Police-public relations—a Chinese view. Aus NZ J Criminol 30(1):87–94
Du W (2007) Gonganjiguan qidong "jingminxiangyuejingwushi" huodong (Police departments launch "Police-Citizens Gather in Police Stations" Program). People's Daily, 11 Feb 2007
Dutton M (2000) The end of the (mass) line? Chinese policing in the era of the contract. Soc Justice 27(2):61–105
Dutton M, Lee T (1993) Missing the target? Policing strategies in the period of economic reform. Crime Delinquency 39(3):316–336
Engel RS, Worden RE (2003) Police officers' attitudes, behavior, and supervisory influences: an analysis of problem solving. Criminology 41(1):131–166
Ernest LN, Arvind V (2008) Dimensions of police culture: a study in Canada, India, and Japan. Policing: Int J Police Strat Manage 31(2):186–209
Eskridge C (1989) College and the police: a review of the issues. In: Kenney DJ (ed) Police and policing: contemporary issues. Praeger, New York, pp 17–25
Eterno JA (2006) Gender and policing: do women accept legal restrictions more than their male counterparts? Women Crim Justice 18(1–2):49–78
Field A (2013) Discovering statistics using IBM SPSS statistics, 4th edn. Sage, London
Fielding NG (1988) Joining forces: police training, socialization, and occupation. Routledge, London

Fleming J, Wakefield A (eds) (2009) The Sage dictionary of policing. Sage, London

Ford RE (2003) Saying one thing, meaning another: the role of parables in police training. Police Q 6(1):84–110

Franz V, Jones DM (1987) Perceptions of organizational performance in suburban police departments: a critique of the military model. J Police Sci Adm 15(2):153–161

Fu HL (1994) A bird in the cage: police and political leadership in post-Mao China. Policing Soc 4(4):277–291

Garcia V (2003) "Difference" in the police department: women, policing, and "doing gender. J Contemp Crim Justice 19(3):330–344

Geertz C (1973) The interpretation of cultures. Basic Books, New York

Geller WA (1997) Suppose we were really serious about police departments becoming learning organizations? Nat Inst Justice J 234:2–8

Ghasemi A, Zahediasl S (2012) Normality tests for statistical analysis: a guide for non-statisticians. Int J Endocrinol Metab 10(2):486–489

Goldsmith A (1990) Taking police culture seriously: police discretion and the limits of law. Policing Soc 1(2):91–114

Goldstein H (1967) Administrative problems in controling the exercise of police authority. J Crim Law Criminol Police Sci 58(2):160–172

Gong H (2004) Status quo and study on non-policing work [feijingwuhuodong xianzhuangshuliyutanjiu]. J Shanghai Police Coll 14(3):27–32

Gong Y (1999) Nulishixian siyousibidechengnuo zhazhashishi tuijin 110 jianshe (Try to realize the commitment of "Four haves and four musts" and promote 110 service). Policing Stud 3:11–13

Gong, Y. (2010). Lun xinshiqi jingchawenhua jianshe [On police culture cultivation in the new era]. *Theory Journal*(6), 101-103

Graves W (1996) Police cynicism: causes and cures. FBI Law Enforce Bull 65(6):16

Greene JR (2010) Pioneers in police research: William A. Westley. Police Pract Res 11(5):454–468

Guo W (2011) The construction of people-oriented police culture (goujian yirenweiben jingchawenhua) Reform Open 16:56

Hagan FE (2006) Research methods in criminal justice and criminology, 7th edn. Allyn and Bacon, Boston

Harris RN (1978) The police academy and the professional self-image. In: Manning PK, Van Maanen J (eds) Policing: a view from the street. Random House, New York

Harrison SJ (1998) Police organizational culture: using ingrained values to build positive organizational improvement. Public Adm Manage: Inter J 3(2):59–71

Hartnell CA, Ou AY, Kinicki A (2011) Organizational culture and organizational Effectiveness: a meta-analytic investigation of the competing values framework's theoretical suppositions. J Appl Psychol 96(4):677–694

Haviland WA (1999) Cultural anthropology, 9th edn. Harcourt Brace, Fort Worth

He T (2006) Chongfen renshi yandafangzhen de lishizuoyong nuligoujian luoshiyandafangzhen de changxiaojizhi (Have a correct understanding of the guiding principle for punishing crime severely and attempts to establish an enduring effective mechanism to implement the guiding principle for punishing crime severely). J Chin People's Pub Secur Univ (Social Sci Ed) 3:1–7

Heidensohn F (1992) Women in control? The role of women in law enforcement. Clarendon Press, Oxford

Herbert S (1998) Police subculture reconsidered. Criminology 36(2):343–369

Hickman MJ, Piquero NL, Piquero AR (2004) The validity of Niederhoffer's cynicism scale. J Crim Justice 32(1):1–13

Hobbs D (1988) Doing the business: entrepreneurship, the working class, and detectives in the east end of London. Clarendon Press, Oxford

Hobbs D (1991) A piece of business: the moral economy of detective work in the East-End of London. Br J Sociol 42(4):597–608

Hu J (2004) Zhongxi jingwumoshi yanjinguocheng zhi bijiao (A comparison of evolution of Chinese and western patterns of police affairs). J Hebei Police Voc Coll 4(1):51–57
Huang Z (2013) Shanghai: zhongguo nvzijingcha faduanzhidi (Shanghai: cradle of Chinese policewoman). Xinmin Evening News.
Ingram JR (2007) The effect of neighborhood characteristics on traffic citation practices of the police. Police Q 10(4):371–393
Ingram JR, Paoline EA, Terrill W (2013) A multilevel framework for understanding police culture: the role of the workgroup. Criminology 51(2):365–397
Ivković SK (2005) Fallen blue knights: controlling police corruption. Oxford University Press, New York
Jaccard J, Wan C (1996) LISREL approaches to interaction effects in multiple regression. Sage, Thousand Oaks
Jenks C (2005) Culture, 2nd edn. Routledge, London
Jia N (ed.) (2012) Women and men in China: facts and figures 2012. Department of Social, Science and Technology, and Cultural Statistics, National Bureau of Statistics, Beijing
Jiang N (2012) Xifang jingchawenhua yanjiu guankui (A brief review of western police culture studies). Policing Stud 7:87–91
Jiao AY (2001) Police and culture: a comparison between China and the United States. Police Q 4(2):156–185
Jiao AY (2001) Traditions and changes of police culture: organization, operation, and behaviour of the Chinese police. In: Messner SF, Liu JF, Zhang L (eds) Crime and social control in a changing China. Greenwood Press, Westport
Johnson RR (2012) Police officer job satisfaction: a multidimensional analysis. Police Q 15:157–176
Johnson SD, Koh HC, Killough LN (2009) Organizational and occupational culture and the perception of managerial accounting terms: an exploratory study using perceptual mapping techniques. Contemp Manage Res 5(4):317–342
Joseph AS, Huebner BM, Byhum TS (2003) Citizen perceptions of police services: race, neighborhood context, and community policing. Police Q 6(4):440–468
Kääriäinen J, Sirén R (2012) Do the police trust in citizens? European comparisons. Eur I Criminol 9(3):276–289
Kappeler VE, Gaines LK (2009) Community policing: a contemporary perspective, 5th edn. Anderson Publishing, Newark
Kappeler VE, Sluder RD, Alpert GP (1998) Forces of deviance: understanding the dark side of policing. Waveland Press, Long Grove
Klockars CB (1985) The idea of police. Sage, Beverly Hills
Klockars CB (1985) Order maintenance, the quality of urban life, and police: a different line of argument. In: Geller WA (ed) Police leadership in America. American Bar Foundation, New York
Klockars CB (1993) The legacy of conservative ideology and police. Police Forum 3(1):155–160
Klockars CB, Kutnjak Ivkovic S, Haberfeld MR (2004) The contours of police integrity. Sage, Thousand Oaks
Knox D (1990) Living sociology. West Publishing Company, St. Paul
Kraska PB (2007) Militarization and policing—its relevance to 21st century police. Policing 1(4):501–513
Kraska PB, Cubellis LJ (1997) Militarizing Mayberry and beyond: making sense of American paramilitary policing. Justice Quarterly 14(4):607–629
Kraska PB, Kappeler VE (1997) Militarizing American police: the rise and normalization of paramilitary units. Soc Probl 44(1):1–18
LaGrange RL (1998) Policing American society, 2nd edn. Nelson-Hall, Chicago
Langworthy RH (1987) Police cynicism: what we know from the Niederhoffer scale. J Crim Justice 15(1):17–35
Leech NL, Barrett KC, Morgan GA (2005) SPSS for intermediate statistics: use and interpretation. Lawrence Erlbaum, Mahwah

Lester D, Brink WT (1985) Police solidarity and tolerance for police misbehavior. Psychol Rep 57(1):326
Lian S (2002) On different thinking modes between China and the West. Foreign Lang Teaching 2:40–46
Liang B (2005) Severe strike campaign in transitional China. J Crim Justice 33(4):387–399
Lin H (2008) On police deviance from the perspective of police subculture (yawenhuashijiaoxia jingchayueguixianxiangsikao). J Chin People's Publ Secur Univ (Soc Sci Ed) 2:152–156
Lindsey B, Lorie F, Shayne J (2012) The link between traditional police sub-culture and police intimate partner violence. Policing: Int J Police Strat Manage 35(1):147–164
Ling Y, Liu Z (2002) Conggangwei yiyuanxuanze jijingwufazhanqushi kannvjing weilaifazhan (Career development of policewoman from the aspect of their selection of positions and trends of policing). Policing Stud 3:52–55
Lingamneni JR (1979) Resistance to change in police organizations: the diffusion paradigm. Crim Justice Rev 4(2):17–26
Liu H (2004) Zhongguo shequjingwu fazhande xinqushi (New trends of community policing development in China). J Chin People's Pub Secur Univ (Soc Sci Ed) 4:18–24
Liu S (2003) Tired China police force. Law Life 2:2–4
Loftus B (2009) Police culture in a changing world. Oxford University Press, Oxford
Loftus B (2010) Police occupational culture: classic themes, altered times. Policing Soc 20(1):1–20
Lotz R, Regoli RM (1977) Police cynicism and professionalism. Human Relat 30(2):175–186
Louis MR (1987) Organizations as culture-bearing milieux. In: Shafritz JM, Ott JS (eds) Classics of organization theory, 2nd edn. The Dorsey Press, Chicago, pp 421–432
Loyens K (2009) Occupational culture in policing reviewed: a comparison of values in the public and private police. Int J Public Adm 32(6):461–490
Luo F, Ruiz J (2012) Comparing police overwork in China and the USA: an exploratory study of death from overwork ('Karoshi') in policing. Int J Police Sci Manage 14(2):177–198
Luo R (1994) Luo Ruiqing lun gongangongzuo (On policing work by Luo Ruiqing). The Masses Press, Beijing
Lurigio AJ, Skogan WG (1994) Winning the hearts and minds of police officers: an assessment of staff perceptions of community policing in Chicago. Crime Delinquency 40(3):315–330
Lv Y (2012) Bianshi butong, yizhongqiutong–luelun zhongxi siweifangshi de chayi yu kuawenhuajiaoji zhongde zhangai (On differences of modes of thinking between China and the West and their influence to cross-cultural communication). Study Explor 12:143–146
Ma Y (1997) The Police Law 1995: organization, functions, powers and accountability of the Chinese police. Policing: Int J Police Strat Manage 20(1):113–135
Ma Y (2000) A research note on the history of the Chinese police. Int J Compar Appl Crim Justice 24(1):115–123
Ma Y (2008) The Chinese police. In: Haberfeld MR, Cerran I (eds) Comparative policing: the struggle for democratization. Sage, Los Angeles
Manning PK (1989) Occupational culture. In: Bailey WG (ed) The encyclopedia of police science. Garland Publishings, New York
Manning PK (1997) Police work: the social organization of policing, 2nd edn. Waveland Press, Prospect Heights
Manning PK (2007) A dialectic of organisational and occupational culture. In: Sklansky DA (ed) Police occupational culture: new debates and directions, vol 8. JAI Press, Oxford, pp 47–83
Manning PK (2007) Occupational culture. In: Greene JR (ed) Encyclopedia of police science, vol 2, 3rd edn. Taylor & Francis, New York
Martin SE, Jurik NC (2007) Doing justice, doing gender: women in legal and criminal justice occupations. Sage, Thousnad Oaks
Mayers A (2013) Introduction to statistics and SPSS in psychology. Pearson Education Limited, Harlow
McLaughlin E (2007) The new policing. Sage, London

Merton RK, Reader G, Kendall PL (1957) The student-physician: introductory studies in the sociology of medical education. Harvard University Press, Cambridge
Meyer ME, Steyn J (2009) Nurturing isolation in the South African police service: a comparison of male and female recruits. Policing: Int J Police Strat Manage 32(1):108–127
Miller LS, Hess KM, Orthmann CMH (2014) Community policing: partnerships for problem solving, 7th edn. Delmar Cengage Learning, New York
Miller LS, Whitehead JT (1996) Introduction to criminal justice research and statistics. Anderson Publishing Co., Cincinnati
Miller S (2010) Integrity systems and professional reporting in police organizations. Crim Justice Ethics 29(3):241–257
Miller SL (1998) Rocking the rank and file: gender issues and community policing. J Contemp Crim Justice 14(2):156–172
Miller SL (1999) Gender and community policing: walking the talk. Northeastern University Press, Boston
Miller SL, Bonistall E (2012) Gender and policing: critical issues and analyses. In: DeKeseredy WS, Dragiewicz M (eds) Routledge handbook of critical criminology. Routledge, Abingdon, pp 315–327
Miller SL, Hodge JP (2004) Rethinking gender and community policing: cultural obstacles and policy issues. Law Enforce Executive Forum 4(4):39–49
Millie A (2014) What are the police for? Re-thinking policing post-austerity. In: Brown JM (ed) The future of policing. Routledge, Abingdon, pp 53–63
Minichiello V, Aroni R, Hays T (2008) In-depth interviewing, 3rd edn. Pearson Education Australia, Sydney
Modaff DP, DeWine S (2002) Organizational communication: foundations, challenges, misunderstandings. Roxbury Publishing Company, Los Angeles
Mollen M, Baer H, Evans H, Lankler RC, Tyler HR (1994) Commission report: commission to investigate allegations of corruption and the anti-corruption procedures of the police department. The Commission, New York
Morabito MS (2010) Understanding community policing as an innovation: patterns of adoption. Crime Delinquency 56(4):564–587
Moser CA, Kalton G (1972) Survey methods in social investigation, 2nd edn. Basic Books, New York
MPS (2002) Guanyu jiaqiang shequjingwu de yijian (The notice of on strengthening the construction of community policing). (Gongtongzi 2002-42), Beijing. Retrieved from http://www.mps.gov.cn/n16/n1991360/n1991447/n2142144.files/n2142143.doc
MPS (2006) Gonganbu guanyu shishi shequhenongcunjingwu de jueding (Decisions on the community and rural policing tactics). (Gongfa 2006-5), Beijing
Muir WK (1977) Police: streetcorner politicians. University of Chicago Press, Chicago
Nhan J (2014) Police culture. In: Albanese JS (ed) The encyclopedia of criminology and criminal justice. Wiley, New York
Niederhoffer A (1967) Behind the shield: the police in urban society. Doubleday, New York
Novak KJ, Paoline EA, Terrill W (2005) The impact of police culture on traffic stop searches: an analysis of attitudes and behavior. Policing: Int J Police Strat Manage 28(3):455–472
NPUC (2015) Undergraduate student enrollment plan of 2015. From http://www.npuc.edu.cn/content.jsp?urltype=news.NewsContentUrl&wbtreeid=1116&wbnewsid=18862
Nunnally J (1978) Psychometric theory, 2nd edn. McGraw-Hill, New York
O'Leary Z (2010) The essential guide to doing your research project. Sage, Los Angeles
O'Loughlin N, Billing P (2000) Positive police culture: correcting perceptions. In: Coady T (ed) Violence and police culture. Melbourne University Press, Carlton South
Oldham S (2006) Proud of the police culture. Law Order 54(5):18–21
Opler ME (1945) Themes as dynamic forces in culture. Am J Sociol 51(3):198–206
Ott JS (1989) The organizational culture perspective. Dorsey Press, Pacific Grove
Packer H (1968) The limits of the criminal sanction. Stanford University Press, Stanford

Pallant J (2005) SPSS survial manual, 3rd edn. McGraw-Hill, New York
Palmiotto MJ (2011) Community policing: a police-citizen partnership. Taylor & Francis, New York
Pan, K. (2010). Quanguo gonganjiguan kaizhan weiqiqigeyue yandazhengzhihuodong (MPS starts strike-hard campaigns that will continue for seven months). China Police Daily, 14 June 2010
Paoline EA (2001) Rethinking police culture: officers' occupational attitudes. LFB Scholarly Publishing LLC, New York
Paoline EA (2003) Taking stock: toward a richer understanding of police culture. J Crim Justice 31(3):199–214
Paoline EA (2004) Shedding light on police culture: an examination of officers' occupational attitudes. Police Q 7(2):205–236
Paoline EA, Myers SM, Worden RE (2000) Police culture, individualism, and community policing: evidence from two police departments. Justice Q 17(3):575–605
Paoline EA, Terrill W (2014) Police culture: adapting to the strains of the job. Carolina Academic Press, Durham
Paoline EA, Terrill W, Rossler MT (2015) Higher education, college degree major, and police occupational attitudes. J Crim Justice Educ 26(1):49–73
Pavalko RM (1971) Sociology of occupations and professions. F. E. Peacock Publishers Inc., Itasca
Peak KJ, Gaines LK, Glensor RW (2010) Police supervision and management: in an era of community policing, 3rd edn. Prentice Hall, Upper Saddle River
Peak KJ, Glensor RW (1999) Community policing and problem solving: strategies and practices. Prentice Hall, Upper Saddle River
Perrott SB, Taylor DM (1995) Crime fighting: law enforcement and service provider role orientations in community-based police officers. Am J Police 14(3):173–195
Petter G, Geoff D, Rune G (2011) Police misconduct and crime: bad apples or systems failure? J Money Laundering Control 15(1):6–24
Pettigrew AM (1979) On studying organizational cultures. Adm Sci Q 24(4):570–581
Phillips SW (2014) Myths, militarism and the police patrol rifle. Policing Soc. doi:10.1080/10439463.2014.922088
Pollock JM (2012) Ethical dilemmas and decisions in criminal justice, 7th edn. Wadsworth Cengage Learning, Belmont
Poole ED, Regoli RM (1979) Police professionalism and cynicism. Crim Justice Behav 6(2):201–206
Poteyeva M, Sun IY (2009) Gender differences in police officers' attitudes: assessing current empirical evidence. J Crim Justice 37(5):512–522
Prenzler T (2009) Police corruption: preventing misconduct and maintaining integrity. CRC Press, Boca Raton
Prokos A, Padavic I (2002) 'There oughtta be a law against bitches': masculinity lessons in police academy training. Gender Work Organ 9(4):439–459
Punch KF (2005) Introduction to social research: quantitative and qualitative approaches. Sage, London
Punch M (2003) Rotten orchards: "pestilence", police misconduct and system failure. Policing Soc 13(2):171–196
Punch M (2007) Cops with honours: University education and police culture. In: Neill MO, Marks M, Singh AM (eds) Police occupational culture: new debates and directions, vol 8. JAI Press, Oxford, pp 105–128
Qu X (2005) An analysis of the strike-hard criminal policy. Contemp Chin Thought 36(3):77–88
Rabe-Hemp CE (2008) Female officers and the ethic of care: does officer gender impact police behaviors? J Crim Justice 36(5):426–434
Raines JB (2010) Ethics in policing: misconduct and integrity. Jones and Bartlett Publishers, Sudbury

Regoli RM (1976) The effects of college education on the maintenance of police cynicism. J Police Sci Adm 4(3):340–345
Reiner R (1985) The politics of the police. Wheatsheaf Books, Brighton
Reiner R (2010) The politics of the police, 4th edn. Oxford University Press, New York
Reiter MS (1999) Empowerment policing. FBI Law Enforce Bull 68(2):7–11
Reuss-Ianni E (1983) Two cultures of policing: street cops and management cops. Transaction Books, New Brunswick
Richards L (2005) Handling qualitative data: a practical guide. Sage, London
Rivera-Vazquez O (2014) Police stress. In: Albanese JS (ed) The encyclopedia of criminology and criminal justice. Wiley, New York
Roberg RR, Novak K, Cordner G (2009) Police and society, 4th edn. Oxford University Press, New York
Robertson I (1989) Society: a brief introduction. Worth Publishers, New York
Rong W (2013) Discussion on expansion of enrollemnt of female students in police universities [kuoda gong'anyuanxiao zhaoshengnvsheng biliwentitaolun]. Retrieved from http://blog.sina.com.cn/s/blog_9ed297970101c2f4.html
Rowe M (2014) Introducton to policing, 2nd edn. Sage, London
Rubinstein J (1973) City police. Farrar, Straus and Giroux, New York
Rumbaut RG, Egon B (1979) Changing conceptions of the police role: a sociological review. Crime Justice 1:239–288
Rydberg J, Terrill W (2010) The effect of higher education on police behaviour. Police Q 13(1):92–120
Sackmann S (1991) Cultural knowledge in organizations: exploring the collective mind. Sage, Newbury Park
Sarantakos S (2005) Social research, 3rd edn. Palgrave MacMillan, Hampshire
Sathe V (1983) Implications of corporate culture: a manager's guide to action. Organ Dyn 12(2):5–23
Sathe V (1985) Culture and related corporate realities: text, cases, and readings on organizational entry, establishment, and change. R.D. Irwin, Homewood
Scaramella GL, Cox SM, McCamey WP (2011) Introduction to policing. Sage, Thousand Oaks
Schein EH (1985) Organizational culture and leadership. Jossey-Bass, San Francisco
Schein EH (1990) Organizational culture. Am Psychol 45(2):109–119
Schein EH (2004) Organizational culture and leadership, 3rd edn. Jossey-Bass, San Francisco
Scoggins SE, O'Brien KJ (2015) China's unhappy police. Asian Surv 55(2)
Scott J, Evans D, Verma A (2009) Does higher education affect perceptions among police personnel? A response from India. J Contemp Crim Justice 25(2):214–236
Scripture AE (1997) The sources of police culture: demographic or environmental variables? Policing Soc 7(3):163–176
Sever M (2008) Effects of organizational culture on police decision making. TELEMASP Bull 15(1):1–11
Shafritz JM, Ott JS (eds) (1987) Classics of organization theory, 2nd edn. The Dorsey Press, Chicago
Shearing CD, Ericson RV (1991) Culture as figurative action. Br J Sociol 42(4):481–506
Shernock SK (1992) The effects of college education on professional attitudes among police. J Crim Justice Educ 3(1):71–92
Shernock SK (2007) Police solidarity. In: Greene JR (ed) The encyclopedia of police science, vol 2, 3rd edn. Routledge, New York
Sklansky DA (2006) Not your father's police department: making sense of the new demographics of law enforcement. J Crim Law Criminol 96(3):1209–1243
Skogan WG (2008) An overview of community policing: origins, concepts and implementation. In: Williamson T (ed) The handbook of knowledge-based policing: current conceptions and future directions. Wiley, Chichester, pp 43–57
Skolnick JH (1986) Justice without trial, 2nd edn. Macmillan, New York

Skolnick JH (2008) Enduring issues of police culture and demographics. Policing Soc 18(1):35–45

Skolnick JH, Bayley DH (1988) Community policing: issues and practices throughout the world. National Institute of Justice, Washington

Skolnick JH, Fyfe JJ (1993) Above the law: police and the excessive use of force. Free Press, New York

Smircich L (1983) Concepts of culture and organizational analysis. Adm Sci Q 28(3):339–358

Sparrow MK, Moore MH, Kennedy DM (1990) Beyond 911: a new era for policing. Basic Books, New York

Steyn J (2007) 'Venus versus Mars': an attitudinal comparison made at the start of South African police service basic training. Int J Police Sci Manage 9(2):145–163

Sun IY (2003) Police officers' attitudes toward their role and work: a comparison of black and white officers. Am J Crim Justice 28(1):89–108

Sun IY, Cretacci MA, Wu Y, Cheng J (2009) Chinese police cadets' attitudes toward police role and work. Policing: Int J Police Strat Manage 32(4):758–780

Sun IY, Sobol JJ, Cretacci M, Phillips SW (2010) A comparison of Chinese and the U.S. police cadets' occupational attitudes. J Crim Justice 38(4):640–647

Sun IY, Wu Y (2009) The role of the people's armed police in Chinese policing. Asian J Criminol 4(2):107–128

Sun IY, Wu Y (2010) Chinese policing in a time of transition, 1978–2008. J Contemp Crim Justice 26(1):20–35

Swanton B (1981) Social isolation of police: structural determinants and remedies. Police Stud 3(4):14–21

Terrell SR (2012) Statistics translated: a step-by-step guide to analyzing and interpreting data. The Guilford Press, New York

Terrill W, Paoline EA, Manning PK (2003) Police culture and coercion. Criminology 41(4):1003–1034

The Knapp Commission (1973) The Knapp Commission report on police corruption. G. Braziller, New York

The People's Police Law of People's Republic of China, Law Press 0228, 1995

Theodorson GA, Theodorson L (1990) Sociology: principles and applications. West Publications Co, St. Paul

Trevaskes S (2003) Yanda 2001: form and strategy in a Chinese anti-crime campaign. Aus NZ J Criminol 36(3):272–292

Trice HM (1993) Occupational subcultures in the workplace. ILR Press, Ithaca

Trice HM, Beyer JM (1993) The cultures of work organizations. Prentice Hall, Englewood Cliffs

Tuffin R (ed) (2008) Dictionary of policing. Willan Publishing, Portland

Tylor EB (1871) Primitive culture, vol 1. J. Murray, London

Van Maanen J (1973) Observations on the making of policemen. Hum Organ 32(4):407–418

Van Maanen J (1975) Police socialization: a longitudinal examination of job attitudes in an urban police department. Adm Sci Q 20(2):207–228

Van Maanen J (1978) The asshole. In: Manning PK, Van Maanen J (eds) Policing: a view from the street. Random House, New York, pp 221–238

Van Maanen J, Schein EH (1979) Towards a theory of organizational socialization. In: Staw BM (ed) Research in organizational behaviour, vol 1. JAI Press, Greenwich

Vander Zanden JW (1996) Sociology: the core. McGraw-Hill, New York

Verma A, Das DK, Abraham M (eds) (2013) Global community policing: problems and challenges. CRC Press, Boca Raton

Violanti JM, Andrew M, Burchfiel CM, Hartley TA, Charles LE, Miller DB (2007) Posttraumatic stress symptoms and cortisol patterns among police officers. Policing: Int J Police Strat Manage 30(2):189–202

Vito GF, Walsh WF, Kunselman J (2005) Community policing: the middle manager's perspective. Police Q 8(4):490–511

Waddington PAJ (1999) Police (canteen) sub-culture: an appreciation. British J Criminol 39(2):287–309
Waddington PAJ (1999) Policing citizens. UCL Press, London
Waddington PAJ (ed) (2008) Dictionary of policing. Willan Publishing, Cullompton
Walker S, Katz CM (2005) The police in America: an introduction, 5th edn. McGraw-Hill, New York
Walker S, Katz CM (2013) The police in America: an introduction, 8th edn. McGraw-Hill, New York
Wang D, Sun Z (2003) Cong yingguojingwugeming kan wogguo gongan gaige redian (On the main points of Chinese policing reform from British policing revolution). J Jiangsu Police Coll 18(5):164–167
Wang N (2011) A survey study on police involvement in non-policing activities among street-level police officers (guanyugonganjiguan jicengpaichusuo canyufeijingwuhuodongqing-kuangde diaochayanjiu). J Jiangxi Police Coll 5:71–77
Wang P (2014) Extra-legal protection in China: how guanxi distorts China's legal system and facilitates the rise of unlawful protectors. Br J Criminol 54(5):809–830
Wang X (2014) Empowering the frontline police officers to cope with police social service role strain in China. Int J Criminol Sociol 3:20–45
Wang X, Wong DS-W (2012) Police social service work in China: community policing with Chinese characteristics. Asia Pac J Police Crim Justice 9(1):34–54
Wang Y, Zheng L, Hu T, Zheng Q (2014) Stress, burnout, and job satisfaction: case of police force in China. Pub Personnel Manage 43(3):325–339
Weber M (1965) Politics as a vocation. Fortress Press, Philadelphia
Wei W, Tom Vander B (2010) Police torture in China and its causes: a review of literature. Aus NZ J Criminol 43(3):557–579
Westley WA (1953) Violence and the police. Am J Sociol 59(1):34–41
Westley WA (1970) Violence and the police: a sociological study of law, custom, and morality. MIT Press, Cambridge
Westmarland L (2001) Gender and policing: sex, power, and police culture. Willan, Cullompton
Westmarland L (2008) Police cultures. In: Newburn T (ed) Handbook of policing, 2nd edn. Willan, Cullompton
White SO (1972) A perspective on police professionalization. Law Soc Rev 7(1):61–85
Wilkins AL, Dyer WG Jr (1988) Toward culturally sensitive theories of culture change. Acad Manage Rev 13(4):522–533
Wilson C, Braithwaite H (1996) Police officer behaviour during interactions with citizens: what distinguishes the "skilled" from the "average" officer?. National Police Research Unit, Payneham
Wilson H (1999) Post-secondary education of the police officer and its effect on the frequency of citizen complaints. J Calif Law Enforce 33:3–10
Wilson JQ (1968) Varieties of police behavior: the management of law and order in eight communities. Harvard University Press, Cambridge
Wong KC (1998) A reflection on police abuse of power in the People's Republic of China. Police Q 1(2):87–112
Wong KC (2001) The philosophy of community policing in China. Police Q 4(2):186–214
Wong KC (2002) Policing in the People's Republic of China: the road to reform in the 1990s. Br J Criminol 42(2):281–316
Wong KC (2007) Studying policing in China: some personal reflections. Int J Sociol Law 35(3):111–126
Wong KC (2009) Chinese policing: history and reform. Peter Lang, New York
Wong KC (2009) A Chinese theory of community policing. In: Wisler D, Onwudiwe ID (eds) Community policing: international patterns and comparative perspectives. CRC Press, Boca Raton
Wong KC (2009) Police scholarship in China. Police Pract Res 10(5/6):503–519

Wong KC (2012) Police reform in China. Taylor & Francis, Boca Raton
Wood JRT (1997) Royal commission into the New South Wales police service: final report. NSW Government, Sydney
Wooden K, Rogers C (2014) Restoring public confidence: perceptions of community police officers. Police J: Theory Pract Principles 87(3):186–194
Worden AP (1993) The attitudes of women and men in policing: testing conventional and contemporary wisdom. Criminology 31(2):203–241
Worden RE (1990) A badge and a baccalaureate: policies, hypotheses, and further evidence. Justice Q 7(3):565–592
Worden RE (1995) Police officers' belief systems: a framework for analysis. Am J Police 14(1):49–81
Worden RE (1996) The causes of police brutality: theory and evidence on police use of force. In: Geller WA, Toch H (eds) Police violence: understanding and controlling police abuse of force. Yale University Press, New Haven
Wu Y, Jiang S, Lambert E (2011) Citizen support for community policing in China. Policing: Int J Police Strat Manage 34(2):285–303
Wu Y, Sun IY (2009) Citizen trust in police: the case of China. Police Q 12(2):170–191
Xiao J, Liu W (2012) Jinshinianlai woguo jingwugaige moshiyanjiu (Research on the modes of policing reform of China in recent ten years). J Fujian Police Coll 3:18–25
Xu W, Zhang L (2008) "Quanguo gonganminjing dazoufang" aiminshijianhuodong quanmianqidong ("Walk through Communities" program commences). Legal Daily, 25 Dec 2008
Xu Z (2008) Zhongguode shequ yu shequjingwu–jianlun zhongguo shequjingwu jianshezhongde ruoganwenti (Chinese community and the community policing). J Shanghai Police Coll 18(5):72–75
Xue X (2010) Yingmei jingchawenhua jiqi yanjiu (Studies of police subculture in the UK and USA). J Jiangsu Police Coll 25(5):142–148
Yang Y (2011) Lun xingjing zhiyewenhua jiqi duizhencha deyingxiang (On the professional culture of the criminal police and its impact on the investigation). J Jilin Public Secur Acad 1:46–50
Ye Y (2011) Study of police culture from the perspective of culture study (wenhuayanjiu shijiao xiade jingchawenhua yanjiu). J Polit Sci Law 28(2):119–123
You W, Xie X (2004) Yanda zhengce de huigu yu kexuedingwei (A review of strike-hard policy and a scientific orientation). J East China Univ Polit Sci Law 1:48–54
Young M (1991) An inside job: policing and police culture in Britain. Clarendon Press, Oxford
Yu N (2011) Jingchayawenhuaxiade yitaixianxiangyanjiu yiyawenhuadefugongnengweishijiao (Research on the heteromorphism in the police subculture-from the view of the dysfunction of subculture). J Jilin Public Secur Acad 2:32–36
Yuan G (2007) Hexieshehuixia woguojingchade juesedingwei (The status of Chinese police in a harmonious social approach). J Chin People's Pub Secur Univ (Soc Sci Ed) 2:127–134
Yuan G (2012) Goujian Gong'anxue Xuekeliluntixi de Fangfayucelue (Methods and strategies to establish the discipline of public security studies). J Chin People's Pub Secur Univ (Soc Sci Ed) 3:31–36
Zhang J (1991) Shilun gonganwenhua jianshe (On public security culture cultivation). J Jiangsu Police Coll 4
Zhang M (2009) Jingwuhuodongyu feijingwuhuodong zhijiefen yigebianzhengdeguandian (Distinction between policing affairs and non-policing affairs: a dialectical point of view). J Shanghai Police Coll 19(6):42–45
Zhang Y, Li G (2006) 20shiji30niandai zhongguonvjingde sheli jiqi zhiyeyingxiang (The establishment of Chinese policewoman in the 1930s and its professional influence). J Zhengzhou Univ 39(6):43–46
Zhang Z (1993) Lun jingchameiyu yu jingchawenhua (On police aesthetic education and police culture). J Henan Pub Secur 13:22–23

Zhang Z (1997) Zhongxijingchawenhua guannianfazhanshulue jibijiaoyanjiu (A brief introduction and a comparative study of police culture studies in China and the West). J Chin People's Pub Secur Univ (Soc Sci Ed) 3:26–28

Zhang Z (2007) Dangdai jingchawenhua lilunyushijian de nandianheredian wenti (Hot issues and difficulties in theories and practice of modern police culture). J Chin People's Pub Secur Univ (Soc Sci Ed) 129:11–16

Zhang Z (2010) Jingcha wenhuaxue (Studies of police culture), 3rd edn. Chinese People's Public Security University Press, Beijing

Zhang Z (2010) Police philoshophy: principles of policing from the perspective of philosophy, 2nd edn. China People's Public Security University Press, Beijing

Zhao W (2010) Xifang jingchayawenhua yanjiu shuping (A review of western police subculture studies). J Shanghai Police Coll 20(6):80–82

Zhao Y (2012) Zhiduhuaxinren yu hexiejingminguanxi jianshetanxi (Institutionalized trust and the construction of harmonious relationship between people and police). J Hunan Police Acad 24(2):143–147

Zhong LY (2009) Community policing in China: old wine in new bottles. Police Pract Res 10(2):157–169

MIX
Papier aus verantwortungsvollen Quellen
Paper from responsible sources
FSC® C105338

If you have any concerns about our products,
you can contact us on
ProductSafety@springernature.com

In case Publisher is established outside the EU,
the EU authorized representative is:
Springer Nature Customer Service Center GmbH
Europaplatz 3, 69115 Heidelberg, Germany

Printed by Libri Plureos GmbH
in Hamburg, Germany